Teaching *Hamlet* in the Twenty-First-Century Classroom

Teaching *Hamlet* in the Twenty-First-Century Classroom

Joseph P. Haughey

ROWMAN & LITTLEFIELD
Lanham • Boulder • New York • London

Published by Rowman & Littlefield
An imprint of The Rowman & Littlefield Publishing Group, Inc.
4501 Forbes Boulevard, Suite 200, Lanham, Maryland 20706
www.rowman.com

86-90 Paul Street, London EC2A 4NE

Copyright © 2024 by Joseph P. Haughey

All rights reserved. No part of this book may be reproduced in any form or by any electronic or mechanical means, including information storage and retrieval systems, without written permission from the publisher, except by a reviewer who may quote passages in a review.

British Library Cataloguing in Publication Information Available

Library of Congress Cataloging-in-Publication Data

Names: Haughey, Joseph P., author.
Title: Teaching Hamlet in the twenty-first-century classroom / Joseph P. Haughey.
Description: Lanham: Rowman & Littlefield, 2024. | Includes bibliographical references and index. | Summary: "Teaching Hamlet in the Twenty-First Century Classroom offers fresh takes on teaching Shakespeare's Hamlet. Each chapter provides learning objectives, guides, discussion questions, film-based strategies, and activities that embrace students' role in meaning-making"—Provided by publisher.
Identifiers: LCCN 2024018480 (print) | LCCN 2024018481 (ebook) | ISBN 9781475871807 (cloth) | ISBN 9781475871814 (paperback) | ISBN 9781475871821 (ebook)
Subjects: LCSH: Shakespeare, William, 1564–1616. Hamlet. | Shakespeare, William, 1564–1616—Study and teaching.
Classification: LCC PR2807 .H424 2024 (print) | LCC PR2807 (ebook) | DDC 822.3/3—dc23/eng/20240501
LC record available at https://lccn.loc.gov/2024018480
LC ebook record available at https://lccn.loc.gov/2024018481

Contents

Prologue: "Begin at This Line"	vii
Acknowledgments	xvii
Chapter 1: "I Could a Tale Unfold": Telling a Good Ghost Story, Bard-Style	1
Chapter 2: "There Is Method in It": Hamlet's Sinking Mental Health—Diving Deep into the Soliloquies	25
Chapter 3: "Words of So Sweet Breath": Listening to Women's Voices—What Ophelia and Gertrude Reveal	51
Chapter 4: "Like the Painting of a Sorrow": Drawing Scenes from Hamlet—Getting Visual with the Text	81
Chapter 5: "I Have Been Sexton/Sixteene Here": How Old Is Hamlet Anyway—Getting Gritty with Textual History	113
Epilogue: "This Business Is Well Ended"	157
Appendix A: "That You Must Teach Me": Additional Hamlet Resources	159
Appendix B: "I Have Some Rights of Memory": A Note on Fortinbras	169
Glossary: "Words, Words, Words"	171
Works Cited	185
Index	189
About the Author	191

Prologue

"Begin at This Line"

To teach *Hamlet* or not to teach *Hamlet*—that is not even a question. *Hamlet* remains today the epitome of the Shakespeare canon, perhaps of the literary canon itself, and to know it well is to have an entry point into a host of cultural knowledge that defines the well-cultured and well-read citizen of our global world. Many consider it the greatest work of the world's greatest author. It remains one of our time's most taught, most performed, and most read works and will undoubtedly remain so through the next generations.

That notion, though, that we study *Hamlet*, or even Shakespeare more generally, because it is something prior generations have always done or because Shakespeare carries a certain cultural capital is an argument that will fall flat for adolescent audiences. And it should. Today's students will (and should) demand better justification. Teachers need instead to teach *Hamlet* for what it provides its careful reader: in a world that can feel like it is collapsing around adolescents today, *Hamlet* provides one schema for building some of the apparatus necessary to work through mental health struggles and to face our own sense of purpose.

Such struggles are both unique burdens that individuals carry alone and collective troubles which we share together. Shakespeare felt them weighing on the world around him, and so has every generation since. It is a crisis from which no generation has been exempt but which today's students know particularly well. At first it may not seem to students that Shakespeare can help. More than four hundred years old, Shakespeare's language and syntax, on first read, feel archaic and toilsome. His are not easy texts. They can puzzle even those who have spent a lifetime poring over their pages and considering their stage and film productions.

To make it worth that effort, teachers today need reasons that will resonate with young people, and the most convincing is that *Hamlet* provides an entry point into our inner thinking regarding the most existential questions we all face. Hamlet does contemplate suicide, and it is an entirely plausible reading in act 3 that he is moments away from taking his own life, but he does not succumb to it. He is, in this, a survivor. True, he does not survive his play—his is a Shakespearean tragedy—but he does survive his crisis, finds some peace in act 5, and makes amends with Laertes.

Above all, he makes it to the end of his story, and that's a victory and a reading worth celebrating. Hamlet does not fall into his own darkness but, rather, into the darkness of Elsinore, which engulfs him. His answer to his proverbial question of "to be or not to be" comes late in the play, in act 5: Hamlet tells Horatio that "the readiness is all" and that what will come will come. His answer to "to be or not to be" is that he will just "let be" (5.2.238).[1] His answer is the affirmative.

Students today face a challenging road ahead as they approach the mid-twenty-first century, and their problems will require new solutions. They will be a philosophical generation, and *Hamlet* remains one of the finest plays for exploring such human philosophy. *Hamlet* is a play meant to teach its readers how to think. Alongside other tools, studying such literature in which characters examine and come to terms with the existential provides places for conversation and analysis as young people wrestle with the nature of their own mortality.

A QUICK NOTE ON THEORY

The discussion of the theoretical underpinnings that guide this book is limited to its endnotes. These begin at the end of this introduction and continue through each chapter. That is not because theory is unimportant but because this book's target audience is secondary and college teachers who want practical guidance in teaching *Hamlet*. It is written for teachers who are just getting started or have some experience but want additional classroom strategies and background knowledge. The endnotes are not exhaustive—far from it—but they do give starting points for a deeper dive.

I hope that through this book, readers do eventually aspire to make that leap—the whole premise is that teachers as much as students benefit from a lifelong relationship with the play—and for readers who are ready for that, the endnotes await. There is some really good stuff there, and the goal is that the notes also make for interesting reading. For teachers, though, who want the practical stuff, read on, and skip the notes for now.

AN EVEN QUICKER NOTE ON RESOURCES

Several resources accompany this book. These include charts, diagrams, paintings, and drawings from museum sites, cue scripts developed by the author, archival clips of original sources, and more—all to be fully described in the following chapters. They are all in the public domain and freely available for educational use. Teachers can photocopy or scan these from the book to share with their students or access them through a resource folder with this link: https://shorturl.at/hBFY3.

FOUR CORE TENETS OF THE BOOK

The *first tenet* of the book is that the goal of a good unit on *Hamlet* is not to cover the play. It is a play that can be neither covered in a unit, a semester, nor even a year. Instead, it is a work to be relished over the course of a lifetime, and the good teacher's ambition should be, through their teaching, to ignite in their students a lifelong love of *Hamlet* that will keep them coming back to it throughout their lives.[2] Virginia Woolf wrote once that she reread *Hamlet* once a year, and in each rereading, she saw something new both in the play and in herself. It served as a mirror she often gazed into.

It can serve students today in the same way as a text they repeatedly return to. For some, it may simply be an echo accompanying them, a few of its lines etched into their minds that they will carry with them. Some will reread it. Some will do so many times. Others will return to it in performance, a Shakespeare in the Park production that brings back fond memories from adolescence. Others may return to it in fragments, a memory of a line that helps them through their day. That students return to the play one day, perhaps repeatedly, is the true marker of a successful classroom *Hamlet* experience. This book is meant to guide teachers as they direct their students toward that lifelong love of *Hamlet*.

To this end, the *second tenet* of the book is that teachers matter. The best teachers focus on higher-order thinking skills as they invite students into the rich world of Shakespearean language and stage play. Adolescents today rarely come to love Shakespeare alone; ask any Shakespeare lover how they first found their love of Shakespeare, and he or she will inevitably tell the story of an English or theater teacher who made a difference, inspiring in them a love of words and stories, and how he or she made the classroom come alive, as well as the ideas that leap from the page to the places inside that Shakespeare speaks to still.

The *third tenet* of this book is that good teachers use class time to focus on what matters most. Students need three layers of instruction: (1) a foundational knowledge of the play's plot, characters, and setting; (2) a fundamental orientation of the play's evolving cultural place in the theatrical and literary canon; and, most importantly, (3) profound, meaningful educational experiences that demand higher-level thinking and engagement with *Hamlet's* text(s). Those first two should be covered quickly; the third should take some time. The book's introduction and first chapter will include several basic activities that address the first two.

The plot itself is not terribly complex—a king has been murdered by his brother and returns as a ghost to call his son to revenge—but students need to master it early in the unit before diving deeply. Similarly, students need some appreciation of just how influential *Hamlet* has been on later literature, popular culture more broadly, and the school curriculum. Both can be accomplished relatively quickly, though, and should not be the end goal of a study of *Hamlet*.

Too many teachers from the past have gotten lost in these weeds and failed to bring their students into the stuff that matters most. Like this book, the bulk of a good *Hamlet* unit will dwell on higher-level thinking activities. Each of its five chapters will build upon students' basic knowledge of the play, established in an opening lesson or two, and then push them into active, project-based approaches for the remainder of the unit, each chapter building on the ones before.

The goal is not coverage of the play but, rather, establishing a variety of ways to engage with *Hamlet* that students can transfer to later encounters with the play after the class, as well as to other literary texts and, more broadly, to other areas of their education and life. In this approach, the study of *Hamlet* through the first two modes is broad and shallow (and quick), but the emphasis in the third is specific and deep (and with time to savor).

The *fourth tenet* of the book is that a meaningful educational experience with any Shakespeare play should be grounded in Shakespeare's language. Through their unique lenses, each chapter of the book is a study of Shakespeare's actual words. This book will not direct students to build models of the Globe or report on the nature of life in London during Shakespeare's time. While these are exciting and important topics, they matter to the study of a Shakespearean play only to the extent they help with understanding Shakespeare's language better.

Knowing the shapes of the original stages, for example—the Globe and the Blackfriars—upon which *Hamlet* would have initially been performed does matter, but only in how it helps students think through how the language might have been originally performed (as well as how it could be performed today) in the way that an actor assigned a part might think through his or her or their lines, as will be addressed in chapter 2.

For example, how might it change the delivery of Hamlet's "Am I a coward? Who calls me villain?" when students know that groundlings would have had their elbows leaning on the Globe stage as they stood and watched? It becomes a different line in performance when the audience is that close, and it sets a different tone if the actor chooses to direct the line directly to a member of the audience, with a pause as if expecting a response, than if it is instead just spoken in the general direction of an abstract audience.[3] The language is everything.

CHAPTER SYNOPSES

Each of the book's five chapters pushes students to consider the work through its specific lens. The structure of each, though, follows the same pattern: each chapter includes ready-to-use learning objectives, suggestions for reading aloud as a class, notes for teachers on language, an anticipatory set activity, a section breaking down biblical and classical references, a film-based activity or two, and a series of discussion questions and writing prompts. Each chapter also culminates in a larger project-based activity that pushes students to think through the play through the chapter's particular lens, as is described in the chapter summaries below.

Chapter 1: "I Could a Tale Unfold": How to Tell a Good Ghost Story, Bard-Style

Chapter 1 establishes an argument for studying Shakespeare through the lens of a *creative writer*. It begins with a close reading of the early ghost scenes, 1.4 and 1.5, in which Hamlet first meets his father's spirit. Students compare film versions of these scenes, analyzing how different directors portrayed Shakespeare's famous ghost story. Students analyze the text, looking for the characteristics Shakespeare incorporates into his storytelling, which they will use as a model for their creative writing work. The chapter's culminating project-based activity has students draft their own ghost story modeled after the version that Shakespeare created: a ghost reveals to students' protagonists a dark secret and urges them to action. Students will incorporate additional elements that they identify from Shakespeare's writing into their own.

Chapter 2: "There Is Method in It": Hamlet's Mental Health, and Diving Deep into the Soliloquies

Chapter 2 establishes an argument for studying Shakespeare through the lens of an *actor*—specifically, an actor working through Hamlet's act 2 soliloquy. The chapter walks teachers and students through the actor's process, analyzing language first through paraphrasing and meaning finding (the dictionary work that actors do as they prepare) and then exploring different vocal techniques and stage strategies (the later rehearsal work as they shape their roles).[4] Students further analyze film versions of the scene, learning from various productions' choices regarding language and delivery as they prepare to create their short production of Hamlet's act 2 soliloquy. The chapter's culminating project-based activity has students cut their version of the second soliloquy script and then record their audio performance.

Chapter 3: "Words of So Sweet Breath": Listening to Women's Voices—What Ophelia and Gertrude Reveal

Chapter 3 establishes an argument for studying Shakespeare through the lens of a *literary critic*. Its language section provides insights into how scholars have deduced what English sounded like in Shakespeare's time and how teachers can use those techniques to get students thinking about how language has shifted over the centuries. The chapter then introduces students to cue scripts, which likewise get students thinking about the historical ways Shakespeare's language has come down through the centuries.

Chapter 3 also emphasizes women's roles in the play, both its two female main characters and the many female actors who have played the title role.[5] One activity has students briefly research and present on the women who have taken up the part. The chapter also considers the interpretations of four female actors who have played Ophelia and has students consider film versions of Ophelia's nunnery scene in terms of their four perspectives.

The culminating activity guides students as they analyze a poem by literary critic Margaret Atwood, who wrote the poem "Gertrude Talks Back," in which she crafts a delicious, villainous reading of Gertrude. Students then write their own version in which they speak as Gertrude, combining their creative and critical writing skills to craft their own reading, providing additional nuance—though still one firmly grounded in Shakespeare's original text—and retell a scene or a moment in the style of Margaret Atwood.

Chapter 4: "Like the Painting of a Sorrow": Drawing Scenes from Hamlet—Getting Visual with the Text

Chapter 4 establishes an argument for studying Shakespeare through the lens of an *artist*. Artists think deeply about textual detail and then juxtapose that detail alongside their own creative impulse. The unit emphasizes Ophelia's flower scene, having students first study how different film versions have handled the difficult scene and then devise for themselves various ways to pass out her flowers as she speaks her lines, giving meaning to each flower as she does. The chapter also has students analyze eight different historical paintings, each inspired by a different moment from *Hamlet*, and culminates in having students explore one of those eight moments—extracting critical visual details from the text that give the passage shape—and then draw or paint their own visual interpretation of their assigned moment.

Chapter 5: "I Have Been Sexton/Sixteen Here": Just How Old is Hamlet—Getting Gritty with Textual History

Chapter 5 establishes an argument for studying Shakespeare through the lens of an *editor*. It builds on students' knowledge of *Hamlet's* place in the literary canon, providing a foundational understanding of the play's textual history. It illustrates the complexity of the editorial work behind a good edition of Shakespeare—how a modern text today comes to us through the three original seventeenth-century source texts (the Second Quarto, the First Folio, and the First Quarto [Q2, F1, Q1]) and how variations in those texts can affect meaning for us as readers and actors—but simplifies the editorial process into a series of introductory, beginner-level activities.

One activity has students examine textual cues in those original texts in the grave digger scene, where they regard Hamlet's age; whether Shakespeare intended Hamlet to be sixteen, thirty, or another age entirely; and how a reading of this question, along with analysis of what scholars and editors have had to say on the matter, affects the understanding of the rest of the play. The chapter's culminating project-based activity has students use digital archival texts of Q2, F1, and Q1 to make editorial choices regarding the passage, teaching them to think carefully about both original source texts and issues of contemporary Shakespeare editing as they make textual choices for their editions of the passage.

NOTES

1. Unless otherwise stated, all line citations in this book are from *The Folger Shakespeare Library Hamlet*, edited by Barbara A. Mowat and Paul Werstine.

2. Rex Gibson explains that this applies as much to teachers as students: "A recognition that one never finishes with Shakespeare . . . an awareness that fresh insights come from active work in the classroom—the students can teach the teacher" (1998, 153).

3. Ralph Alan Cohen provides an example of this from a 2007 American Shakespeare Center (ASC) production: in 3.3, when Claudius attempts to pray, Ben Curns, who played Hamlet, directed his question "And shall I kill him now?" to one of the students sitting on one of the gallant stools on the stage. In Shakespeare's time some audience members actually sat on stools onstage during performances, and the ASC recreates this in their Blackfriars Playhouse. Cohen (2019) explains that "the young man, quite visibly and emphatically nodded gravely. As the audience laughed, Curns took seriously the young man's answer . . . and added . . . 'When he is purging of his soul?' The young man nodded again. Curns turned the next clause to another question: 'making his way for heaven?,' and the young man said quite audibly, 'He's got to die.' Again, before the boy's vocalized response could disrupt the moment, Curns quickly argued Hamlet's case: 'This is a benefit / And not revenge.' Then Curns said 'No,' as if he were finally rejecting the young man's advice" (175). Cohen summarizes, "In this moment Curns forced the production as near to improv as possible without changing the words. He was relying not on the text as it is set in a film or on a page but as an actor can make it work in a theater" (176). Such practice happens often at the ASC. I recall seeing an ASC production of *Midsummer* where a young boy, about ten, sat upon one of the gallant stools as well. When Puck was trying to remedy his error in act 4 and put the love potion on the sleeping Lysander's eyes, he looked to the boy for help as to which of the two men was Demetrius. The boy pointed and said, "That one," helping prevent Puck from applying the flower juice to the wrong Athenian again.

In a similar moment, I recall a 2016 Globe performance of *Macbeth* in London, where I stood in the yard, elbows on the stage, and where I could not see behind me as the murderers entered through the audience to kill Banquo. One put his hands on both my shoulders to make me move so he could leap to the stage. I did so. Seconds later, he had killed Banquo and nearly killed Fleance too. It's a jarring feeling in that space, even if it is not real, to have been touched by a man who moments later commits a murder before your eyes.

4. The idea of teaching Shakespeare through performance-based methods—having the students think about the play as a script, as actors would—is not new. Some of the earliest contributors to *English Journal* in the first decade of the twentieth century suggested such strategies (Haughey 2012, 60–66). Performance-based methods became popular in the 1970s, 1980s, and 1990s through the work of scholar-educators such as David Bevington, Rex Gibson, Robert Hapgood, and numerous others. Peggy O'Brien led a series of summer teacher workshops at the Folger Shakespeare Library beginning in the late 1980s, which culminated in the *Shakespeare Set Free* series,

three books that outline performance- and language-based units that have been the gold standard for decades and remain popular in revised editions; the second of these, first released in 1994 and then in revised form in 2006, addresses *Hamlet* and *1 Henry IV*. In the current century, many teachers have built on this performance tradition. Ralph Alan Cohen ([2006] 2018) makes the case for teaching Shakespeare through performance in *ShakesFear and How to Cure It: A Complete Handbook for Teachers*: "Take it apart and play with it in your classroom, secure in the knowledge that your class's irreverent handling of the play is perfectly in keeping with Shakespeare's process *and* with the best contemporary critical theory" (15). Edward Rocklin (2005), in *Performance Approaches to Teaching Shakespeare*, offers performance-based strategies for teaching *Taming of the Shrew*, *Richard III*, and *Hamlet*; he eloquently explains, "Just as the dramatic script is the actor's cue for invention, so too when we teach Shakespeare's plays we can design our own pedagogic scripts to offer our students cues for invention in the classroom" (363). Mary Dakin Ellen (2009), who participated in the Folger workshops and later wrote *Reading Shakespeare with Young Adults* and *Reading Shakespeare Film First*, both rooted in performance-based methods, provides useful strategies and lessons. More recently, Kevin Long and Mary T. Christel (2019) outline a performance-based method for teachers called the *Folio* technique, a name which they credit to Barbara Gaines (197). Their method teaches students to analyze language clues from the First Folio (65–89). The list of performance-based teachers is long—too long to properly credit here.

5. Performance-based approaches, while effective, are not the be-all and end-all for teaching Shakespeare; they are just one set of tools in a teacher toolbox: Thompson and Turchi (2016) explain that, in teaching Shakespeare in the twenty-first century, "theatre-based classroom techniques . . . are only one dimension of the active approaches appropriate for advanced learners" (2). Based on work in New Media Literacies by Henry Jenkins and James Gee, they outline four pedagogical frameworks for teaching Shakespeare that encapsulate but extend beyond performance-based methods: (1) "participation in informal learning communities," (2) "explicit explorations of identity," (3) "divergent paths to knowledge," and (4) "innovative performances of their knowledge" (3–6). Wendy Beth Hyman and Hillary Eklund (2019) recently edited a collection of essays, *Teaching Social Justice through Shakespeare: Why Renaissance Literature Matters Now*, that builds on this type of thinking: "Shakespeare perhaps more than any other literary figure, has been trotted out as a symbol of white cultural supremacy. It [is] incumbent upon us to call out and correct this dangerous lie . . . insists instead on the centrality of literary and humanistic studies to fostering the prudent discernment required for civic participation" (2–3). Though limiting such theoretical discussion to the endnotes—which keeps my writing style in the actual chapters more fluid and approachable—my intention is that the activities in my book form a praxis that also aligns with and builds upon the frameworks Thompson and Turchi have established.

Acknowledgments

There are so many people to acknowledge that writing an acknowledgment becomes a necessary albeit infeasible impossibility. Years ago, when I taught middle and high school, I was always searching out new and better methods, and now, as I work to prepare future teachers, I emphasize that our best teachers take the great ideas they see and make them their own. I still follow that advice. Every insight or teaching strategy I've ever employed is rooted in an exchange with a colleague or student. Some of these start in the great books on teaching, and my endnotes hopefully point to some of those. But most come from my experiences in a classroom. All the best teaching (and learning too) weaves and tangles itself into a single pedagogical fabric, making it nearly impossible, some twenty years into a teaching career, to distinguish where any one thread started.

With that said, these two pages will prove my attempt to recall some of those early inspirations that were influential in instilling in me a love of Shakespeare without which this book would never have been written: Sharon Whitehill, at Grand Valley State, who fanned a spark into a flame when she took us out to read *Midsummer* in the Shakespeare Gardens; Grace Tiffany, who opened to me the world of graduate-level Shakespeare study; Tony Ellis, whose dedication to my work and success meant more to me than I ever got a chance to tell him; Edward Rocklin, who took me under his wing at my first-ever Shakespeare Association of America (SAA) annual meeting and has mentored me ever since; and perhaps most of all of these, Allen Webb, my dissertation advisor, who became something of a father to me, and who taught me far more than just about Shakespeare.

I also extend a hearty thanks to my many colleagues in the SAA and the National Council of Teachers of English (NCTE), who all continue to inspire in every annual meeting and in the interactions between them. Those two organizations and the many friendships formed through them have inspired me, enriching my intellectual life in countless ways. I also thank my colleagues in the Language, Literature, and Writing Department at Northwest

Missouri State University for providing a collaborative and nurturing academic home in which I could do this work. I owe particular thanks to Heather Hill for providing feedback on concepts of transfer in my writing prompts and to Jenny Rytting for taking the time to read early drafts and catch some errors that had made their way into my thinking and writing.

And no acknowledgment page is complete without ending with thanks given to the family and friends who helped see a project through. I owe special thanks to Harry Peers for reading drafts of my work and providing feedback. I am indebted to my daughters, Ryan and Dakotah, for their patience and love. Dakotah let me include some of her art in the book, and you will see her handwriting in several of the student exemplars. She spent hours putting those together. And countless thanks, too, go to my partner, Brandy Haughey, for our endless conversations about teaching, which is just one ongoing, larger conversation that takes just brief pauses for work and sleep; without her, this book would still be half formed in my mind, not in print. She is the love of my life, but she is also my daily intellectual sounding board. There's probably not a single important thought I've had in our twenty-four years of marriage that didn't originate from one of our conversations in some way.

Chapter 1

"I Could a Tale Unfold"
Telling a Good Ghost Story, Bard-Style

One of the joys of teaching *Hamlet* is that, at its core, it is a ghost story, and most students—and most teachers too, for that matter—love a good ghost story. The play's opening words, "Who's there?" establish a foreboding tone: something is wrong. Denmark is on edge (1.1.1). It is frigid cold. It is the middle of the night. And above all, the two guards—who speak the play's first lines but never appear again after the first act—have seen the ghost of the former king silently roaming the castle walls.

By the time Hamlet meets his father's ghost, audiences have already learned that Hamlet's father, who was also (somewhat confusingly) named Hamlet, had died just shortly before the start of the play. His wife was Gertrude (and young Hamlet's mother), and she married again immediately after her husband's death. Even worse, she married her brother-in-law, the young Hamlet's uncle. If that sounds just a bit icky to students, they are already well on their way to getting inside Hamlet's head. Ask students to imagine how they would feel if their mother married one of their uncles. The king's top advisor, Polonius, is convinced that Hamlet's melancholy is rooted in his love for Ophelia, though, who is Polonius's daughter, but the truth is that Hamlet grieves for his father and is disgusted with his mother's marriage.

When Hamlet meets his father's ghost, he is unsure whether it is his actual father or, rather, a "goblin damned" bent on tricking him into committing regicide (1.4.44). To wrongly murder his uncle would damn his own soul to hell. At the same time, if the ghost is telling the truth, then ignoring his call for revenge would leave his father unavenged and Denmark in the hands of a fratricidal murderer. It is a moral conundrum that Hamlet will wrestle with until act 3.

Shakespeare can be confusing to first-time readers. Thus, the first goal of a good *Hamlet* unit should be to establish these essential plot elements early. It is a Shakespearean tragedy, and all the major characters (except Horatio) will be dead by the end; there's no need to keep that spoiler a secret from

Chapter 1

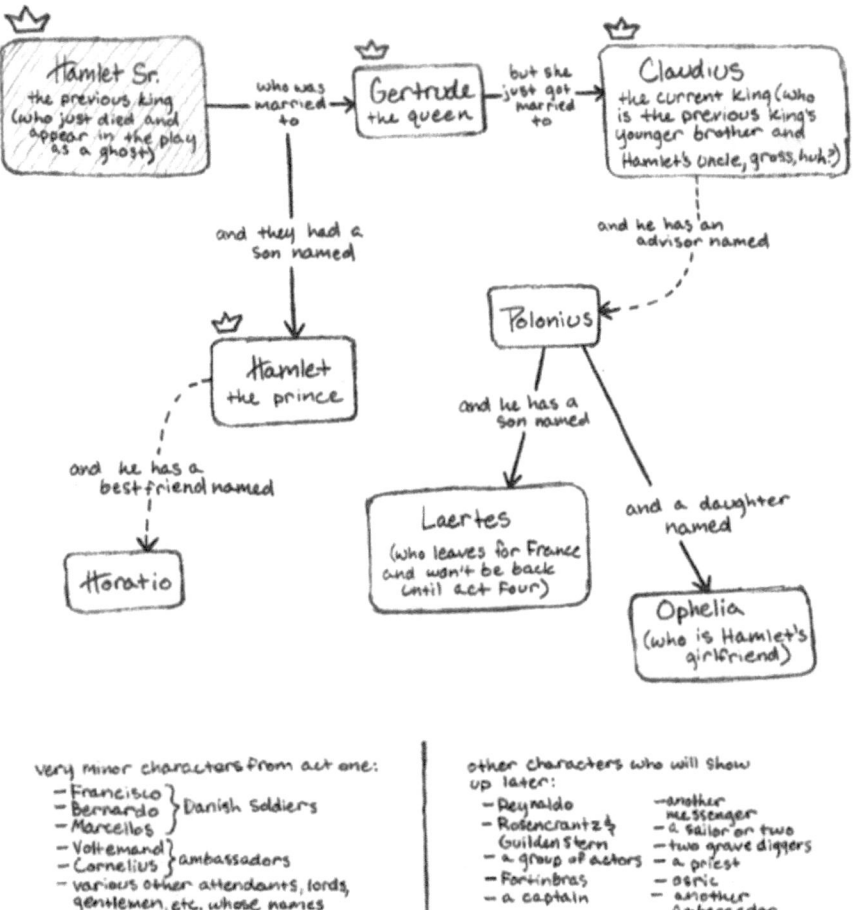

Figure 1.1: An example of student notes from an introductory Hamlet lesson maps out its eight main characters and lists its several minor characters.

students. Once teachers have clarified the play's story elements in their first lesson—spending ten to fifteen minutes drawing a character diagram on their board and walking students through the eight main characters—they can use the bulk of the unit to delve deeper into Shakespeare's rich language and poetry. If students know those eight characters and their relationships, they have a firm foundation for study.

This first chapter provides learning objectives for the play's first act that teachers can use in their planning, suggestions for reading aloud as a class, strategies for teaching second-person familiar pronouns (though, thee, thy, thine, ye), a series of discussion questions and writing prompts, and a culminating project in which students write their own ghost story inspired by Shakespeare's original.

In this closing activity, students will approach the play as a creative writer would, blending their ideas into Shakespeare's mold. Teachers need not follow every activity precisely as laid out but, rather, are encouraged to let these ideas inspire them as they adapt them to their students' needs.

ACT ONE LEARNING OBJECTIVES

1. Students will recall *Hamlet's* basic plot, setting, and character elements.
2. Students will describe how Shakespeare's second-person familiar pronouns (thou, thee, thy, thine, and ye) function in his writing and analyze how their use affects meaning.
3. Students will compare film versions of the ghost scenes (1.4 and 1.5) from *Hamlet* and evaluate how the productions' choices affect their reading(s) of the scenes.
4. Students will, like a creative writer, analyze the structure of the ghost story elements of the opening ghost scenes of *Hamlet* and then synthesize those elements in writing their own ghost story inspired by act 1 of *Hamlet*.

READING SCENES OF ACT 1 TOGETHER

Most students will benefit from reading the play aloud together in class. It is a good use of class time, as few students will successfully read the play independently.[1] It is essential that teachers set a relatively quick pace while reading aloud. Spend some time providing definitions for challenging vocabulary, but emphasize that students need not understand every line or word. It is okay if words or even whole passages elude them.

This is true for teachers too. Many brilliant Shakespeare scholars have spent their whole careers attempting to untangle some of the complexities of *Hamlet* without ever arriving at any definitive answer. That is okay; the joy is in the untangling. It is rather far more critical that, on their first (or even second or third) reading of *Hamlet*, students have a positive experience with the play than that they tackle every nuance of language and meaning. There will be time in the future to return for deeper study. The study of *Hamlet* is a marathon, not a sprint.

With that said, energize the time spent in class reading, and strive to make it pleasurable. Have students read on their feet. Have them read either from their devices or easily handled single-play paperbacks, not from heavy anthologies. Or make photocopy scripts from open-source, online sources. Make sure they read from something they can hold open in one hand. Free their bodies (and at least one hand) to move with the action.

Instruct students as they read to keep track of which characters are on stage together in a scene, when and where they enter and exit, who they are talking to, and what tone of voice and volume they would use to deliver their lines. Ask them about what changes when they try an opposite approach; instead of being fearful of the ghost, for example, what happens if their tone expresses confidence? Try both versions aloud, and decide which best suits the lines as a class. Direct students to think about the play as though they might someday be actors preparing to perform it before an audience.

Because *Hamlet* is a long play—performing the modern text on stage without any cuts takes four hours—reading it in its entirety aloud together as a whole class is not feasible in most classrooms. Unlike a play such as *Macbeth*, which has almost half as many lines, one of the difficulties of teaching *Hamlet* can be its unwieldy girth. To keep the pace of the unit, teachers should select some scenes (or parts of scenes)[2] to read aloud and some to summarize for students.[3] This will vary depending on the needs of the class.

One strategy for act 1 is to emphasize Hamlet's interactions with his father's ghost, which then will prepare students for the act 1 culminating project at the end of the chapter:

- 1.1: The play's first scene is short and essential reading to any study of *Hamlet*. Emphasize how Francisco's "Tis bitter cold" helps establish the setting. What other lines and words reveal details about the setting and mood? Have students brainstorm ways the silent ghost could be portrayed and how his appearance changes how the other characters deliver their lines.
- 1.2: The play's second scene introduces many of the play's main characters: Claudius, the (new) king; Gertrude (the old and new) queen; Polonius, the king's advisor; Laertes, his son; and the young Prince Hamlet. Spend time reading the first half, but Hamlet's lovely soliloquy in the middle need not be scrutinized too closely in a first reading; rather, gloss over it quickly—Hamlet is melancholy about his father's death—and save its deeper analysis until later. Likewise, summarize Horatio's revelation of the ghost for your in-class reading.
- 1.3: The third scene features Polonius and his children, Laertes and Ophelia. Emphasize Laertes's advice to Ophelia in its first fifty lines;

what do these tell us about the brother and sister? Polonius's advice to Laertes in the second half can be read in at least three different ways: one, as sage advice from a wise parent to his child; another, as empty maxims from a befuddled old man spouting nonsense; and yet another, as the plotting of a conniving toady who cares more about his position at court than his children. If time allows, ask students to evaluate if they think his life advice to his son is valuable.
- 1.4: The last two scenes of act 1 are essential in-class reading in establishing the play as a proper ghost story. In the fourth scene, emphasize the second half. Why does Horatio try to stop Hamlet from leaving alone with the ghost? What does it say about Hamlet that he insists on being allowed to talk to the ghost alone? What tension does it create for an audience when he does? What must happen on stage to achieve this tension?
- 1.5: Shakespeare's ghost story comes together in the fifth scene. It is essential that students can recall the details of the king's murder: his brother secretly pours poison in his ear while he sleeps in the garden, but nobody else knows the truth except young Hamlet now. Likewise, it is essential that students realize Hamlet cannot be sure if the ghost really is his father or is lying to him. Make a list of characteristics Shakespeare incorporates into his ghost story for students to use later in the culminating project, when they write their own.
  - Special note for 1.5—Pay particular attention to Hamlet's last two speeches in act 1; he is telling Horatio and the others that he will "put an antic disposition on"—that is, that he will pretend to be mad for the rest of the play but that he is not (1.5.192). Many students (and some teachers) get confused over whether Hamlet is actually mad or just pretending, but he makes it clear in these lines that he is only pretending. Students must understand this detail.

SOME NOTES ON SHAKESPEARE'S LANGUAGE: SECOND-PERSON FAMILIAR PRONOUNS

As students read through *Hamlet*, teachers should provide guidance for tackling Shakespeare's challenging language. In each chapter a section like this one will provide insight into one aspect of teaching Shakespeare's language, with specific examples from the corresponding act. These language skills will build upon one another as the book progresses and are integrated into activities, discussion questions, writing prompts, and culminating projects.

For act 1, begin by teaching students to translate, in their minds, Shakespeare's singular, familiar second-person pronouns (thou, thee, thy,

Table 1.1

		First-Person Pronouns	Second-Person Pronouns		Third-Person Pronouns
			Familiar	Formal	
as the *subject* of the sentence	singular	I	thou	you	he / she / it
	plural	we	thou	you	they
as the *object* of the sentence	singular	me	thee	you	him / her / it
	plural	us	you	you	them
as a *possessive adjective*	singular	my / mine*	thy / thine*	your	his / her / its
	plural	our	your	your	their
as a *possessive pronoun*	singular	mine	thine	yours	his / hers / its
	plural	ours	yours	yours	theirs

* Substitute forms are used before a noun beginning with a vowel.

thine) to their more recognizable formal counterparts (you, your, yours). The grammatical terms initially make the concepts seem much more complex than they are. If students know, though, that these old-fashioned-sounding pronouns in today's English mean "you," "your," and "yours" and can translate them in their minds as they read, they will find Shakespeare's pronouns easier to grasp than before. And that is an excellent first step.

When reading aloud, teach students to speak Shakespeare's actual words and get comfortable with Shakespeare's exact language but to make the substitution internally in their minds. The point is not to paraphrase Shakespeare's language into something more modern-sounding—though that sometimes, too, can be a helpful activity in their study of *Hamlet*—but, rather, to make these pronouns feel more natural for students and to get them used to saying them aloud. Even if students never puzzle out the more subtle (and fun) complexities of familiar and formal pronouns, they will have already taken significant strides to simplify a challenging concept for many students.

For more advanced study, though, teachers can delve into how pronouns were in flux in Shakespeare's time. In the years just before Shakespeare, familiar second-person pronouns were part of everyday speech, but in Shakespeare's time, they were already fading from use. Shakespeare continued to use them in his plays, though, for the nuance they gave to his characters' speeches. Understanding how they work adds an extra layer to understanding his plays.

Familiar second-person pronouns (thou, ye, thee, thy, thine) are informal. When they were used in English, they were directed toward people of lower rank, such as a king speaking to a subject. They also, though, could carry a familial intimacy—words spoken between family members or even between lovers. Ironically, though, they can also be insults. They are like nicknames today; with family and friends, nicknames can express tenderness, but when hurled at a stranger or enemy, they can be rude.

Teachers should also know that the familiar second-person pronouns above are used only when a person is talking to an individual, not to a group. There is no plural version of the familiar second-person pronoun. That makes sense, though: a necessary formality takes over when somebody must address a group. Familiarity is reserved for words directed at an individual.

On the other hand, the formal second-person pronouns (you, your, yours) carry a weight of formality. They express respect. In their initial reading of a scene, students in their minds should exchange familiar pronouns for formal ones, but once they have established the primary context of a scene, they can analyze what characters' pronoun choices reveal about their relationships with other characters. And this is where understanding the pronouns gets interesting.

For example, Hamlet uses formal pronouns with Horatio and Marcellus, indicating some distance between the three, but when the ghost of his father appears, Hamlet switches to familiar pronouns:

> Be *thou* a spirit of health or goblin damned,
> Bring with *thee* airs from heaven or blasts from hell,
> Be *thy* intents wicked or charitable,
> *Thou* com'st in such a questionable shape
> That I will speak to *thee*. I'll call *thee* "Hamlet." (1.4.44–49, emphases added)

Hamlet's change in pronoun use suggests a change in tone, a familiarity with the ghost that has been lacking with the other characters. It is the first time in the play, in fact, that Hamlet employs familiar pronouns; even with his mother earlier, he had opted for formal pronouns. One possible reading of this shift is that Hamlet genuinely believes the ghost from the beginning to be his father and, as a family member, one to be addressed with familiar second-person pronouns. Another potential reading, though, is that Hamlet, as a royal prince, sees the ghost as one beneath his station, one to be addressed as a subject. Reinforcing this second reading, note that Horatio, a courtier, had also used formal pronouns in the first scene when with the guards and up until the ghost appeared. Then he, too, reverted to familiar pronouns.

There is no definitive answer as to which of the two is correct. Both could be. There are other possible ways as well to interpret these shifts, and teachers can build on these competing interpretations through performative reading activities with their students. For example, have students take turns reading the whole passage in pairs when Hamlet first meets the ghost (1.4.43–62). First, have them together highlight all the second-person pronouns in the passage. Then, have one student read aloud, emphasizing each highlighted pronoun with a touch of familial tenderness to create a Hamlet who immediately believes the ghost to be his father.

Next, have the second student reread the passage but, this time, giving each pronoun an air of superiority. Instruct them to craft a Hamlet who believes the ghost is not his father but an inferior, one that the royal prince Hamlet sees as a subject. Afterward, have students evaluate which reading they prefer. Analyze how the decision in performance would affect the tension between the living characters and the ghost as the act proceeds. Readers can entertain both readings, but in performance, actors must decide on a single reading that they will privilege in their production.

There are other examples from earlier in act 1 that teachers can have students read aloud and analyze Shakespeare's pronoun choices. Choose one or more of the following scenes, and have students, in pairs, highlight familiar pronouns in one color and formal pronouns in another and then read them aloud together:

- In 1.1 have students analyze which pronouns Horatio and the guards use with each other and with the ghost; the pattern is like Hamlet's pronoun use before and after meeting the ghost.
- In 1.2 have students analyze Claudius's speeches first to Laertes and then to Hamlet. He switches from formal to familiar with Laertes, suggesting a switch to tenderness as he gives him permission to leave for France. With Hamlet, though, he uses only formal pronouns.
- In 1.3 have students analyze Polonius's conversations with his two children. With Laertes, he uses familiar pronouns, but with Ophelia, he uses formal pronouns, suggesting a tenderness with his son that he withholds from his daughter.

It is worth noting to students that it is an anomaly that English lost its familiar second-person pronouns. Many world languages still retain them alongside their formal second-person pronouns. Spanish, for example, still has both: *tú* and *tus* (familiar) and *usted* and *ustedes* (formal). So do the other Romance languages (French, Italian, Portuguese, and Romanian), as well as the Slavic languages (Russian, Ukrainian, Polish, Czech, etc.). Greek and Japanese also have second-person familiar pronouns. Students who speak these languages may already be quite comfortable with the concept of familiar second-person pronouns, and teachers should draw on this expertise where available and appropriate.[4]

A QUICK NOTE ABOUT THE ROYAL WE

In Shakespeare's plays, kings often use plural first-person pronouns instead of singular ones: "we" instead of "I," "our" instead of "my," and so forth. This is known as the *royal we*, and it has long been the linguistic practice of kings and monarchs in real life too. Claudius opens the play's second scene with the royal we:

> Though yet of Hamlet *our* dear brother's death
> The memory be green, and that it *us* befitted
> To bear *our* hearts in grief, and *our* whole kingdom . . .
> That *we* with wisest sorrow think on him
> Together with remembrance of *ourselves*. (1.2.1–7, emphasis added)

The king is saying that he bears the whole kingdom's sadness but also remembers the need to take care of pressing matters of state too. Since the office of the monarch encompassed the entire realm, Shakespeare's kings (just like real kings did) use plural first-person personal pronouns for themselves. They speak not just for themselves but for their entire kingdom. Take a few minutes to explain this to students; once they get used to it, it is not difficult to translate the plural to the singular in their minds and recognize the extra formality and weight it adds to the speech of kings.[5]

ANTICIPATORY SET ACTIVITY: MAPPING DENMARK AND EUROPE

Hamlet takes place entirely in Denmark—specifically, in Elsinore, which is the Anglicized name for Helsingør. This city still exists today and is less than an hour's train ride north of Copenhagen. Note how similar Elsinore and Helsingør sound when said aloud. In Shakespeare's time Helsingør was a thriving trade city that governed the lucrative Øresund Strait, the closest point between Denmark and Sweden.

Danish royal coffers grew rich from the levy charged to pass through the straight, and Danish merchants grew rich from the many ships required to make port there to pay it. While Shakespeare never visited Helsingør or its Kronborg Castle, which also still stands tall today, he would have heard stories of the place from merchants who had seen it, stories that inspired him to use it as his backdrop for *Hamlet*.

For a warmup activity, have students explore the region in Google Maps to answer the following questions:

- How close is Elsinore/Helsingør to Sweden? Is it closer to Sweden or the Danish capital, Copenhagen?
- How far is it from France (where Laertes attends university)? How long would it take to sail to France on a ship?
- How far is it from Wittenberg (where Hamlet and Horatio attended university)? How long would you guess it would take to travel there?
- How far is it from Norway (to where the king, in 1.2, has sent ambassadors regarding the Fortinbras matter)?

In act 4, teachers can revisit the mapping activity, having students do a follow-up anticipatory set activity for when Hamlet is sent away to England. How far is Elsinore/Helsingør from England? How long would it take to get there, or partially there, and then back? How far would it be for Fortinbras to trek from Norway, across Denmark, to get to Poland?

Note: While a modern map conveys a sense of the places mentioned in *Hamlet*, be sure to teach students that the borders have shifted since Shakespeare's time. The borders of England, Denmark, Norway, and France have shifted only a little, but Germany (where Wittenberg is located) was not yet a unified nation when Shakespeare wrote *Hamlet*.

ACT 1 BIBLICAL AND CLASSICAL REFERENCES: PURGATORY

Hamlet is filled with biblical and classical references, and while there are far more than can be discussed in this volume, each chapter will have a brief section that points out a reference or two that are helpful in teaching the play. Though it is certainly not necessary to master every such reference—even the greatest scholars have been left puzzled trying to riddle out some of their complexities—some knowledge of these can enrich both teachers' and students' understanding of *Hamlet*.[6]

One such biblical concept is purgatory. Purgatory is a place where souls go after they die to be purged of sin before they can enter heaven. It is not hell. Souls in hell had no hope of redemption, but souls in purgatory all eventually get to go to heaven, though some must spend many years—some, even thousands of years—suffering hell-like torments before being allowed to move on.

By Shakespeare's time the Protestant Reformation had formally removed the idea of a Catholic purgatory from the official English Church doctrine. That process had started decades before Shakespeare was born, when Henry VIII split from the Catholic Church, but it was a complicated and messy process. In Shakespeare's youth Queen Mary I, daughter of Henry VIII, had reintroduced Catholicism as the state religion for her five-year reign. And when Elizabeth I, another daughter of Henry VIII, took her place, she made England Protestant again. It was whiplash. The old belief, though, in a place between heaven and hell lingered still, as can be seen in Horatio's lines to the ghost in the first scene of the play:

> If there be any good thing to be done
> That may to thee do ease and grace to me,
> Speak to me. (1.1.142–44)

Catholic doctrine stated that those still alive could affect how long a soul was sentenced to purgatory. Prayer and gifts to the Church on behalf of a soul could reduce their suffering. If a person loved their ancestor enough and had enough money, they could help them buy their way out of purgatory. Horatio is making a very Catholic-like offer to the ghost in offering to help ease his pain.

The ghost reaffirms to Hamlet later in act 1 that he indeed does spend his days suffering in a purgatory-like place but that he cannot reveal its torments to the living:

> And for the day confined to fast in fires
> Till the foul crimes done in my days of nature
> Are burned and purged away. But that I am forbid
> To tell the secrets of my prison house,
> I could a tale unfold. (1.5.16–20)

That Shakespeare creates a ghost that spends his days in purgatory speaks to the underlying, religious tension in England between Protestants and Catholics at the end of the sixteenth century. That tension cannot be understated. In Shakespeare's time it was a crime to practice Catholicism, and many suffered gory executions for their faith. That tension had permeated English life for some hundred years before *Hamlet*, and it would continue to do so for centuries afterward. Echoes of it still reverberate in everyday life today throughout the United Kingdom and Ireland.

Students need not know all the details of that history to enjoy *Hamlet*, but teachers should have at least a rudimentary knowledge of it, and students should have a definition of purgatory in their minds as they read the ghost's lines.[7] Such details are a fascinating study of their own, both in terms of Shakespeare and how that history—not just in England but across the continent—affected how people believed and lived the past six hundred years, of which *Hamlet* is but one artifact.

INCORPORATING FILM: THE GHOST ON SCREEN

This book draws on six excellent film versions of *Hamlet*, and teachers ideally should attain classroom access to all of these for their teaching. Activities throughout the book are based on these six, but they can be easily adapted to others. At the back of the book, in the teacher resources appendix, the six are described in more detail, though teachers should update this list based on what is available to them or as new productions are released.

One premise of this book is that it is an inefficient use of classroom time for students to spend two or three class periods just watching a film from beginning to end; instead, teachers should incorporate short scenes from multiple films, preferably at least two film versions of the same scenes, throughout their lessons.[8] Students do not need to see any one film in its entirety but, rather, need appropriate scaffolding interspersed throughout as they balance watching and reading. It is also vital that students do not think of any single *Hamlet* performance as definitive, whether it be stage or film, but rather that they learn that *Hamlet* has and will continue to manifest itself in countless interpretations.

These sometimes even compete and disagree with one another, such as in the activity earlier in the chapter, when students differently emphasized familiar pronouns to craft different performative interpretations. This is one of the beauties of Shakespearean performance: that new modes will always exist through which students can make its language their own. To this end, five of the six are English-language films, but the 1964 Russian-language Kosintsev *Hamlet* is also included to provide a global perspective, as critics largely agree it is one of the finest *Hamlet* films ever made. It is one every *Hamlet* lover should see.[9]

Another premise of this book is that students see more in a film when they are assigned specific tasks to complete while watching. With that said, have students analyze the ghost in one or more film versions of 1.4 and 1.5. Such analysis is an ideal starting point for explaining how much creativity a particular performance can insert into a production. Make groups of four and assign the following roles:

- *Casting and costumes director:* Pay special attention to the choices regarding the actors who play Hamlet and the ghost. How old are they? What costumes do they wear? What does the production do regarding the ghost's voice? Does the production make the ghost seem like a regular person, or does it do something special to give it a ghost-like quality? How does Hamlet react to the ghost's news?
- *Set and props designer:* Pay special attention to the production's decisions regarding the sets and props. Where are Hamlet and the ghost when

they talk? What is the mood? Are there any special props? Are there flashbacks, and if so, what special sets and props are used for these?
- *Special effects manager:* Pay attention to how the production handles special effects. Remember to consider when a production was filmed; some special effects seem lackluster by today's standards but were groundbreaking in their own time. How does the production give Shakespeare's ghost story a supernatural vibe? How does the ghost appear and disappear?
- *Camera operator:* Pay special attention to the camera angles the production utilizes. How much of the scene is built on close-ups? How much on long- and mid-distance shots? Does the camera move or stay still throughout the scene? From whose gaze do viewers see the scene?
  - *Note on assigning the roles:* Print slips for the four roles, and distribute them to students. To randomize groups, write the group number on the back of each slip, and then shuffle the slips before passing them out to students. (Or create the groups yourself based on class needs.)

Watch one film version of 1.4 and 1.5 to start, give five minutes for discussion, and then watch the same scenes from one of the other films. Afterward, lead a classroom discussion comparing the two versions based on the questions embedded in the watching roles above. Start and end times are listed in table 1.2.

Table 1.2

Laurence Olivier as Hamlet; John Gielgud as Ghost (1948)	Act 1.4 begins at **28:45**, 1.5 ends at **43:00** (14 minutes)
Innokentiy Smoktunovskiy as Hamlet; Ghost uncredited (Russian-language film with English captions, 1964)	Act 1.4 begins at **20:10**, 1.5 ends at **28:00** (8 minutes)
Mel Gibson as Hamlet; Paul Scofield as Ghost (1990)	Act 1.4 begins at **22:40**, ends at **36:00** (14 minutes)
Kenneth Branagh as Hamlet; Brian Blessed as Ghost (1996)	Act 1.4 begins at **34:55**, 1.5 ends at **51:15** (16 minutes, includes a brief suggestive scene near the beginning, with Claudius and Gertrude in the bedroom; this can be skipped by instead starting at **36:00**)
Ethan Hawke as Hamlet; Sam Shepard as Ghost (2000)	Act 1.4 begins at **20:30**, ends at **27:30** (7 minutes, makes some significant cuts and rearrangements to the script)
David Tennant as Hamlet; Patrick Stewart as Ghost (2009)	Act 1.4 begins at **28:15**, and 1.5 ends at **43:05** (15 minutes)

DISCUSSION QUESTIONS AND WRITING PROMPTS

Each chapter will include discussion questions and writing prompts that teachers can adapt to their needs. Depending on class structure and needs, these can be used to guide whole-class or small group discussions or as writing prompts for quick writes or longer essay questions:

1. Why is the ghost silent in 1.1 but not in 1.5? Why does he speak only with Hamlet and not with anybody else? What could this mean for an actor playing the ghost?
2. Claudius permits Laertes to return to university in France but does not allow his nephew Hamlet to return to university at Wittenberg (in Germany). Why do you think Claudius wants Hamlet to stay at home in Elsinore in Denmark? What purpose does it serve him to keep his nephew close?
3. Analyze the advice that Polonius gives to Laertes in 1.3. Reread it. Go through the list of ten "precepts" Polonius offers his son; do you think they are good advice? Is it how you think you should live your life? Pick one of the ten, and analyze it carefully; then explain why you think it is good or bad advice.
4. Hamlet does not know whether or not to believe the ghost is his father. What would be the consequences if the ghost were not his father but some evil spirit tricking him into committing regicide?
5. In 1.4 and 1.5, Hamlet uses formal pronouns (you, your, yours) with Horatio, Barnardo, and Marcellus, but when he speaks alone with his father, he switches to familiar pronouns (thee, thy, thine). What is the significance of this change? What does it suggest about the relationship between Hamlet and his father?

ACT 1 CULMINATING PROJECT: WORKING THROUGH THE PLAY LIKE A CREATIVE WRITER

In this project students will analyze how Shakespeare constructs his own ghost story in the first act of *Hamlet* and then draft and edit their own ghost story from his model.[10] Creative writers have long tinkered with the *Hamlet* story to turn it into something new.[11] Many students will be familiar, for example, with Disney's *The Lion King*—both the animated and live-action versions—in which the young prince Simba (the Hamlet character) witnesses his uncle, Scar (the Claudius character), murder his father, Mufasa (the ghost character). Then he spends the remainder of the film brooding and searching within himself for what to do next. It is one of many works in a long tradition of riffing on *Hamlet*.

Over the past four centuries, countless other movies, novels, and plays have borrowed from Shakespeare's masterpiece. Many recent young adult authors in the twenty-first century likewise have found inspiration in *Hamlet*, including books like *Monster*; *The Steep and Thorny Way*; *Forgive Me, Leonard Peacock*; and *Ophelia* (see the appendix at the back of the book for a brief synopsis of each of these). It is not a tradition, though, reserved only for published authors; it is also a tradition in which students can and should take part.

First, brainstorm a list of the characteristics that Shakespeare incorporates into his narration that students will then use as guidelines for constructing their own ghost stories. That list might include the following:

- A group of three minor characters on a cold night, shortly after midnight, see a ghost and decide to alert the main character.
- The main character, who comes from an elevated socioeconomic status, is related in some way to the ghost.
- On a second night, the main character is tempted away by the ghost and the minor characters try unsuccessfully to prevent the main character from speaking alone with the ghost.
- The ghost character reveals something awful and troubling, and the main character decides to believe it.
- It is not entirely clear whether the ghost is really who it claims to be or even if it is telling the truth

The class should compile some five to ten such characteristics together, either in small groups or together as a whole class (with guidance from the teacher), then students individually choose from which elements they will borrow for their own writing; they need not incorporate every element from the list, but they can pick and choose as they make their story their own creation. Shakespeare's inspiration should echo in their writing but leave them enough room to remain playful. They can set the scene in modern or historical times, making it about people they know or fictional characters they have created.

The writing project can be flexible. If time is tight, students can draft a paragraph-length version in class in fifteen to twenty minutes, which they then share in small groups with a classmate or two. If more time is available, students can take multiple classes to expand this initial draft and revise it into a full three-to-five-page short story. Adapt the project based on students' needs.

For an extra challenge, have students revise their final drafts and convert some second-person pronouns from formal (you, your, yours) to familiar (thee, though, thine) as appropriate. In Shakespeare's original, Hamlet uses formal second-person pronouns with Horatio and the guards, but when he is alone with the ghost, he reverts to familiar second-person pronouns, as would be appropriate for a father and a son speaking alone. Instruct students to adhere to this same usage, having their main characters use formal pronouns before the ghost appears, then familiar when they are alone with their ghost character. This will also provide extra practice in getting comfortable with these otherwise challenging pronouns.

REFLECTING ON WRITING

Good writing, like good teaching, requires reflective practice. Research has demonstrated that to transfer newfound writing skills into other writing domains, students need explicit instruction about how those skills can be used in other rhetorical situations.[12] Thus, each chapter's culminating project in this book will conclude with students reflecting on how they can apply what they have learned in other writing spaces.

For this assignment, instruct students to reflect on modeling creative writing from another writer's work. Ask them to think carefully about their writing process and how that process can be transferred to other kinds of writing they will be asked to do in the future:

> Reflect on how you wrote your ghost story. Which story elements from Shakespeare did you decide to build into your own story (a scene set on a cold night, a ghost that reveals a terrible secret, a family connection, not knowing whether or not to trust the ghost, etc.)? Which elements did you decide not to include? How did you decide? How does this work in other writing assignments? How do you decide which elements to include and which not to include? How can you use what you learned about writing from this assignment in your future writing?

Brainstorm together aloud as a whole group for five to ten minutes. Then have students write silently, without worrying about spelling or punctuation, for five to ten more minutes. If time is short, have them sum up their ideas in just one sentence. If time is not short, follow up afterward with further discussion to close the activity.Figure 1.2: This example from the ghost story culminating project sets the action at a schoolyard basketball court in which the ghost of a student's father, who used to be the principal, emerges from the shadows.

> Manny dribbled the ball and took his shot. The ball flew over the hoop and beyond the court, crackling into the leafless hedge that bordered the school playground and the convenience mart. Sarah trotted after it across yellowing grass. Most of the trees had lost their leaves about a month ago, but the grass had persistently stayed green until last week. Now everything just seemed like it'd given up on whatever warmth of summer it had been clinging to.
>
> Sarah approached the hedge's shadows hesitantly, seeming unsure of what might be lurking in the shadows. She picked up the ball, lunged an impossible shot from behind the hoop, and airballed it. A breeze shivered in the darkness as the ball bounced across the asphalt to Phillip's feet at half-court. He glanced over his shoulder at her as she meandered back. School grounds were off-limits to students after dark but not to Manny. And by default, not to his friends either. Unlike on the streets, Manny could leverage his dad's protection here. Or at least he used to be able to.
>
> That had been one of the few perks of having a dad for a principal, and even though it was technically probably wrong, his dad had let him come here late with friends to play as long as he made sure it stayed secret. It'd started in middle school on the nights his dad worked late. He'd liked it better when Manny was close to him rather that out on the streets. And then even on nights he didn't work late, he'd trusted Manny to let him stay with his friends out on the courts. The hedges were high, and nobody ever knew.
>
> His dad used to be principal — before he died two months ago — and he'd set the security cameras not to record the school's two outdoor courts at night anymore. Nobody else knew that, though. At some point, someone would figure things out and end these midnight games.

Mrs. Clench, the new principal, had taken over his dad's job, and his office, and it seemed almost every other thing in his dad's life. Almost everything. Manny still had his dad's key fob to the school, though, and they hadn't deactivated his dad's code yet either. So this basketball court was still Manny's turf, one space that belonged just to him. To him, but to Sarah and Phillip too, and he wasn't going to surrender it to Mrs. Clench until he had to.

"You're sure you saw this thing? If this is all some joke, then so help me, you all are the worst friends ever." Manny still couldn't bring himself to imagine what they'd said was true. It didn't matter how long his dad had been gone, though; it still hung as fresh as if it'd been yesterday.

Phillip just nodded and kept looking around. Sarah's murmur assured Manny they were being real with him, "Yeah. Twice. Like we said. The two nights you were in Trenton." Manny had let them borrow the fob and play without him. It was his kingdom and his to share with his friends when he decided to.

Manny picked up Sarah's missed shot, dribbled deliberately toward the hoop, faked out an imaginary defender, and took an easy layup. Picking up his own shot, he tried to calm his nerves. There was thunder in the distance. "You think you'll get those new Jordans? They'll be cheaper on Black Friday."

Even sneaker talk didn't relax Phillip, though. He just muttered robotically, "Maybe. I get paid Wednesday."

"Yeah." Manny passed to him, but he just let it bounce off his elbow like he'd forgotten what you were supposed to do with a basketball.

There was a long pause, another distant roll of thunder, and then Phillip jumped back in fright. "There it is!" He pointed shakily toward the other side of the court, and there it was indeed. A figure had emerged out of the murk, a man, and he took one step toward them. Then he took a second and then a third, one foot methodically in front of the other. But then it stopped just under the hoop. And he just stared.

It wore his dad's blue blazer, the one mom had bought him last Christmas. She had bought him most of his clothes. It had his glasses too, the black, round ones. Its hair was salt and pepper. Everything about it has his dad's look. Even that half-smile his dad always wore when he gave Manny a hello. It had to be his dad. The ghost lifted its arm and motioned to Manny to follow him back into the school — that same half-smile easing Manny's fear — but as Manny stepped forward, Phillip grabbed his arm, "No. Don't go." It was a whisper. Phillip didn't want the ghost to hear, but he also feared for his best friend. It didn't feel right to let him go off alone with whatever this thing was.

"But it wants to talk with me! Let go! I swear, let go!" Manny raised his fist, and Phillip stepped back. He had never threatened anybody before, especially not Phillip or Sarah.

His dad waved at him again. "I'll go."

And he took one step forward but stopped. His dad waved to him once more. "I'll go." And this time, he said it loud enough so his dad could hear him from across the court. Manny walked deliberately, step by step, staring at the ghost's chest until he was a foot away. Then, he bit his lip and tilted his head up finally to look right into the ghost's face, and as he did so, the ghost slowly, so as not to startle him, put both his arms around Manny and pulled him in. It was the first hug Manny had allowed since the funeral. His dad's touch wasn't cold. I was warm. He breathed deeply. It was like the way his dad embraced him just before he'd told him about Grandma's cancer. It was exactly the same. And that's how Manny knew this was real.

"There's something I need to tell you son. Let's go into the school and talk."

Figure 1.2: This example from the ghost story culminating project sets the action at a schoolyard basketball court in which the ghost of a student's father, who used to be the principal, emerges from the shadows.

NOTES

1. Very few secondary students will successfully read *Hamlet* independently, and even many college readers will require significant in-class scaffolding. Mary Ellen Dakin (2009) emphasizes this point too: "By almost no means can Shakespeare be considered independent reading for young adults" (ix). Ayanna Thompson and Laura Turchi (2016) explain, "We believe that students should be given the plot and characters . . . that teachers can introduce the bare bones of the plot and allow students to have a starting place for recognizing who is who in the drama" (25).

2. Shakespeare did not divide his plays into acts; he divided them into scenes, and even these divisions were inconsistent: in *Hamlet*, Q1 and Q2 have no act and scene divisions, and the First Folio marks only 1.1, 1.2, 1.3, 2.1, and 2.2. Later editors divided each play into acts and scenes, which is convenient but can create artificial breaks that did not exist before (Dakin 2009, 88; Rocklin 2005, 262; also see textual notes from the *Riverside Shakespeare*). Russ McDonald suggests that readers should think of scenes as locations; the action remains in the same location for a scene and shifts to a new location for each new scene (quoted in Dakin 2009, 88).

Several teacher-scholars have suggested students work like editors in rethinking traditional act and scene divisions. Rex Gibson ([1998] 2016) suggests breaking Shakespeare into "sense units": these are "section[s] of language that comprises a thought, a coherent unit of dramatic language"; he then provides methods for having students work through a scene sense unit by sense unit (166–72). Edward Rocklin (2005) has students analyze the entire play for overarching arcs to create new divisions (262–66; he cites work from Hapgood, 96–131). Rocklin (2005) explains, "The point is not for students to discover some correct division. Rather, in redividing the play, they will discover new aspects of its interlocking patterns that are one source of its theatrical power" (264). Later he provides two activities in which students further subdivide individual scenes and speeches; in the first of these activities, they decide where the breaks should occur in *Hamlet*'s first 175 lines; students generally find some four to twelve such breaks. Later he has students divide Hamlet's first soliloquy into three or four units and analyze their results (286–90).

Dakin (2009) terms these divisions "beats" and defines them as often occurring "at the points within a scene where characters exit and enter"; she has her students "chunk" scenes into these beats and provides the first sixteen lines of *Hamlet* as an example of the play's first "beat"; and students then give each beat its own title (95–98). Gibson ([1998] 2016) similarly chunks Barnardo, Francisco, and Horatio's opening lines and provides staging questions: "What will be the first thing the audience sees? Is Francisco on sentry duty, patrolling the stage, before the first members of the audience enter?" (147–49). Dakin (2009) also provides two further lessons for chunking *Hamlet* 2.2 and breaking down "to be or not to be" into three parts (88–90, 92–95).

3. Ralph Alan Cohen warns that teachers should have students read through a few lines at a time with frequent informational asides: "You must always be building a theatre in their minds, and to do that you must frequently interrupt yourself and comment on the text" (28).

4. For additional resources on teaching second-person familiar pronouns, see Dakin (2009, 52–57), Gibson ([1998] 2016, 83–84), Gibson and Field-Pickering (1998, 61), Snyder ([1994] 2006, 9–15), Long and Christel (2019, 70–72, 82–85).

5. Dakin, together with her students, noticed that while Claudius uses the royal we in the first half of the speech, he switches to the more personal singular pronouns when he addresses Hamlet directly: "But now, *my* cousin Hamlet, and *my* son" (1.2.64). Some of her "students wondered if Claudius deserved Hamlet's scathing reply . . . since Claudius seemed to have dropped his big-shot voice for the voice an ordinary man who loves his grieving stepson" (50). She also includes a stand-alone lesson that walks through Henry V's speech as he switches between the royal we and the singular first-person pronoun (50–52). Susan Snyder ([1994] 2006) notes how Hamlet uses "psychological attacks on his uncle" to "destabilize Claudius's royal pronouns"; after the mousetrap, "a jittery Claudius . . . jumbles the person and the ruler" as he haphazardly switches from the singular "I" to the royal "we" and back again (13). Long and Christel note that in F1, Shakespeare sometimes uses "we" and sometimes "wee"; modern editors all modernize these to just "we," but they argue that Shakespeare intended the "wee" spelling to indicate a stronger emphasis than the "we" spelling (67–68). A search at internetshakespeare.uiv.ca reveals that the "we" spelling occurs in F1 *Hamlet* 113 times, but the "wee" spelling appears just seven times—and never by Claudius. The "wee" spelling does not appear at all in Q2, but it appears sixteen times in Q1 (including three times by Claudius). Regarding the royal we, also see O'Brien ([1994] 2006, 80).

6. Gibson ([1998] 2016) writes that "each mythological allusion illustrates some aspect of character, story or theme"; he goes on to provide the example of Niobe from *Hamlet*: "When Hamlet speaks of Gertrude as being 'like Niobe, all tears,' he is thinking of Niobe, Queen of Thebes who wept for her dead children even when she was turned to stone. This image of everlasting sorrow ironically comments on Gertrude's short-lived grief for her dead husband" (223). Rocklin (2005) also makes the case for using classical allusions as resources for teaching; "although at first students may see this resource as an obstacle," teachers should provide scaffolding "to work these allusions for students to grasp the precise way in which they indicate the contours of Hamlet's thought" (290).

7. For teachers who want more on how Shakespeare straddled Protestant and Catholic belief in Hamlet, Stephen Greenblatt's *Hamlet in Purgatory* provides the best starting point. Greenblatt gives background to how the Catholic notion of purgatory functioned in literature before and during Shakespeare's lifetime in his first four chapters, and then he makes the case in his fifth and final chapter for a Protestant Hamlet with a Catholic father: "A young man from Wittenberg, with a distinctly Protestant temperament, is haunted by a distinctly Catholic ghost" (2002, 240; 2019, 282). Rocklin adds that "many of the original spectators would have been well aware of the divergent theological understandings of the afterlife" and that "students will come to recognize that the play's design is deeply equivocal about whether its universe is governed by Catholic or Protestant theology" (309–10). The underlying theological conception of Christian afterlife in Hamlet is inconsistent—it lurks somewhere between

Protestant and Catholic—but upon deeper study, these conflicting contradictions add richness to the play rather than detract from it.

8. Other teachers similarly make the claim that it is better to watch films in chunks (not a whole film at once) and to watch two or more film versions of a scene rather than just one. O'Brien ([1994] 2006) has teachers choose two film versions of the nunnery scene (105–6) and the mousetrap scene (109–10). Gibson ([1998] 2016) explains that "one essential principle governs the use of the video: *active, critical viewing*. This involves close study of particular scenes, actions or speeches . . . one video version of a play should be compared and contrasted with another" (200–1). Cohen overall is wary of film, believing it inferior to live stage productions, but does concede its value; he argues, though, that clips should be short and that teachers should show at least two versions of a scene: "If you show a video version, say of Oliver's *Hamlet*, to your students, that interpretation is likely to become their *Hamlet*. But if they see Zeffirelli's Hamlet as well, then they will know without your telling them that there is no single *Hamlet*" (2006, 27; 2018, 22–23). Dakin (2012), as another example, asserts, "One of the best ways to help students begin to see that every performance is a reading is to key up two or more film productions of a scene students have reread and analyzed for the ways in which the Shakespearean text supports multiple and even contradictory readings of a character" (143–44). Dakin's second book is entirely devoted to using film to teach Shakespeare; in it she makes the case that "we need to learn with our students how to read Shakespeare in triplicate, as the stuff of transformative literature, theater, and film. The combined effect will be greater than the sum of its parts" (xix).

9. Emily Griffith Jones, based on her experiences teaching *Hamlet* in Singapore, encourages teachers not to just show the Kosintsev *Hamlet* but also to balance it with other non-English *Hamlet* films. She makes the case for "comparing parallel moments across global productions"; these help "students see Hamlet as more than the angry, melancholic man Anglo-Americans assume they know. In Kosintsev's Soviet moment, he rises beyond his own preoccupations—possibly beyond his original creation by Shakespeare—to discover that justice for his family and freedom for himself matter chiefly because they mean freedom and justice for his neighbors" (2019, 57). Other non-English and global *Hamlets* can be found digitally and free of charge through the MIT's Global Shakespeares Video and Performance Archive, which Jones helped develop as part of her teaching and research (59).

10. Thompson and Turchi (2016) suggest that teachers incorporate frames in their Shakespeare instruction, defining a frame as a "delimited, intentional and focused approach" (23). They explain, "A teacher must choose and prioritize from such topics in order to create a frame . . . this delimiting decision organizes her materials, discussions, assignments and assessments toward the purpose: building student facility with complex texts" (26). They offer five possible frames for *Hamlet*: (1) "familiar relations," (2) "remembrance," (3) "revenge," (4) "purpose of playing"; and (5) "the problem with women" (26–27). Building on their framework, this chapter has made a frame for the first act of "telling a ghost story." From the activities explaining biblical and classical references to the culminating project, this idea of the first act as a ghost story serves as the organizing frame for the first chapter. Later chapters similarly build

around their own frames: Hamlet's mental health in chapter 2, what the women say in chapter 3, visual art in chapter 4, and editing and textual history in chapter 5.

11. Gibson ([1998] 2016) suggests a similar strategy for having students write their own point of view narratives, ones in which they "tell the story from the point of view of one of the characters in the play" (104). He also discusses teaching staging options for the ghost's entrances: "What does the Ghost look like? How does the ghost enter: slowly? Suddenly? with particular gesture? Any accompanying sound effects? How might he leave the stage?" (140). He thinks this opening scene is particularly apt for acting out with students in the classroom (162–63). The chapter 3 culminating project builds on Gibson's methods by having students retell their story from Ophelia's or Gertrude's point of view. Winston (2015), who lauds Gibson's work (41–44), later explains that teachers can have students write back stories for minor characters; he bases his idea on work the Royal Shakespeare Company (RSC) did in a recent *Hamlet* production in which RSC actors created "a back story for their character which they worked on through improvisation over two or three days of the rehearsal period" (63). O'Brien ([1994] 2006) provides additional performance-based strategies for the play's first eighty lines (76–78), as well as the later act 1 ghost scenes (88–89).

12. One entry point to the research on transfer is *Writing Across Contexts: Transfer, Composition, and Sites of Writing* by Kathleen Yancey, Liane Robertson, and Kara Taczak (2014), who explain that questions of transfer ask "how we can support students' transfer of knowledge and practice in writing; that is, how we can help students develop writing knowledge and practices that they can draw upon, use, and repurpose for new writing tasks in new settings" (2). Theirs is a focus on transfer in college-level composition courses, but transfer is a pedagogical concept that crosses into other disciplines as well as beyond traditional school settings. It pushes students to plan how they will use new skill sets in other rhetorical contexts. Yancy, Robertson, and Taczak propose a first-year college composition course in which "reflection, as both theory and practice, is also a key feature of the course that students engage in before, during, and after their writing assignments . . . which allows for the development of a theory of writing—or a framework of writing knowledge they can apply to new writing contexts—both within the course and beyond it" (73). To this end, each chapter's culminating project in this book will conclude with such a transfer-based reflection, starting with students evaluating the skills required for writing a *Hamlet*-inspired ghost story that will transfer to future writing contexts.

Chapter 2

"There Is Method in It"

Hamlet's Sinking Mental Health — Diving Deep into the Soliloquies

In act 2 *Hamlet* shifts. What started as a ghost story in act 1 has become something else. Some two months have passed, and Hamlet is breaking. He made it clear in act 1 that he would only pretend to be mad, to feign "an antic disposition," but his mental health seems to be cracking for real (1.5.192). Beneath the weight of his father's murder, he wrestles with the monumental task of determining whether the ghost was telling the truth and, if so, how to carry out the revenge demanded of him.

New characters appear as well in act 2. The king has called Rosencrantz and Guildenstern, two of Hamlet's schoolfellows, to court to act as spies to discover what troubles Hamlet. The king does not realize that Hamlet knows of the murder, believing his monstrous misdeed is still his secret. Hamlet immediately sees through Rosencrantz and Guildenstern, though, calling them out as the king's agents and outdueling them in a lexical contest of wits. They never enter his good graces, and fairly or unfairly, which will be a conversation for chapter 5, they become tangled in and destroyed by the rottenness that consumes Elsinore.

A troupe of actors also appears in act 2, though to a much warmer greeting than Hamlet's schoolfellows. Arriving shortly after Rosencrantz and Guildenstern, they are to perform at court. Hamlet loves theater, a fitting attribute for the most profound character of England's most renowned playwright, and he basks in their presence. For a moment the players give Hamlet a respite from the grinding disquiet of his own mind. He snaps back to his old self, the better version of himself, from when his father still lived. Perhaps that is what good theater does; it makes us, for a moment, again into our best versions of ourselves.

The lead actor, whom Hamlet had known before the play, performs a speech at Hamlet's request. The speech tells the story of a murdered king—his name is Priam (more on him later in the chapter)—and touches Hamlet deeply. It inspires Hamlet to instruct the players to perform the story of another murdered king, this one named Gonzago, before his uncle and the rest of the court later that evening.

Hamlet has them add some "dozen or sixteen lines" so their play will depict Claudius's exact crimes: pouring poison in the king's ear, marrying his wife, and stealing his crown (2.2.567). Hamlet will watch his uncle's reaction, which he hopes will prove whether or not the ghost told the truth. That will be the stuff of act 3.

As act 2 closes, though, Hamlet soliloquizes to theatergoers his steadfast resolve to avenge his murdered father. This chapter will have students spend significant time working through that closing soliloquy. In it Hamlet argues that if a mere actor can stir himself to such passion over the murder of a fictional king, then he should be able to do much more for his very real king-father. Perhaps that is also what good theater does; it calls us to act against injustice. The injustices we face are different—none of us have been tasked with revenging a murdered father-king—but injustices of similar and greater scale nonetheless surround us, and Shakespeare reminds us of theater's capacity to spark action.

This second chapter follows a similar format as chapter 1, providing learning objectives, suggestions for reading aloud as a class, some notes on Shakespeare's language, a series of discussion questions and writing prompts, and a culminating project in which students analyze, paraphrase, and cut Hamlet's closing soliloquy, preparing it for performance as a director or an actor would. Teachers are encouraged to adapt these ideas based on their students' needs.

ACT 2 LEARNING OBJECTIVES

1. Students will distinguish Shakespearean verse and prose; identify examples of enjambment, shared lines, and blank verse; and analyze Shakespeare's use of verse and prose regarding character and tone.
2. Students will define unfamiliar vocabulary from *Hamlet*.
3. Students will compare film versions of Hamlet's act 2 closing soliloquy and evaluate how choices the productions made affected their reading(s) of the speech.
4. Students will paraphrase line by line the closing soliloquy of Hamlet in act 2 into modern-day, contemporary English.

5. Students will (like an actor or director) create their own audio or video production of the *Hamlet* act 2 soliloquy, analyzing appropriate cuts/edits and determining proper vocal pitch, tone, and so forth.

READING SCENES OF ACT 2 TOGETHER

Act 2 is shorter than act 1, with only two scenes. There are some bits that can be skipped over, but make sure students see that what happens here places the foundation for what is to come in act 3.

- 2.1: Teachers can summarize or skip the first seventy-one lines of act 2. Polonius meets with Reynaldo, who disappears entirely from the play after his short part here, and instructs him to travel to Paris to spy on his son, Laertes. Such backhanded espionage against his son reveals Polonius as either conniving or foolhardy—both are valid readings—but can be skipped over on students' first readings.
  - The second half of the short scene, on the other hand, is fundamental to later scenes; teachers should spend some time in the second half. Ophelia reveals to her father that an enraged Hamlet has just burst into her closet, which, in Shakespeare's time, was another word for a small private study or sewing room, something like a modern-day bedroom but without a bed. The bed would have been in a separate room. Hamlet's dress and demeanor had alarmed Ophelia. She explains to her father that he had grabbed her by the arm and stared coldly into her eyes. This wrongly convinces Polonius that Hamlet's behavior is rooted in an unrequited love for Ophelia, and he rushes off to report this to the king.
- 2.2: The second scene is long and complex, with over five hundred lines. Rosencrantz and Guildenstern receive instructions from the king to learn what is troubling Hamlet. They exit, and Polonius rushes onto the stage with the news that he (incorrectly) has figured out what has been bothering Hamlet, but he defers to the two ambassadors who have just returned from their trip to Norway; they'd been sent just in act 1, which tells the audience that some two months have passed since act 1.
- Much of what transpires next sets up the third act. Polonius concocts a plot to have Ophelia interact with Hamlet while he and the king secretly watch, which becomes the action of 3.1. Next, the players arrive, and Hamlet asks them to perform a scene before his uncle in which a king is murdered by his brother in the same way that the old king Hamlet was murdered; Hamlet hopes that such a performance will cause his uncle to react and prove the ghost true. This will be the action of 3.2.

SOME NOTES ON SHAKESPEARE'S LANGUAGE: VERSE AND PROSE

Many students struggle to hear the difference between Shakespeare's verse and prose, but editors have made it easy to see the difference when it is written out. Shakespeare's verse looks different on the page than prose. Each line of verse begins with a capital letter, so there is a straight line of capital letters going down the page at the left margin. Further, verse on the page is divided into lines, usually *iambic pentameter*, giving it a truncated appearance. After ten syllables (or so), the line ends, even though it has not yet reached the right margin.

This gives it a different appearance than prose, which uses capital letters only at the beginning of actual sentences and where it is appropriate for proper nouns. The text goes from the left margin to the right and appears more like a modern paragraph in a novel. The paragraphs in this book are all written as prose, though they could be converted to appear as verse, like this:

> Shakespeare's verse looks different on the page
> Than prose. Each line of verse begins with a
> Capital letter, so there is a straight
> Line of capital letters going down
> The page at the left margin. Further, verse
> On the page is divided into lines,
> Usually iambic pentameter,
> Giving it a truncated appearance.

Alongside distinguishing verse and prose, students should also be able to identify when Shakespeare incorporates *enjambment* and *shared lines* in his verse. Enjambment is when a poet continues a sentence without pause beyond the end of a line; Shakespeare frequently uses enjambment. A shared line is when two different characters split a single line of verse; it indicates that the characters should speak the line without any pause quickly upon the heels of one another. A final term that students should be familiar with as part of their study of verse is *blank verse*. Blank verse is verse that does not rhyme; Shakespeare's best verse rarely rhymes. Very little of Shakespeare's verse in *Hamlet* rhymes. Though hearing it is far more difficult than seeing it, verse also sounds different from prose when spoken aloud. Shakespeare composed in iambic pentameter (more to come on teaching iambic pentameter in the anticipatory set activity in the next section). Some describe it as the rhythm of a beating heart. Others describe it as the natural cadence of spoken English. Though it is more challenging than seeing it visually on the page, when a student speaks it aloud, she should be able to hear the rhythm as well as see it.

Have students practice distinguishing verse from prose and emphasizing the rhythm when reading verse aloud. Historically, actors accentuated the verse in performance to a degree that would seem unnatural today. Nowadays, though, actors strive to find a naturalistic rhythm that does not overstress the accented, or stressed, syllables. In their initial readings of *Hamlet*, it is enough that students know that lines of iambic pentameter are made up of ten syllables and can be visually recognized on the page.

Shakespeare uses verse and prose for different purposes, and much in the way that understanding how Shakespeare uses familiar and formal second-person pronouns to establish relationships and infuse additional meaning (as discussed in the previous chapter), students can glean additional meaning when a character speaks in verse or prose.

Verse is heightened language, so characters of noble birth speak in verse. Both kings—the dead ghost-father and the current brother-murderer—speak exclusively in verse. So does the queen. They never speak in prose. It is generally only the everyday characters who speak in prose, and since the cast of *Hamlet* consists primarily of noble characters, most of the play is in verse. In fact, all of act 1 is in verse.

The most interesting analysis is of the characters that use both verse and prose at different points in the play, as Hamlet does. He switches to prose in act 2—the first time audiences hear prose in the play—when speaking alone with Polonius. Both are noble, but Hamlet changes the mood by pretending to be a madman to trick Polonius into believing him insane, and the move so befuddles Polonius that he, too, is dragged down into prose along with Hamlet.

Hamlet maintains prose when he first speaks with Rosencrantz and Guildenstern, and they follow his lead (even though, earlier in the scene, they had been speaking in verse with the king and queen). Using prose, Hamlet again establishes a lowbrow tone for the conversation, which he plays upon further with bawdy jokes regarding "the secret parts of fortune" (2.2.253).

When the players enter, Hamlet continues to speak with them in prose. Actors were lowborn in Shakespeare's time and expected to speak in prose, though they switched to verse when beginning their parts. Once the player becomes a king, his language must befit the role he takes on as much as his costume does. In truth, the player king is no more a royal than the real-life actor playing Claudius. Both are just actors playing parts. There is a delicious metatheatrical irony in the idea of an actor playing an actor who is playing a part, one that Shakespeare richly exploits in several plays, but particularly here, in *Hamlet*.

Teach students to pay attention to whether they are reading verse or prose. It is easy to see the difference on the page, and when students can distinguish between the two, it provides additional context clues about characters and tone. Teach students to pay attention to characters who use both at different points in the play as well as the reasons for the shift. Hamlet switches from verse to prose to take control of the scene's tone. Polonius, Rosencrantz, and Guildenstern do so to follow Hamlet's lead. On the other hand, the player king switches from prose to verse as he shifts into character to play his royal part.

In later acts, have students continue to pay attention to when Shakespeare chooses verse and when he chooses prose. Since the play is mostly in verse, it is easiest to pay special attention to when Shakespeare uses prose instead. In act 3, Hamlet will again impose prose on Polonius, Rosencrantz, and Guildenstern—but also on Ophelia; his choice to speak prose to her indicates that he will pretend to be mad with her, too, and that he will not bring her into his confidence. Later in act 3, he speaks entirely in verse with his mother, confirming that he is not actually mad but only pretending. In act 4, Ophelia has the only lines of prose, and she speaks them from a broken mental place; one reading of acts 2, 3, and 4 is that prose throughout reveals such broken mental places.

In act 5 the two gravediggers—the most lowborn of all characters in the play—speak prose to one another. And when Hamlet and Horatio enter, they speak prose with the gravedigger for some of the most profound philosophical passages of the play. Prose may be the language of the lowborn, but that does not mean that Shakespeare uses it only for jokes and jests; he plumbs the deepest depths of philosophy in prose, too, when he so chooses.

ANTICIPATORY SET ACTIVITY: ACTING OUT IAMBIC PENTAMETER

This anticipatory set activity sets a foundation for the culminating project at the end of the chapter, when students will complete a close reading of the act 2 closing soliloquy. The activity can contract or expand to meet classroom needs. The whole activity, as described, takes some fifteen minutes, but teachers can reduce the activity to five minutes by just using the cards described below and cutting the analysis of the soliloquy's first eight lines. It can also be expanded into a longer lesson, where students work through the whole soliloquy instead of just the first eight lines. It can also be adapted as an anticipatory set in later lessons to any of Hamlet's soliloquies.[1]

The idea of *iambic pentameter* can seem complicated at first, and rightfully so. Its intricacies have stumped scholars, actors, and even editors. At its simplest level, though, students on a first or second reading need only to understand that a typical line of iambic pentameter is made up of ten syllables in a ba-BOOM, ba-BOOM, ba-BOOM, ba-BOOM, ba-BOOM pattern. In poetry terms, each ba-*boom* represents one iambic foot: an unstressed syllable followed by a stressed syllable. Five iambs together make up a single line of iambic pentameter.

For this activity create two sets of ten color-coded cards, twenty cards in total. These can be made in a few minutes with basic construction paper. For the first set, make two red cards, and in black permanent marker, write "ba" in lowercase letters on the first and "BOOM" in uppercase letters on the second. Make it big enough to read from the back of the room. Then make two more orange cards in the same way, then two yellow cards, two green cards, and two blue cards.

ba BOOM | ba BOOM | ba BOOM | ba BOOM | ba BOOM

For the second set, use the same color combinations, but this time, use the opening line of Hamlet's act 2 soliloquy; write the unstressed syllables again in lowercase letters and the stressed syllables in uppercase letters, as shown above. Each color-coded pair represents one iambic foot. The five feet together represent a single line of iambic pentameter.

In class, line up ten students at the front of the room, and give each a color-coded card in order. Speak the syllables aloud first from the back of the room, modeling appropriate volume and pitch, emphasizing the ba-BOOM, ba-BOOM cadence. Pat your chest as you speak, ba-BOOM, ba-BOOM, in the rhythm of a human heartbeat. Next, have students read their syllables aloud, embodying the rhythm themselves. Students with a "ba" card should speak their syllable softly and unstressed. Students with a "BOOM" card should speak their syllable with emphasis. Have the ten students read through their cards two or three times, praising them as they find a rhythm together. Next, pass out the cards with Shakespeare's actual syllables and have the ten students read them aloud using the same rhythm they have already established. Have them repeat the line several times, until they gain confidence in the rhythm.

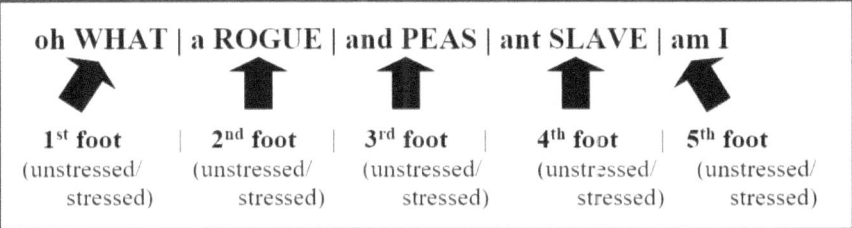

Figure 2.1: Iambic Pentameter.

Last of all—and, if needed, this part can be cut to save time—have students return to their seats and practice in pairs reading aloud the first eight lines of the soliloquy through to "For Hecuba," (2.2.585) overemphasizing the rhythm. Have them read through these lines three or four times, getting used to speaking Shakespeare's language and rhythm aloud.

> oh WHAT | a ROGUE | and PEAS | ant SLAVE | am I
> is IT | not MON | strous THAT | this PLAY | er HERE
> but IN | a FIC | tion, IN | a DREAM | of PAS sion,
> could FORCE | his SOUL | so TO | his OWN | con CEIT
> that FROM | her WORK | ing ALL | the VIS | age WANNED
> tears IN | his EYES | dis TRACT | ion IN | his AS pect
> with FORMS | to HIS | con CEIT | and ALL | for NO thing.
> For HEC | u BA.

Students will notice that three lines have eleven syllables instead of ten. This is still iambic pentameter because each foot still has an initial unstressed syllable followed by a second stressed syllable. This is Shakespeare jamming one extra syllable into each line. He generally does this to add extra oomph to a line. In act 3, the first line of the "to be or not to be" speech is perhaps the finest example of this technique; it adds one more unstressed syllable to the end of the last foot.

Students will also notice that the last line has only four syllables (two iambic feet). Traditionally, most actors would take this as a cue from Shakespeare to give a six-beat pause before continuing into the next line.[2] Pay special attention to verse that strays from the ten-syllable template; it is one of Shakespeare's ways of giving his actors directions on how to read the line.

Sometimes Shakespeare adds an extra syllable to "-ed" and "-est" words that are not there naturally. In modern editions these appear with an accent mark when the "éd" or "ést" is to be pronounced as a separate syllable and without an accent mark when it is to be combined with the previous syllable.[3] Consider Ophelia's example when she is describing Hamlet's unkempt appearance to her father:

FOUR ADDITIONAL NOTES FOR TEACHERS TO KNOW ABOUT IAMBIC PENTAMETER

Studying Shakespeare's verse and iambic pentameter can be a rabbit hole for teachers. At one point in history, such study made up the bulk of many students' study of Shakespeare. It should remain a part of their classroom study still today—a rudimentary understanding of the basics of Shakespeare's

Table 2.1

My lord, as I was sewing in my closet,	
Lord Hamlet, with his doublet all *unbraced*,	*unbraced* is two sylla-
No hat upon his head, his stockings *fouled*,	bles: un-braced
Ungartered, and *down-gyvéd* to his ankle,	*fouled* is one syllable
Pale as his shirt, his knees knocking each other,	*ungartered* is three, but the
And with a look so piteous in purport	accent mark indicates that so is
As if he had been *loosèd* out of hell	down-gyvéd
To speak of horrors—he comes before me.	*loosèd* has an accent, so it's two
(2.1.87–94, emphasis added)	syllables

language sets students up for more advanced study—but students in the twenty-first century, on their first or second reading, really need only to be able to distinguish between verse and prose; identify examples of enjambment, shared lines, and blank verse; and analyze possible implications of Shakespeare's verse and prose regarding character and tone. With that said, here are a few advanced details teachers may find helpful to know regarding verse and iambic pentameter:

- Much can be discovered by breaking down a line into its stressed and unstressed syllables. This work is called *scansion*. Proper scansion, or scanning, involves graphically marking each unstressed syllable with a *breve*, which looks a bit like a small, flattened u, and each stressed syllable with a *slash*, like those in the table below. Other than the chart (see table 2.2) below, though, this book will use combinations of lower- and uppercase letters to signify unstressed and stressed syllables, which can be a bit easier for the novice to interpret.[4]

Table 2.2

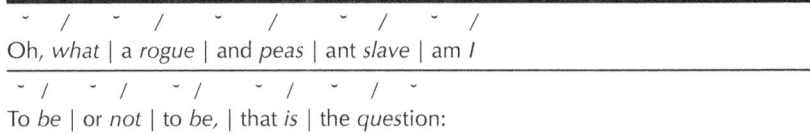

- In English, words with more than one syllable always have one stressed syllable: most two-syllable nouns are stressed on the first syllable, and most two-syllable verbs are stressed on the second syllable. If unsure of the scansion, say the word aloud and listen for the stressed syllable. If still unsure, consult a dictionary for help.
- Shakespeare and his contemporaries often wrote in iambic pentameter—the poetic rhythm that sounds most like speech in English—but there are

other kinds of metrical feet. Their names of the feet are a mouthful, but teachers should be aware of the four most common in English poetry:

Table 2.3

two syllables	**Iamb (iambic):** One unstressed syllable followed by one stressed syllable (and sometimes an additional unstressed syllable) (ba-BOOM)	be-LONG
	Trochee (trochaic): One stressed syllable followed by one unstressed syllable (BOOM-ba)	O-ver
three or more syllables	**Anapest (anapestic):** Two unstressed syllables followed by a stressed syllable (ba-ba-BOOM)	un-der-STAND
	Dactyl (dactylic): One stressed syllable followed by two unstressed syllables (BOOM-ba-ba)	PROM-i-nent

- A line with just one foot is *mono*meter, a line with two feet is *di*meter, three feet is *tri*mester, four feet is *tetra*meter, five feet is *penta*meter, and so on. The prefix is based on the Greek number root. Edgar Allen Poe, for example, in "The Raven," weaves together lines of eight trochaic feet, or trochaic octometer:

ONCE up | ON a | MID night | DREAR y, | WHILE i | PON dered | WEAK and | WEAR y

ACT 2 BIBLICAL AND CLASSICAL REFERENCES: JEPHTHAH AND DIDO

Shakespeare incorporates two references in the second act of *Hamlet* that are lost on most audiences in the twenty-first century: (1) when Hamlet refers to Jephthah, and (2) when Hamlet asks the lead player to tell the story of Priam and Hecuba (from Dido's tale to Aeneas in the *Aeneid*). Students need not necessarily know the intricacies of these two allusions on their first or second reading, but teachers should be familiar with their basics.

Jephthah, Judge of Israel

In 2.2 Hamlet insults Polonius, calling him "Jephthah, judge of Israel" (2.2.427). Polonius is taken aback because he gets the biblical reference. Shakespeare's audiences would have too. In the Bible, in Judges 11, Jephthah has been made general of the army and promises God that in exchange for victory in battle, he will offer as a burnt sacrifice the first living thing he encounters upon his return home. He likely thought it would be a sheep or ox that he would see first.

God grants him the victory, but when Jephthah returns home, it is no sheep or ox but his only daughter who first comes out to greet him. He keeps his promise to God, though, and offers up his daughter as a sacrifice. Through the allusion, Hamlet accuses Polonius of playing a game in which his daughter, Ophelia, has become a pawn. The well-known Jephthah story had been turned into a ballad in Shakespeare's time; Hamlet's following lines quote from its first stanza:

> I have read that many years agoe,
> When Jeph[th]ah, judge of Israel,
> Had *one faire daughter and no moe,*
> *Whom he loved passing well.*
> *And as by lot, God wot,*
> It came to passe, most like it was,
> Great wars there should be,
> And who should be chief but he, but he. (Child 199, emphasis added)

And Hamlet is right. He is more right than even he knows. Polonius is dragging his daughter into his spy network to spy on Hamlet for the king, and she will soon be dead as a result.

Dido's Tale: Priam and Hecuba

Hamlet's reference to the slaughter of King Priam, briefly introduced in this chapter's introduction, likewise would have been familiar to Shakespeare's original audiences. Priam's story is best told, as Hamlet points out, in book two of Virgil's *Aeneid*—when Aeneas weaves the tale of how the Greeks sacked Troy—but other versions appear in various forms throughout myth, including plays by Sophocles and Euripides. Like the end of Shakespeare's speech, these dramas emphasize the suffering of his wife, Hecuba. Priam was an old man—defeated, unable to lift his sword, and clinging to a holy household altar for protection.

Any honorable Greek warrior would have left the old king alone out of piety to the gods and respect for ancient fathers, but Pyrrhus hesitates only a moment, holding his sword high over the old man's head for just a second, and then hacks him to death—bringing his sword down relentlessly on Priam's "milky head," like a blacksmith's hammer on the anvil—while his queen, Hecuba, watches ("milky" because of the old man's white hair; 2.2.503). The moment in both Shakespeare and Virgil is brutal.

By Shakespeare's time Hecuba's suffering had become an allegory for the fickleness of fortune. Everybody in Shakespeare's original audiences would have known who Priam and Hecuba were. Before the Trojan War, Hecuba had been perhaps the most blessed woman in antiquity. She was wealthy beyond imagination, had raised many children, and led the most privileged life, but afterward, she was reduced to abject slavery. Two times in the scene, Shakespeare calls Fortune a "strumpet" (2.2.254, 518). Hecuba witnesses both her husband's slaughter and her many children being killed, often before her eyes, or taken into slavery. It would take a most callous person not to pity Hecuba's suffering.

Through the player's performance, Hamlet feels the call to action. The player had so embodied Hecuba's suffering that he altered his appearance: his face changed color, tears filled his eyes, and his voice broke. Polonius is not impressed: "Look whe'er he has not turned his color and has tears in's eyes. Prithee, no more" (2.2.545–46). Hamlet, on the other hand, is moved:

> All his visage [face] wanned [turned pale],
> Tears in his eyes, distraction in his aspect [facial expression],
> A broken voice, and his whole function suiting
> With forms to his conceit [performance]. And all for nothing!
> For Hecuba! (2.2.581–85)

Hamlet is moved because the player has made Priam's suffering real, and it mirrors Hamlet's own grief. Theater can do that.

Hamlet can see himself both in Pyrrhus and Hecuba. Whether right or wrong, Pyrrhus had been decisive. He had killed Priam to avenge his own dead father, who had died at Trojan hands. Hamlet wants to be more like that. But he also sees himself in Hecuba. He has witnessed his king murdered and knows who did it (or, at least, has been told by the ghost who did it), but he has been unable to bring justice upon the killer.

Hamlet is broken. He is both Pyrrhus and Hecuba, but he has not acted yet because he does not know whether the ghost has told him the truth. As he makes clear to his audience at the end of act 2, the way to fix what is broken is to see if the players can stir the same kinds of emotion in his uncle as they did him. If they can activate his uncle's guilt, Hamlet will know how to proceed.

The Jephthah reference is often cut in performance. The Hecuba reference sometimes is too. Olivier cut them both. So did Gibson and Hawke. They preferred their film audiences not trip over complex biblical and classical allusions. Branagh and Tennant, on the other hand, who are going for a complete telling of *Hamlet* with fewer cuts, keep them. Teachers should explain the Hecuba reference at least. Understanding her story brings Hamlet's soliloquy

Figure 2.2: *The Death of Priam* by Jules Lefebvre (oil on canvas; 1861; image in public domain); in the foreground Pyrrhus hesitates momentarily, just as described by Shakespeare: Pyrrhus's sword "seemed i'th'air to stick; / So as a painted tyrant Pyrrhus stood" (2.2.504–5). Hecuba, on the right in the shadows, looks away in horror.

Source: https://en.wikipedia.org/wiki/The_Death_of_Priam_(Lefebvre)#/media/File:Lefebvre_La_mort_de_Priam.JPG.

at the end of act 2 to life and is also essential for the chapter's film activity and culminating project.

INCORPORATING FILM: HAMLET'S HECUBA SOLILOQUY

This section introduces two film activities designed to get students thinking deeply about Hamlet's act 2 closing soliloquy. Both are designed to prepare students for a deep dive into Shakespeare's language in the chapter's culminating project.[5] Teachers can opt to teach just one—they can function individually as standalone lessons—or they can teach both, as they complement one another.[6]

FIRST VIEWING ACTIVITY: BUILDING VOCABULARY THROUGH FILM

The first activity, which takes approximately forty-fifty minutes, focuses on building valuable vocabulary for the culminating project. Have students watch the Branagh and the Tennant film version of Hamlet's second soliloquy in their entirety. The Branagh version takes some four minutes. The Tennant version takes some five minutes. These two film versions work for this activity, whereas the others do not, because both keep the soliloquy intact. The others cut significant parts of the text, including the challenging language the activity seeks to illuminate. Those cuts will be helpful in the second viewing activity but remove too much of the rich vocabulary on which this activity focuses.

Like in the chapter 1 film activity, divide students into groups of four, and assign students in each group one of the four following watching roles:

- *Casting director:* Pay special attention to the choices regarding the actor who plays Hamlet. Does he seem younger or older than you expected Hamlet to be? How does he use gestures and facial expressions to convey meaning?
- *Set and props designer:* Pay special attention to the production's decisions regarding set and props. Where is Hamlet when he delivers the soliloquy? What is in the background? Does it make you feel like you are in the present or back in time?
- *Costume manager:* What kind of costume does Hamlet wear? Is it modern or old-fashioned? Does it look like something a wealthy prince would wear or something more like a regular person would wear?
- *Camera operator:* How much of the scene is built on close-ups? How much on long- and mid-distance shots? Does Hamlet move around much? Does Hamlet ever look directly into the camera at the audience?

As always, edit the activity to fit classroom needs. For example, the activity can work with just one of the film versions instead of both. The start and end times are listed in the table 2.4:

Table 2.4

Kenneth Branagh as Hamlet (1996)	Hamlet's soliloquy begins at **1:26:40** and ends at **1:30:25** (4 minutes)
David Tennant as Hamlet (2009)	Hamlet's soliloquy begins at **1:21:45** and ends at **1:26:22** (5 minutes)

After watching discuss the different pacing each actor employs. Ask students whether they prefer Branagh's faster or Tennant's slower pace. Also, discuss how each uses the camera: Branagh never looks directly into the camera, while Tennant does. Which do students prefer? Does a soliloquy work better on film when an actor looks directly into the camera? Would the same be true with a stage performance? Do students think an actor should look directly at the audience in a live performance?

The questions regarding Hamlet's age set up a textual question that will be the crux of the book's last chapter. Students may be surprised to find that the mustached Branagh was thirty-six when he filmed *Hamlet* in 1996, while the clean-faced Tennant was actually two years older, aged thirty-eight, when he filmed *Hamlet* in 2009. The best textual clues to Hamlet's actual age will come in act 5, but they are ambiguous: the most common reading, when students come to it later in their study, is that Hamlet is thirty years old, but some scholars have interpreted those same lines to read that Shakespeare intended Hamlet to be just sixteen. More on that in chapter 5.

After discussion choose one of the film versions, and play it again. Instruct students to individually write down at least five unfamiliar words and phrases as they watch. Be sure the closed captions are on as they watch. Next, have students in their groups of four take fifteen to twenty minutes to combine their words into one list.

Then, using a historical online dictionary, such as the *Oxford English Dictionary* (*OED*), have them write out, as a group and in their own words, a brief, student-friendly definition for each unfamiliar word and phrase. Some words have archaic meanings, which have evolved over time. The advantage of a historical dictionary is that it lets students see these changes. Each group should produce at least twelve definitions. As they compile these, have each group write them into a shared Google document.

Alternatively, if there is a free whiteboard in the classroom that need not to be erased for a few days, have students write out their words and definitions there, which the teacher will save for the culminating project. As a whole class, collapse repeats of the same word or phrase into a single definition. For example, if multiple groups have the word "malefactions," then discuss the different definitions, and turn them into just one entry. If the class has made their glossary on the whiteboard, have students take photos of the whiteboard on their phones for their notes.

The collective class document—a student-centered, student-created glossary—will serve as a resource for the chapter's culminating project, so teachers should keep it so that students can access it in later class sessions. This document, whether digital or on a whiteboard, can also cross multiple sections, with students collaborating across different classes. Teachers should "make a copy" in Google Docs or take photos of the whiteboard for their notes if the original becomes corrupted (a custodian accidentally erases it, a prankster sabotages the online document, etc.).

Close the viewing activity by rewatching both versions of the soliloquy once more with their now-improved vocabulary.[7] If time is tight, choose just one. As an exit pass, ask students to write one or two sentences explaining something they understood better in their second viewing. Table 2.5 provides most of the words that modern readers find unfamiliar:

Table 2.5

rogue—a dishonest person	**peak**—to mope about, brood, languish	**treacherous**—describes somebody guilty of betrayal or deception
player(s) – stage actors	**John-a-dreams**—an idle dreamer who never accomplishes much	**lecherous**—having excessive sexual desire
conceit—an artistic expression of brilliance; the player's performance is stellar and moving	**unpregnant**—not pregnant, empty; in this case, Hamlet feels empty because of how little he has accomplished in getting his revenge	**drab**—another word for a prostitute
visage—a person's face	**pate**—a person's head; to break somebody's pate is to strike them on the head	**Fie upon't! foh!** – an exclamation of disgust; perhaps something today like "OMG! Ugh!"
wanned / wan—to turn pale or white	**plucks my beard**—to pull a hair out of somebody's beard, a sign of disrespect	**scullion**—a servant assigned the most menial kitchen tasks; some editors choose **"stallion"** from Q2 here, which means a male prostitute.
aspect—his facial expression; i.e., the player has a distracted look on his face	**tweaks me by the nose**—to twist or pull something sharply, another sign of disrespect	**malefactions**—criminal acts; evil-doing
Hecuba—an ancient queen who lost her husband, children, and all her wealth	**lie i' th' throat**—a lie that comes from the throat is a small lie; a lie that comes from deeper, from the lungs, is a much worse kind of lie.	**tent him**—to probe into a wound

cue—a signal to an actor to enter the stage for their part	**Swounds**—short for "God's wounds," or Jesus's wounds, an old-fashioned swear word in Shakespeare's time, a way of taking God's name in vain.	**to the quick** – "quick" often means "alive" in Shakespeare; in this case, it means down deep in a wound, deep into the living body
cleave—to split something into two	**Pigeon-livered**—weak-hearted, having the liver/heart of a pigeon	**blench**—to flinch; to make a sudden movement out of fear or pain
appall—to horrify somebody with terrible news	**gall**—a kind of venom inside you; if you lack gall, then you lack the fortitude to do terrible things, like commit murder	**melancholy**—a feeling of sadness, typically with no apparent cause
confound—to confuse somebody with something unexpected	**fatted**—to have fed something and made it fat	**potent**—having great power
faculty/faculties—a person's mental abilities	**kites**—meat-eating birds; ravens, crows, etc.; always an ill omen in Shakespeare	**grounds**—factors forming a basis for action, such as "grounds" for a person's arrest.
muddy-mettled—sluggish, slow-witted, not very smart	**offal**—the internal organs and intestines of an animal	**relative**—in proper proportion to something else, having "grounds more relative" means having good enough evidence to justify believing the ghost

SECOND VIEWING ACTIVITY: THINKING ABOUT HOW PRODUCTIONS CUT *HAMLET*

For this second viewing activity, have students watch the Gibson and Hawke film versions of Hamlet's act 2 soliloquy: "Oh what a rogue and peasant slave am I" (2.2.577). At some two and half minutes each, these are shorter than the Branagh and Tennant versions because they make significant cuts to Shakespeare's script. Divide students again into groups of four, and assign the same watching roles from the previous activity.

They will find that the Gibson version sets the scene in a medieval castle and dresses Hamlet in old-style medieval clothes. The bit beforehand, with Priam and Hecuba, has been cut, but Hamlet's seeing the players in the courtyard midspeech sparks his idea for the mousetrap play-within-a-play. (Regarding Hamlet's age, Gibson was forty when he filmed his *Hamlet* in 1990).

The Hawke version has a big-city, turn-of-the-twenty-first-century vibe as its backdrop. Hawke is watching actors on television—the bit with the players has been completely cut—as the idea to set the mousetrap comes to him at the beginning of the speech. Instead of players performing a scene, Hawke's mousetrap is a video production that he creates and projects for his uncle in a special screening. (Hawke was just thirty when he played Hamlet in 2000; he was the youngest Hollywood Hamlet so far.)

Next, have students watch both film versions a second time. This time, using either an online document or a printed script of the soliloquy, have them highlight in yellow which lines Gibson keeps from Shakespeare's original. Next, have them highlight in green (or whichever color of highlighters is available) the lines Hawke keeps from Shakespeare's original. Have them underline and draw a box around those lines that both keep (i.e., those that are double highlighted) and cross out those that neither keep.

Students will notice that Gibson cuts almost the entire first half of the soliloquy and keeps most of the second half; some 50 percent of the speech remains. Hawke cuts quite a bit more; he keeps a little more than a third of the lines. Hawke keeps most of the first twelve lines, cuts out the middle, and then keeps most of the last quarter of the speech. Neither Gibson nor Hawke keep anything, though, that would require audiences to know who Hecuba is, but both keep some ten of the same lines, which students will have underlined, including the lovely rhyming couplet at the end: "The play's the thing / Wherein I'll catch the conscience of the king" (2.2.633–34).

These closing two lines are also the only lines that Olivier keeps. The Russian-language Smoktunovskiy version also reduces the speech to less than a minute. Because these two cut so much, their versions are not useful for this viewing activity (or the previous one); it is worth mentioning to students, though, just how much these two versions cut; they should know that there is a broad spectrum of choices film directors (and stage directors too!) have made when deciding how to cut lines from *Hamlet*. (Smoktunovskiy was thirty-nine when he filmed his Hamlet. Olivier was forty.)

Table 2.6

Mel Gibson as Hamlet (1990)	Hamlet's soliloquy begins at **1:00:45** and ends at **1:03:20** (3 minutes, cuts most of the first half of the speech)
Ethan Hawke as Hamlet (2000)	Hamlet's soliloquy begins at **45:40** and ends at **47:15** (2 minutes, cuts about half the lines)

After students have finalized their marked-up scripts, have one or two volunteers read aloud the versions as presented in the film. Analyze together as a whole class what is missing now. What remains? Which lines are most essential (i.e., are never cut)? What challenging vocabulary do both productions opt to cut? Do students agree with the cuts? Is there anything they would put back if they were to make their own film version of the soliloquy? Is there anything they think they would remove that the film versions kept?

Teacher Tip

Teachers do not need to retype out Shakespeare's scripts for activities like these. There are several reliable online, open-source Shakespeare editions, and teachers (and students) can copy and paste from these to bring longer passages from *Hamlet* into their work. The text below originated from open-sourceshakespeare.org (and then it was edited to match the Norton *Hamlet*, remove the line numbers, and fit on one page).

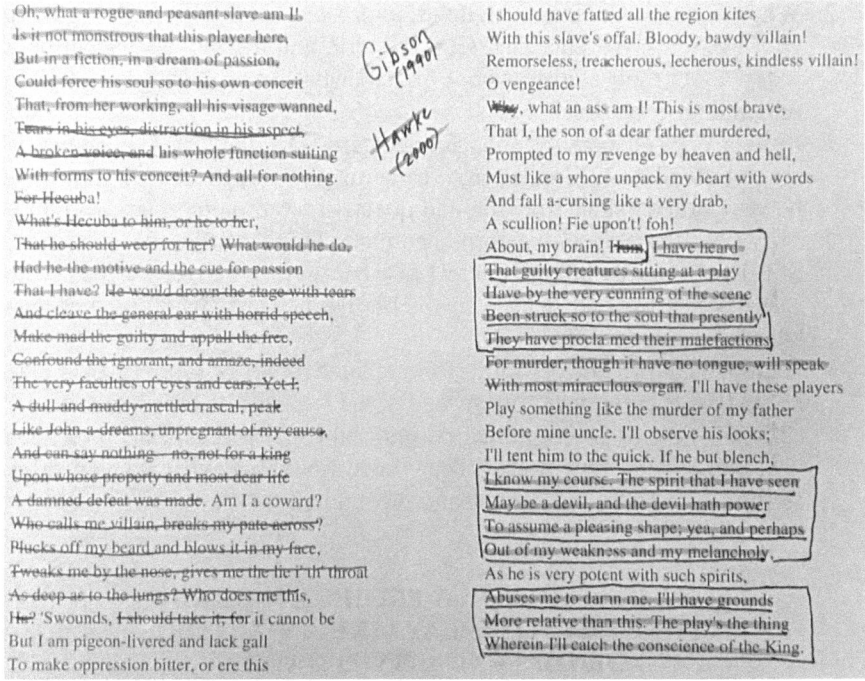

Figure 2.3: This example of marked-up script compares Gibson's and Hawke's cuts to Hamlet's act 2 closing soliloquy. The lines they both cut are crossed out, and the lines they both keep have a box around them.

DISCUSSION QUESTIONS AND WRITING PROMPTS

Like the questions from the previous chapter, the questions below can be adapted for various uses. They can guide the discussion, or teachers can use them as free-writing or assessment questions.

1. In the second half of 2.1, Ophelia reports to her father that Hamlet came before her while she "was sewing in [her] closet" (2.1.87). It happens off-stage, and audiences do not get to see it, only to hear Ophelia describe what happened.
   - First, describe what happens. According to Ophelia, how is Hamlet dressed? How does he behave?
   - Second, analyze why Hamlet acts the way he does. Is Polonius right? Do you think he is genuinely frustrated with Ophelia for ignoring him? Or does Hamlet do it to trick Ophelia into thinking he is mad? Could it be a combination of the two? Does he do it because he is hurting inside?
2. Why do you think Hamlet switches to prose in act 2 when he's speaking with Polonius, Rosencrantz, Guildenstern, and the players? What does it say about their status? About his? In what ways does it lend to him pretending to be mad?
3. Reflect on Rosencrantz and Guildenstern. Did they have a choice to spy on Hamlet? Is Hamlet right to be angry with them? Or should he be sympathetic since the king and queen ordered them to spy on him?
4. Why does the player's performance move Hamlet? Why does the story of Priam's murder affect Hamlet? In what ways is he like Pyrrhus (who is Achilles's son)? In what ways is he like Hecuba (who sees her husband/king murdered)?
5. Hamlet asks the players to perform "The Murder of Gonzago," a play he had seen previously, but to add some "dozen . . . or sixteen lines" (2.2.567–68). (It is not an actual play but one Shakespeare pretended was real.) Audiences do not hear those lines, but what do you think Hamlet adds to the play to ensnare his uncle?

ACT 2 CULMINATING PROJECT: WORKING THROUGH THE PLAY LIKE AN ACTOR OR DIRECTOR (TWO DAYS)

In this project students will get creative as they prepare a miniproduction of Hamlet's act 2 soliloquy. On the first day of this two-day project, in wrapping up their study of *Hamlet*'s second act, students will paraphrase Shakespeare's original words, finding meaning in his text, like an actor might do in preparing for a part. Directors and actors put careful thought into how they will transform Shakespeare's script into their own productions. *Hamlet* has been performed countless times across four centuries and by the greatest theater minds ever. To do it right, modern theater companies need to make *Hamlet* their own and do something that stamps the production with their own unique genius.

On the second day, students will cut the script to some three-quarters its original length, like a director would, and then take turns recording themselves reading their finished scripts aloud. To do the whole of *Hamlet* takes some four hours. It is too much, so most directors make cuts to make it palatable to a modern audience, carving away at least a quarter of the text, preferably a little more. Twenty-first-century Shakespeare productions rarely last more than three hours. Some theater companies prefer to keep their Shakespeare productions closer to two hours.

Day One: Paraphrasing

On the first day, students paraphrase Hamlet's words into their own.[8] Before a director or an actor can perform, they must understand every word. Students do too. A core tenet of this book is that students need not understand every word or phrase in the play to appreciate *Hamlet*, but they should practice doing so with a passage or two, a skill that they can apply to other passages.

Have students work together in pairs to craft their own line-by-line paraphrase of the entire speech. This will take some time. Some students may need to be reminded of the difference between a summary and a paraphrase. A summary would shorten the speech to just its main ideas. On the other hand, paraphrasing demands that students include the same level of detail as the original but in their own words. The first ten lines of the speech might become something like this:

> My gosh! I can't believe what a poor bum I am!
> Isn't it just wild to think that a mere actor
> Just in doing a play, getting himself all worked up for his part,
> Can get himself so into his character,
> That he can make his face turn completely white,
> Bawling and crying, all emotional,
> His voice breaking, and everything about him
> All turned into passion? And all for no real reason,
> Just for some fictional character named Hecuba?

If students completed the earlier watching activity in which the class compiled a glossary of unfamiliar words from the speech, have them consult it as they work. Alternatively, if they did not, teachers can copy out the definitions from that earlier section and provide them to students. They can also use an online dictionary or web search for unfamiliar words and phrases.

Students need not try to write in iambic pentameter or use familiar second-person pronouns (thee, thou, etc.). Their work should look and sound like their own everyday speech, but it also should be a line-by-line, word-by-word translation from Shakespeare's original. After pairs have completed their paraphrase, have them partner with another pair. In these groups of four, have them compare their work line by line. Which turns of phrase are they most proud of? Were there lines that still confused them? Provide clarification, and spend the remainder of the class working with students toward fully comprehending the speech.

Teachers should make their own model or use the one provided here. If time allows, close class by asking volunteers to share their work aloud, having two to three groups each read out loud what they came up with in their own words. As an exit pass, ask students to write out the one line from their paraphrase that they are most proud of.

Day Two: Cutting and Recording

For the second day of the project, in their original pairs from the previous class, have students return to the original soliloquy and, side by side with their paraphrase, reduce it by at least a quarter. The original is fifty-six to fifty-seven lines, depending on the version of the text. Their edited version should be no more than forty-two lines. Students should cut lines and words but add none of their own. Everything that remains must be entirely from Shakespeare.[9]

As they cut, teachers should roam the room, discussing students' decisions. Have they kept or cut the lines referring to Hecuba? If they have cut them, they are leaning toward a production that will be easier for a modern audience to understand. That is perfectly all right. What have they done with the unfamiliar words and phrases? How did they decide what to keep and what to cut?

They will also need to decide how the soliloquy will fit into the broader structure of the play; has Hamlet already formed his plan for act 3 before he speaks the soliloquy, or does the idea come to him while he is talking? Do they imagine the actor giving the speech directly to the audience? Or do they imagine him speaking it aloud to himself? Or a combination of the two? Also fundamentally important, does what is left after cutting still make grammatical sense when read aloud?

Original	Paraphrase
Oh, what a rogue and peasant slave am I!	Ugh. I can't believe what a loser I am!
Is it not monstrous that this player here,	It is absolutely insane to me to think that this actor here
But in a fiction, in a dream of passion,	Just in doing a play, getting himself all worked up for his part
Could force his soul so to his own conceit	Can get himself so into his character
That, from her working, all his visage wanned,	That he can make his face turn all pale,
Tears in his eyes, distraction in his aspect,	Bawling and crying, all emotional,
A broken voice, and his whole function suiting	His voice breaking, and everything about him
With forms to his conceit? And all for nothing.	All turned into passion? And all for no reason,
For Hecuba!	Just for some fictional character named Hecuba?
What's Hecuba to him, or he to her,	What is Hecuba to him, why should he care about her,
That he should weep for her? What would he do,	Why weep for her? What would he do
Had he the motive and the cue for passion	If he actually had a reason to get upset
That I have? He would drown the stage with tears	Like I do? Ugh, he would drown the stage with tears
And cleave the general ear with horrid speech,	And make every single person listen to his words.
Make mad the guilty and appall the free,	He'd make the guilty go mad, and the innocent furious,
Confound the ignorant, and amaze, indeed	Confuse all the idiots, and completely shock
The very faculties of eyes and ears. Yet I,	All our eyes and ears. But me,
A dull and muddy-mettled rascal, peak	A damned fool, I mope about
Like John-a-dreams, unpregnant of my cause,	Like a sleepy toddler, doing nothing for my father
And can say nothing—no, not for a king	Who can't say anything; no, say nothing for a king
Upon whose property and most dear life	A king whose kingdom and life
A damned defeat was made. Am I a coward?	Were stolen. What am I? A coward?
Who calls me villain, breaks my pate across?	Who out there would dare punish me, accuse me,
Plucks off my beard and blows it in my face,	Dare challenge me to my face or threaten me?
Tweaks me by the nose, gives me the lie i' th' throat	Who would say I was wrong or call me a liar?
As deep as to the lungs? Who does me this,	And the worst kind of liar too!? Who!?
Ha? 'Swounds, I should take it; for it cannot be	If they actually were to call me that, I'd have to take it.
But I am pigeon-livered and lack gall	I'm clearly a yellow-bellied chicken, and lack courage
To make oppression bitter, or ere this	To step up for what is right. Man, a long time ago
I should have fatted all the region kites	I should have fed to the buzzards
With this slave's offal. Bloody, bawdy villain!	This dummy's guts. Murdering, perverted monster
Remorseless, treacherous, lecherous, kindless villain!	Black-hearted, dangerous, violent dummy-head!
Why, what an ass am I! This is most brave,	My god, I'm worthless! Look how brave I am,
That I, the son of a dear father murdered,	The son of a murdered father,
Prompted to my revenge by heaven and hell,	Ordered by god and the devil both to revenge my dad,
Must like a whore unpack my heart with words	Stand here like a tramp chatting and chatting,
And fall a-cursing like a very drab,	Cussing him out, fighting with only words like a woman,
A scullion! Fie upon't! foh!	I'm just a nobody. My god!
About, my brain! Hum, I have heard	I could just pull out my hair! Hey, wait a minute, I've heard
That guilty creatures sitting at a play	That guilty people when they go to a play
Have by the very cunning of the scene	Have sometimes, when they see a scene,
Been struck so to the soul that presently	Got themselves so emotional, that suddenly
They have proclaimed their malefactions;	They confess all their sins:
For murder, though it have no tongue, will speak	For murderers don't tell us what they've done literally
With most miraculous organ. I'll have these players	But they tell us with actions! I'm going to have the actors
Play something like the murder of my father	Do a play that resembles the murder of my father
Before mine uncle. I'll observe his looks;	For my uncle to see. I'll watch how he reacts,
I'll tent him to the quick. If he do blench,	And see if it gets to him. If it does,
I know my course. The spirit that I have seen	I'll know what I need to do. That ghost I saw
May be a devil, and the devil hath power	Actually have been a devil, and devils have the power might
To assume a pleasing shape; yes, and perhaps	To look like they are angels, yah, and just maybe
Out of my weakness and my melancholy,	Because I've been feeling so sad,
As he is very potent with such spirits,	This devil has such an ability to do so,
Abuses me to damn me. I'll have grounds	And he is just trying to send me to hell. No, I'll figure out
More relative than this. The play's the thing	Better proof than just the ghost – the play's opportu—
Wherein I'll catch the conscience of the King.	Where I'll finally be able to see through the king

Figure 2.4: In this example of the paraphrase activity, Shakespeare's words are converted to a modern-day text. While professional paraphrasing texts are not very useful, students' making of them themselves can help teach close reading.

Students should do as they please with the script—Shakespeare penned it with the idea that a production would messy it up a bit—but they should be able to explain why they made the decisions they did. Sometimes it is as simple as liking how something sounds; many directors have made decisions based on their own aesthetic sense. Other times, their choices may be rooted in a deeper purpose, such as removing some of Hamlet's misogynistic language and crafting a more feminist Hamlet.

With the last ten to fifteen minutes of class, have students take turns reading their speech aloud and making recordings on their phones or on the devices they will submit. Before recording, students should practice reading aloud two to three times. They should look up how to pronounce words they are unsure of. These can be either audio or video recordings, though the emphasis on such a short production should be the words. If it's video, students should not think about costume or set. Each student in each pair should complete their own recording, taking turns doing the reading, then submitting.

Above all, they should give their reading their own voice; each production of Shakespeare is its own creation: the genius of its actor (standing on the shoulders of the countless other members of the cast and production team) blended into the genius of Shakespeare to make something new each time.

Ask student volunteers to play their recordings aloud to close the class if time permits. As an exit pass, ask students to summarize their work by finishing the following sentence: "One thing that makes my version of *Hamlet* different is that _____
_____."

> One thing that makes my version of Hamlet different is that we focused on making it as easy as possible to understand in today's English.

> One thing that makes my version of Hamlet different is that we got rid of all the lines that speak badly of women.

> One thing that makes my version of Hamlet different is that we tried to imagine it as a soliloquy that Hamlet was saying directly to the audience as he talked.

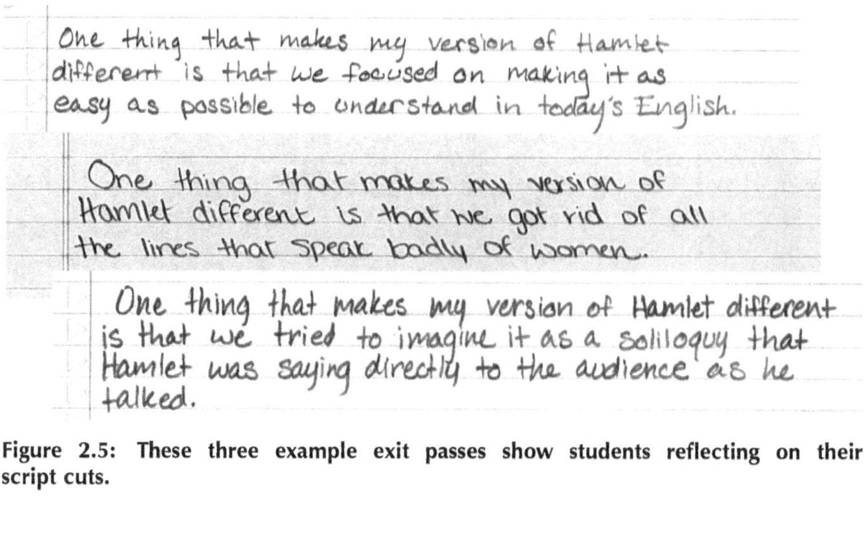

Figure 2.5: These three example exit passes show students reflecting on their script cuts.

REFLECTING ON WRITING: TAKE TWO

Like they did at the end of the act 1 culminating project, students should reflect on their writing. Ask them what they learned from this paraphrasing work that they can apply in other writing contexts:

> Reflect on your work with paraphrase. How did you work through each line as you wrote? What did you do when you came across words you did not know? How closely did you match the original words to your replacement words? Why is paraphrasing an important skill? Where do you think you will use this skill in the future?

First, brainstorm as a whole group, then take five to ten minutes for students to freewrite without worrying about punctuation or spelling. Save a few minutes at the end, after everybody has written, to share further. Adapt, though, as needed to fit the available class time.

NOTES

1. Kevin Long and Mary T. Christel (2019), as part of the *Folio* technique, offer teachers a suite of activities for teaching verse, shared lines, iambic pentameter, and other aspects of Shakespeare's language (90–112). In one of these for learning iambic pentameter, instead of just holding cards and emphasizing stress, like in my activity above, students tap dance out the rhythm; they "engage with the rhythm of the language through the physical use of their bodies . . . On each unstressed syllable of the line, they should 'step.' On each stressed syllable, they should drop their 'heel'" (107).

2. Edward Rocklin (2005) points out the natural silences in act 1, when Horatio first speaks to the ghost; four times, he pleads with the ghost to explain, and all four times, the ghost stays silent: "Imagine what must happen when you implore another creature, whether natural or supernatural, to speak—namely, you pause to allow time for a response . . . the short line can indicate a pause [like it does at the end of the Hamlet soliloquy too] . . . and the length of pause can be equivalent to the missing syllables . . . we begin to see how Shakespeare sought to control the way the actor playing Horatio speaks at this critical moment" (273).

3. Long and Christel (2019) have students return to F1 to decide whether "to voice or not to voice ending syllables" (69). The F1 punctuation is a bit different, though, from modern editions. Long and Christel explain when Shakespeare wants his actors to voice the extra syllable; instead of adding an accent mark, he writes out the letters, such as in "banished," "knowest," "throned," "seest," and so forth—these would all be pronounced as two-syllable words. But when Shakespeare wants them to leave these words unvoiced, he writes them as a contraction: "banish'd," "know'st," "thron'd," and "see'st"; these would all be pronounced as just one-syllable words (69–70).

Teachers should know that modern editors do not always agree with F1 punctuation; in the Ophelia example above, using Long and Christel's *Folio* technique would have "ungartered" be four syllables and "loosed" be two syllables.

4. Mary Ellen Dakin (2009) makes the case, too, that using capitalization to indicate stress is an easier system for students: "The capitalized syllables not only help students to immediately see stress, but to begin to see meaning . . . students have told me that handouts [using capitalization to indicate stressed syllables] . . . help them to understand what the speaker is saying because 'the most important words' and word-parts 'stand out'" (195). There are several other resources for learning about and teaching Shakespearean verse and prose, as well as rhythm and meter (Cohen [2006] 2018, 45–50; Duggan 2008, 18–22; Gibson [1998] 2016, 66–73; Gibson and Field-Pickering 1998, vi–vii, 28–45; Mellor 1999, 11–12).

5. Peggy O'Brien ([1994] 2006) suggests assigning "one student to read the [Hecuba] passage while three others mime the actions of Pyrrhus, Priam, and Hecuba, . . . the students can see the emotion the player creates and Hamlet's response" (93).

6. O'Brien ([1994] 2006) also offers teaching methods for comparing different film versions of the Hecuba speech and then having students paraphrase it into their own words (95–98).

7. Dakin's (2009) first five chapters address strategies for making Shakespeare's vocabulary accessible to students. Her premise is that most of Shakespeare's vocabulary is still accessible in the twenty-first century. She provides hands-on lessons for tackling the difficult words: "These activities show students the small percentage of Shakespeare's archaic words is surrounded by recognizable, modern words and that context clues and vocal inflection are natural tools for understanding them" (18). Cohen (2006/2018) similarly argues that teachers should "remind . . . students of the original 'fun' of Shakespeare's linguistic inventiveness" and provides strategies for tackling the vocabulary (55). Other excellent resources for teaching Shakespeare's vocabulary include Gibson and Pickering (1998, 135–37).

8. Ayanna Thompson and Laura Turchi (2016) warn against "translation-performance exercises: read the text, translate it into 'modern' English and perform the rewritten scene"; they explain that "while this activity does prompt a type of close reading, it does not allow the class as a whole to grapple with the dynamism of Shakespeare's language" (53). I agree. The first day of the culminating project outlined above would be insufficient by itself. Students should not just paraphrase and perform; rather, this work on day one of the activity is meant to prepare students to think like actors about to cut texts, setting them up for success in the next day's work as well as for the act 5 culminating project, when they will think like editors, making decisions regarding text, including cutting.

9. Mellor (1999) provides further discussion and activities for cutting *Hamlet* (96–98).

Chapter 3

"Words of So Sweet Breath"

Listening to Women's Voices — What Ophelia and Gertrude Reveal

Acts 2 and 3 occur in the same temporal space on the same day. Where there had been some two months between *Hamlet*'s acts 1 and 2, there is no break at all between acts 2 and 3. Polonius's and Hamlet's scheming from act 2, comes to fruition immediately in act 3: Polonius uses his daughter, Ophelia, as a pawn in 3.1, just as he said he would, and Hamlet has the players perform the mousetrap scene in 3.2, adding the requested lines to gull the king into revealing his guilt.

If the story of *Hamlet* is a battle of wits, though, a contest of who plays spy the best, then Hamlet wins in act 3. He recognizes and thwarts Polonius and the king's plot, realizing they are eavesdropping on him from behind the arras, but he pulls his own mousetrap off brilliantly. By the end of act 3, Hamlet also knows, without doubt, that the ghost told the truth and that his uncle is a murderer. So does Horatio. And to be sure there is no confusion for audiences, Shakespeare twice has the king explicitly confess his guilt in soliloquy—first, in an aside in 3.1 and then, again, with more detail as he tries but fails to pray in 3.3. Hamlet knows the truth, and playgoers do too.

Act 3 is also where audiences meet the women of the play, which this chapter will emphasize. In earlier scenes the two women of the play appear tangentially, but in act 3, their characters take center stage: Ophelia in 3.1 and Gertrude in 3.4. These raw scenes bare both women's souls. Ophelia does not get many lines, but her onstage presence during and immediately following Hamlet's "to be or not to be" speech and how an actress chooses to portray her in this pivotal scene provide the texture for the remainder of the play.

Similarly, later in act 3, Hamlet's bombast outshouts Gertrude's, but she likewise provides a counterbalance to Hamlet that reverberates through the rest of the play. Audiences are reminded through both women (as they were

52   Chapter 3

in act 2 through the players) of an alternative kind of Denmark that existed before the play, under the old king, and that could still have been under different circumstances.

This third chapter, in a similar format as the previous two, will provide learning objectives for the play's third act that teachers can use in their planning, suggestions for reading aloud as a class, a series of discussion questions and writing prompts, and a culminating project in which students create a critical reading of Gertrude—they get to choose whether to do so through an analytic or creative lens—thinking like a literary critic as they engage with the play. Teachers are always encouraged to adapt these ideas to meet their classroom needs.

ACT 3 LEARNING OBJECTIVES

1. Students will analyze Shakespeare's treatment of Ophelia and Gertrude and develop their own critical framework for reading the two heroines.
2. Students will identify changes in pronunciation since Shakespeare's time by analyzing rhymed couplets that no longer rhyme in modern English.
3. Students will compare competing perspectives of Ophelia's characterization by analyzing historical actresses' and critics' writings.
4. Students will compare film versions of Ophelia and Gertrude and evaluate their director's choices in portraying the two women.
5. Students will (like a literary critic) write a critical interpretation of Gertrude as a creative essay.

READING SCENES OF ACT 3 TOGETHER

Act 3 is long, and while it includes Shakespeare's most well-known speech, Hamlet's "to be or not to be," it also has several passages often cut from performance. As described below, teachers can safely gloss over some passages:

- 3.1 (the nunnery scene): The first scene opens with some fifty-five lines of the king scheming with Polonius, Rosencrantz, and Guildenstern (and a silent Ophelia in the background). The latter two exit, and the king and Polonius hide just out of sight as Hamlet enters. This opening can be summarized, so the class can start reading at line sixty-four.
  - Hamlet delivers his famous "to be or not to be" speech. Ophelia is also onstage, perhaps where Hamlet can see her, perhaps not. One classic

question a production (and a class) must answer is whether she hears it or not, and if so, whether he knows she hears it. It is different if he says it while knowing she is listening than if he's saying it just for the audience. Another classic question is at what point Hamlet knows he is being spied on. It changes everything if Hamlet knows it when he enters rather than if he figures it out later in the scene.
- The second half of the scene is the nunnery scene in which Hamlet belittles Ophelia and orders her to live her life chastely as a nun. The scene is filled with performative choices to be made that determine meaning and are a delight to puzzle through. It is worth careful reading and is the focus of the film analysis activity later in the chapter.
- As the scene closes, the king devises a plan to send Hamlet away to England, which will happen in act 4. Polonius suggests, though, that the king first allow him to spy on Hamlet one more time; this time he will hide himself in Gertrude's closet and listen as the mother and son speak, which will come to pass in 3.4.
- 3.2 (the mousetrap scene): The second scene is the mousetrap scene. It is the play-within-a-play that Hamlet orchestrated in act 2. The first forty-eight lines provide some wonderful metatheatrical fodder: Hamlet instructs the players on how to act. Audiences can almost hear Shakespeare chiding his own actors, teaching them how to best perform his words naturally, without overdoing them.
  - After this, Hamlet confides in Horatio his plan to dupe his uncle; the two will observe the king to see his reaction when he sees a version of his misdeeds performed onstage. The others then all enter—every major character is onstage for the mousetrap—and Hamlet decides to sit with Ophelia, making bawdy jokes as he does so. His lines to Ophelia in 3.2 will need to be handled delicately in some classrooms. Rather than explicitly explaining these here, curious students (and teachers) can rely on Google or their text's footnotes.
  - Next, the players act out the murder of the king. At line 280, though, it is the player king's *nephew* who pours poison in his ear, not his *brother*. Students must notice this difference. This alarms the king—the mousetrap is the story of a *nephew* killing a king—and the king recognizes the implicit threat, calls for light and for the show to stop, then storms off. Hamlet and Horatio are convinced by his reaction that the ghost has been an honest one.
- 3.3: The third scene is less than a hundred lines, but it is essential. The king attempts to pray but cannot. Hamlet sees him and contemplates killing him but decides to wait for a better time. Hamlet believes that if he kills the king while praying, he will send his soul to heaven, but he wants to make sure he sends his soul to hell instead.

- 3.4: In the closet scene, Hamlet goes to his mother as requested and rebukes her for having remarried. He twice goes too far in his chiding. When his mother cries out the first time, Polonius, who is hiding behind a curtain again, starts to come out, and Hamlet stabs him through the curtain, thinking it is the king. The second time, a bit later, the ghost appears, chiding Hamlet not to forget his purpose, and has him comfort his mother.
  - After the ghost departs, Hamlet reveals to Gertrude that he is not mad but only pretending and pleads with her not to go to bed with the king again. Then he exits, pulling Polonius's dead body offstage.

SOME NOTES ON SHAKESPEARE'S LANGUAGE: ORIGINAL PRONUNCIATION AND RHYMING COUPLETS

Shakespeare's English is not nearly as different from today's as students might think. It is still relatively easy, with some effort, to make out his language, at least compared with understanding the older versions of English that came before Shakespeare. Linguists call the English of Shakespeare's time Early Modern English. It was the version of English spoken some four hundred years ago, from roughly the late fifteenth century through the late seventeenth century. If one goes back in time just two hundred years before Shakespeare, though, to when Geoffrey Chaucer was writing, it would be far more challenging to understand the English people spoke then.

Linguists label the English of Chaucer's time Middle English, which lasted from roughly 1066, when the Normans took control of the English monarchy, until 1476, when William Caxton established the first printing press in England. Such labels are arbitrary, but Chaucer's language certainly would be harder for a twenty-first-century reader to decipher than Shakespeare's. And if an English speaker today went even further back, before 1066, they would not be able to converse with English speakers of the past at all; it would be like trying to speak with somebody in an entirely different language. Linguists label this Old English.

With that said, though, *Hamlet*'s language is still a challenge, and there have been significant pronunciation changes since Shakespeare's time. There are, of course, no audio recordings from Shakespeare's time to help, but scholars and actors have unraveled some pronunciations from the past. One way they have done this is by looking at examples of rhymed couplets in Shakespeare that no longer rhyme. The player king and queen provide eight such examples in 3.2. They speak exclusively in rhymed couplets, or, at least, they had rhymed originally in Shakespeare's time. Consider the player queen's first lines: "So many journeys may the sun and *moon* / Make us again count o'er [over] ere [before] love be *done*" (3.2.182–83, emphasis added). Four hundred years ago, "moon" and "done" rhymed. "Done" was pronounced then more like "dune" is today.

Another example comes in the first lines of her third speech: "The instances that second marriage *move* / Are base respects of thrift, but none of *love*" (3.2.205–6, emphasis added). In Shakespeare's time "move" was pronounced more like "muhv"; it rhymed with "love." There are five other examples in the player king's and queen's lines, which serve as clues to help with understanding how pronunciation in English has shifted: "sheen"/"been," "speak"/"break," "propose"/"lose," "flies"/"enemies," and "try"/"enemy." Teachers can work through the passages of the mousetrap for themselves, finding and highlighting these examples, or use it as another brief language activity with their students.

One joke seen later, in 3.2, is when Hamlet starts to spout a ditty that would have rhymed in his own time. He changes the last word, though:

> *Hamlet:* For thou dost know, O Damon dear,
> This realm dismantled was
> Of Jove himself, and now reigns here
> A very, very—pajock [peacock].
> *Horatio*: You might have rhymed. (3.2.307–11)

If Hamlet had rhymed, his last word in the ditty would have been "ass." Linguists know that "was" in Shakespeare's time was pronounced "whass." Back then, it rhymed with "ass." Teachers will have to decide whether to share this witty wordplay's behind-the-scenes function.

Theatergoers in Shakespeare's original theaters would have expected the naughty rhyme, though, and delighted in Hamlet's linguistic sleight of hand. Hamlet's father had been a "Jove"—one of the Roman names for Zeus—but his "realm" was "dismantled," and the current king, who "now reigns here," is nothing more than an "ass," or, rather, a peacock, which itself was no compliment. People in Shakespeare's time perceived peacocks as violent and lust-filled birds.[1]

ANTICIPATORY SET ACTIVITY: LOOKING UP THE WOMEN WHO PLAYED HAMLET

In this activity students will take twenty to twenty-five minutes to research and discuss the many women who have played Hamlet over the past two centuries. Some played it as men. Other productions made Hamlet a woman.

Some ignored gender. Whichever direction, though, there is a long tradition of female Hamlets that stretches across continents and centuries, and students should be aware of that rich heritage. This activity also provides a foundation for the chapter 5 culminating project in which students will build upon questions of gender and age as they analyze the play through the lens of an editor.

One woman who mastered the part was Sarah Bernhardt, in 1899. After playing the part onstage in a Paris run, she became the first person ever to play Hamlet on film. It is a silent film, less than two minutes total to the last scene. Online clips are readily available in the public domain and can be introduced to students to get a sense of the earliest Shakespeare work on film. In her time Bernhardt was one of the greatest actors in the world, and her production of Hamlet was the talk of Europe at the close of the nineteenth century.[2]

The 2019 play *Bernhardt/Hamlet*, written by Theresa Rebeck, tells the story of that production. Rebeck's fictional Bernhardt in that play makes the case that Hamlet should be portrayed as an adolescent between seventeen and nineteen. To this end, he should be played by a mature female actor—Bernhardt was fifty-four when she played Hamlet—who can pull off the voice and demeanor of a younger man but with the maturity that comes with age:

> [Hamlet] is a passionate, confused boy with the mind of a man of forty. A young actor, of what, twenty cannot understand the philosophy of Hamlet. An older actor no longer looks the boy, nor has he the ready heart of the woman who can combine the light carriage of youth with the mature thought of the man. The woman more readily looks the part and feels the part, yet has the subtleness of mind to grasp it. (16–17)

While it does not work textually for Hamlet to be nineteen—the three source texts leave room to make him either sixteen or thirty, but no other age (more on that in chapter 5)—her case that the part should be played by a woman who can look like a young man is a good one. (With that said, it is okay, too, for productions to cast blind to an actor's age; seventy-year-olds have played the thirteen-year-old Juliet on the professional stage before.)[3]

Bernhardt was not the first famous woman to play Hamlet. Before her, Sarah Siddons had played the part in multiple performances in the eighteenth and early nineteenth centuries.[4] And after her, a host of other notable women have succeeded in the role: Alice Marriott (1859, 1864), Charlotte Cushman (1861), Lillian Lawrence (1890s), Charlotte Compton (1899), Janette Steer (1900), Adelaide Keim (1905), Asta Neilsen (1921), Eve Donne (1923, the first ever to play Hamlet on radio), Yaeko Mizutani (1933, 1935), Frances de la Tour (1980), Leea Klemola (1995), Eie Asama (1995), Rebecca Hall

(1997), Angela Winker (2000), Maxine Peake (2014), Michelle Terry (2018), and many others.

For this activity, have students in pairs complete online research into one of the female Hamlets listed above. First, model by giving students a brief description of Sarah Bernhardt. Next, group students in pairs, assign each pair one of the women Hamlets listed above, and then instruct them to conduct preliminary research to find the following:

1. What year(s) she played Hamlet; what year she was born; and from these, calculate her age(s) when she played Hamlet
2. In what city and country she played Hamlet
3. Whether she played as a male, female, or nonbinary Hamlet
4. An online photo of their assigned female Hamlet
5. One interesting fact they can find about the production or her performance

Give each pair five to ten minutes for research, and then put the pairs into larger groups of four to six students for five to ten additional minutes, having each pair present their female Hamlet to the rest of the group. After the pairs have shared within their larger groups, bring the class together for whole-group discussion:

- What interesting things did you learn about your female Hamlet?
- Does it matter if an actor looks the right age for their part? Does it matter in the case of Hamlet? Should an audience be expected to use their imagination, or is a production better if it casts somebody who is the right age?
- Who do you think is better suited to play Hamlet, a female or male actor? Why?
- At one point Hamlet mentions his beard: who "plucks off my beard and blows it in my face"; it is part of the soliloquy students studied in-depth in chapter 2 (2.2.600). Would it be wrong for a production to cut that line so they could make Hamlet younger?

Teachers should let students know that the class will pick up these conversations when they get to act 5, which has some lines, depending on which source texts editors look at, clearly stating that Hamlet is either thirty or possibly just sixteen years old. It is a bit complicated, but it is a joy to puzzle through. More on that is to come in the last chapter.

ACT 3 BIBLICAL AND CLASSICAL REFERENCES: JULIUS CAESAR

There are some lovely biblical and classical references in act 3. The back-and-forth between Hamlet and Polonius, with its Julius Caesar reference, just before the mousetrap, though, is perhaps the most delicious in the whole play:

> *Hamlet:* You played once i'th'university, you say?
> *Polonius:* That did I, my lord, and was accounted a good actor.
> *Hamlet:* What did you enact?
> *Polonius:* I did enact Julius Caesar. I was killed i'the Capitol; Brutus killed me.
> *Hamlet:* It was a brute part of him to kill so capital a calf there.
> (3.2.105–12)

What makes it delicious, beyond the lovely turn of phrase Hamlet pulls off with "brute" and "capital," is the strong likelihood that the same two actors on Shakespeare's original stage who played Hamlet and Polonius also played Brutus and Julius Caesar in Shakespeare's *Julius Caesar* a year or so before. *Caesar* was first performed in 1599, and Hamlet was performed in 1600. And the onstage stabbing in that play's act 3 would still have been fresh in audiences' minds. It will parallel the stabbing to come in this play's act 3, when the actor playing Hamlet once more acts out the stabbing of the actor playing Polonius.

For those unfamiliar with Shakespeare's *Julius Caesar*, it retells the history of how Brutus and a group of like-minded senators, some two thousand years ago, in the name of democracy and freedom, assassinated Julius Caesar to keep him from becoming emperor of Rome. The idea was to protect the Roman Republic, but it did not work, since it led to a civil war and an eventual line of emperors who would rule for centuries. In Shakespeare's time everybody would have been familiar with Julius Caesar and the line of emperors who followed him.

Later in the same scene after the mousetrap, Hamlet mentions one of those later Roman emperors, Nero, who came to power a few decades after Julius Caesar. Alone onstage, Hamlet steels himself to see his mother:

> Soft, now to my mother.
> O heart, lose not thy nature! Let not ever
> The soul of *Nero* enter this firm bosom.
> Let me be cruel, not unnatural.
> I will speak daggers to her but use none. (3.2.425–29, emphasis added)

Nero is not remembered well by history. Under his watch, fires in Rome raged for days while he did nothing to stop them. He is also remembered for having had his own mother murdered. Hence, when Hamlet hopes that the "soul of Nero" will never "enter" his heart, he is reminding himself that he is not to kill his mother, which would be "unnatural." It is against nature's laws for any child ever to harm their own parent.

Earlier in 3.2, Hamlet also references Termagant, an imaginary Muslim deity prone to violence; then, a few words later, Herod, the king of Judea from the Gospel of Matthew, who, in hopes of killing baby Jesus, orders the execution of all male children under age two in Bethlehem: "I would have such a fellow whipped for o'erdoing Termagant. It out-Herods Herod. Pray you, avoid it" (3.2.13–15).

Because of the evil they symbolize, both characters were prone to being exaggerated in performance. Both appeared in fifteenth- and sixteenth-century morality plays as over-the-top villains. Hamlet instructs the players just before the mousetrap to avoid such excessiveness in their acting. Their acting should be subdued. Because of their obscurity in the twenty-first century, the Nero, Termagant, and Herod references are often cut in performance. Likewise, teachers should share the Julius Caesar bit with students, but they can save their knowledge of Nero/Termagant/Herod in case students ask about them.[5]

One last reference from act 3, which also often gets cut but that teachers should know, is Hamlet's reference to Vulcan's stithy. It also comes just before the mousetrap, as Hamlet is unveiling to Horatio his plan to reveal the king's guilt:

> If his occulted [hidden] guilt
> Do not itself unkennel [show] in one speech [the one that Hamlet has had the actors insert into the play],
> It is a damnèd ghost that we [Hamlet and Horatio] have seen,
> And my imaginations [delusions] are as foul [dirty]
> As Vulcan's stithy. (3.2.85–89)

Vulcan was the Roman blacksmith god of fire and metalwork. In Greek myth he was called Hephaestus. "Stithy" is an old-fashioned word for an anvil, or forge, upon which Vulcan would have pounded out weapons and armor. It would have been covered in soot from the work. Working it would have dirtied his hands with sediment. If the ghost has lied to Hamlet and Horatio, their plotting against the king has been as "foul" as the blacksmith god's ash-covered "stithy."

WHAT'S HAMLET BEEN READING?

Hamlet had been reading a book back in 2.2. When Polonius asks what he is reading, Hamlet never tells him, confounding him by replying, "Words, words, words" (2.2.210). Audiences never find out what Hamlet is reading, which becomes an open question for actors and readers to ponder. It is lovely to imagine, though, that Hamlet has been reading *The Aeneid* since his father's death. It is at least plausible: Hamlet reveals in 2.2 that his book features an older man, which could be Priam. Dido's "Tale to Aeneas," which is the stuff of book 2 of *The Aeneid*, as described in the previous chapter, had been on Hamlet's mind when he requested the players act out its story for him later in the scene.

Books 3 and 4 of *The Aeneid* also fit thematically into Hamlet's obsession with his mother's remarriage. In book 3 Aeneas narrates the rest of his years-long journey, and his heroism enchants Dido. In book 4 Dido confesses to her sister that Aeneas's tale kindled her longing to make him her second husband, even though she had sworn never to remarry after the murder of her first husband:

> Since the death of poor Sychaeus [her first husband], . . . this man [meaning Aeneas] alone has moved my heart and made me waver. I recognize the traces of that flame I felt before. But I'd sooner have the depths of earth gape open, and almighty Father [meaning Jupiter/Zeus] hurl me down to Hades with his bolt . . . before I disobey my conscience or its laws. The man who first married me still has my love. Let him guard it in his grave. (4.19–29)

Dido never stood a chance, though. Back in book 1, Venus had instructed Cupid to infect her with love. Cupid sat on her lap, disguised as Aeneas's little son, while Aeneas spent two books spinning his adventures. Dido fell utterly in love with him.

Their love starts well but ends badly. During a hunt a sudden storm comes on, brought about by the gods, and Aeneas and Dido get separated from the rest of their group. They take shelter alone in a cave, where they make love. Dido is convinced they are now married, but Aeneas sees things differently. Several months pass and, urged on by the gods, Aeneas chooses duty over love—he has been destined to found Rome—and abandons Dido at the end of book 4 to travel north to the site of what would one day be Rome. Overcome by his betrayal, she dies by suicide as he sails away.

Hamlet would have read it as a grave warning against remarriage. It may even be these lines from Dido that inspired Hamlet's additions to the mousetrap scene, the "dozen or sixteen lines" he had the players add to their

Figure 3.1: *Aeneas Tells Dido of the Sack of Troy*, Pierre-Narcisse Guerin (1815; image in the public domain, original in the Louvre Museum in Paris). Cupid, disguised as Aeneas's son, infects Dido with love as she listens to Aeneas tell of his adventures. Dido's sister listens from behind.

Source: https://en.wikipedia.org/wiki/Aeneas#/media/File:Gu%C3%A9rin_%C3%89n%C3%A9e_racontant_%C3%A0_Didon_les_malheurs_de_la_ville_de_Troie_Louvre_5184.jpg.

production (2.2.567–68). They echo the player queen's protestations against remarriage:

> Such [second] love must needs be treason in my breast.
> In second husband let me be accurst. . . .
> The instances that second marriage move
> Are base respects of thrift, but none of love.
> A second time I kill my husband dead
> When second husband kisses me in bed. (3.2.201–8)

READING ACTIVITY: INTRODUCING STUDENTS TO CUE SCRIPTS—THE NUNNERY SCENE

In this activity students will pair up to read Hamlet and Ophelia, looking for details that cue scripts reveal. Plan for fifteen to twenty minutes. It is designed to be completed after students have read 3.1, the nunnery scene, and have gained a surface-level understanding of its plot and thematic elements. It can then flow directly into the film activity that follows. Depending on the class, the two activities can be squeezed together into one fifty-minute lesson.

Alternatively, they also can nicely fill a longer block-schedule class or be spread across two fifty-minute classes. This activity can be modified to fit many scenes from Shakespeare. Cue scripts will also be provided in chapter 5 to guide students through the act 5 back-and-forth between Hamlet and the gravedigger.

In Shakespeare's time actors preparing their parts did not have access to an entire script. Instead, they just had their lines written out, along with the last line or part of the line before theirs, which was their cue. As a result, scholars now call these *cue scripts*, and they have spent considerable time thinking about how reading from a cue script is different from reading from a modern script.[6] Recreating and working from cue scripts allows today's students to explore these scholarly ideas about performance.[7]

One difference that students will notice is that they will need to pay careful attention as they listen to the other parts; they will need to hang on to every line, never quite sure how long it will be until their turn. That attention affects performance in subtle ways. Shakespeare sometimes even seems to have built miscues into his scripts, lines that lead an actor to interrupt when it is not yet their turn, creating a realistic dialogue where actors stumble over one another as real people do in actual speech. There are examples of this in the nunnery scene: Hamlet four times gives a variation of the line "to a nunnery, go," which is Ophelia's cue to speak her closing passage too soon; he also twice says, "Farewell," which are also two separate cues.[8]

Have students read through the scene twice, once as each character.[9] Do not let students get caught up with gender; every student should read Hamlet once, and every student should read Ophelia once. Make it a practice in your class to have students read lines that do not match their gender; when this happens in the theater, it is called gender-blind casting. In addition to the many notable women who have played Hamlet, some men have played Ophelia. Instruct students as they read to highlight unfamiliar vocabulary.

Have them use the definitions and context to help them understand what they are saying. When Hamlet chides Ophelia, "I have heard of your paintings," he is referring to women wearing makeup, which people in Shakespeare's time disagreed about. Some thought it was immoral for women to wear makeup, but many women felt they needed to meet the standards of youthful beauty required of women, a similar standard that women still struggle against.[10] Ask students how such standards today affect their choices about makeup and clothes. Ask them how they think Hamlet should deliver the line to be more cruel. How would they deliver it to be more gentle? What different reactions might Ophelia have in response?

After reading through the cue scripts twice, lead students in further discussion: What did they see in the scene?[11] How did they listen differently when they did not know precisely how long until their line? Which character gets more lines? Which words did they highlight that they need help defining? Would the scene make more sense if the actress playing Ophelia wore makeup? What if she was not? How did the context information in the cue scripts help them make sense of what they were saying?

"The Nunnery Scene" from 3.1: Hamlet's Cue Script
(Your lines are in bold; helpful notes are in italics.
Highlight words you don't know; listen closely for your cues.)

[YOU START] The fair Ophelia! Nymph, in thy orisons

orisons = prayers

Be all my sins remembered.

... for this many a day?

I humbly thank you; well, well, well.

... now receive them.

No, not I! I never gave you aught.
aught = anything

... There, my lord.

Ha, ha! Are you honest?
honest = virtuous

... My lord?

Are you fair?
fair = beautiful or pretty

... means your lordship?

That if you be honest and fair, your honesty should admit no discourse to your beauty.

... have better commerce than with honesty?

Ay, truly; for the power of beauty will sooner transform honesty from what it is to a bawd than the force of honesty can translate beauty into his likeness. This was sometime a paradox, but now the time gives it proof. I did love you once.

Some definitions and context:

- A "bawd" is a pimp, a man who brokers illicit encounters with prostitutes. Hamlet here is saying that women's beauty is like a pimp (i.e., their beauty turns them into whore)s. Virtue, though, lacks this "power"; being virtuous cannot protect women from their own beauty. The "paradox," then, is that women cannot be both beautiful and virtuous. His "proof" is mother, who was both beautiful and virtuous before, but who he now thinks of as a whore because she has married his uncle.

>...you made me believe so.

You should not have believed me; for virtue cannot so inoculate our old stock but we shall relish of it. I loved you not.

>...I was the more deceived.

Get thee to a nunnery! Why wouldst thou be a breeder of sinners? I am myself indifferent honest, but yet I could accuse me of such things that it were better my mother had not borne me. I am very proud, revengeful, ambitious; with more offenses at my beck than I have thoughts to put them in, imagination to give them shape, or time to act them in. What should such fellows as I do, crawling between earth and heaven? We are arrant knaves all; believe none of us. Go thy ways to a nunnery. Where's your father?

>...At home, my lord.

Let the doors be shut upon him, that he may play the fool nowhere but in's own house. Farewell.

>...you sweet heavens!

If thou dost marry, I'll give thee this plague for thy dowry: be thou as chaste as ice, as pure as snow, thou shalt not escape calumny. Get thee to a nunnery. Go, farewell. Or if thou wilt needs marry, marry a fool; for wise men know well enough what monsters you make of them. To a nunnery, go; and quickly too. Farewell.

>...heavenly powers, restore him!

I have heard of your paintings too, well enough. God hath given you one face, and you make yourselves another. You jig, you amble, and you lisp; you nickname God's creatures and make your wantonness your ignorance. Go to, I'll no more on 't. It hath made me mad. I say, we will have no more marriage. Those that are married already, all but one, shall live. The rest shall keep as they are. To a nunnery, go. [Hamlet exits.]

Some definitions and context:

- *"Calumny" (pronounced cal-uhm-nee) is a bad reputation. Hamlet is saying that no matter how chaste Ophelia is, she will always be thought of as a whore.*

- *When Hamlet accuses women of painting themselves another face, he is talking about makeup. Makeup was a thing back in Shakespeare's time, just like today, but some people did not think women should wear it, and Hamlet apparently agreed.*

"The Nunnery Scene" from 3.1: Ophelia's Cue Script
(Your lines are in bold; helpful notes are in italics.
Highlight words you don't know; listen closely for your cues.)

. . . all my sins rememb'red.

Good my lord, how does your honor for this many a day?

. . . thank you; well, well, well.

My lord, I have remembrances of yours that I have longed long to re-deliver. I pray you, now receive them.

* "remembrances" means gifts; Ophelia says for a long time she has been meaning to return Hamlet's gifts. . . . never gave you aught.

My honored lord, you know right well you did, and with them words of so sweet breath composed as made the things more rich. Their perfume lost, take these again; for to the noble mind, rich gifts wax poor when givers prove unkind. There, my lord.

. . . Are you honest?

My lord?

Are you fair?

What means your lordship?

. . . admit no discourse to your beauty.

Could beauty, my lord, have better commerce than with honesty?

. . . I did love you once.

Indeed, my lord, you made me believe so.

Some definitions and context:

- When Hamlet originally gave the gifts, he gave her "sweet breath" (i.e., he said "sweet" words to her), but that "perfume" has faded (i.e., he doesn't give her kind words anymore). "Wax" here means becomes; the gifts are poor because Hamlet has "prove[d] unkind."

                                                            . . . I loved you not.

I was the more deceived.

                                                            . . . Where's your father?

At home, my lord.

                                                            . . . but in's own house. Farewell.

O, help him, you sweet heavens!

                                                            . . . go; and quickly too. Farewell.

O heavenly powers, restore him!

                                                            . . . To a nunnery, go. [Hamlet exits.]

O, what a noble mind is here overthrown!
The courtier's, scholar's, soldier's, eye, tongue, sword,
Th' expectancy and rose of the fair state,
The glass of fashion and the mold of form,
Th' observed of all observers, quite, quite down!
And I, of ladies most deject and wretched,
that sucked the honey of his musicked vows,
Now see that noble and most sovereign reason,
Like sweet bells jangled, out of tune and harsh;
That unmatched form and feature of blown youth
Blasted with ecstasy. O, woe is me
T' have seen what I have seen, see what I see! [LAST LINE]

                            ecstasy = madness, insanity

Some definitions and context:

- In her last lines here, Ophelia is upset at seeing Hamlet's fall, how he has descended from being handsome and well respected into what seems to her like madness. Hamlet was once a "noble mind," and he had "sovereign reason," but now he is a "youth" who has been "blasted with ecstasy."

INCORPORATING FILM: FOUR CRITICAL APPROACHES TO OPHELIA

Actresses and critics alike have taken different approaches to Ophelia over the years. In this activity students will compare four historical readings of Ophelia from four different women and then apply those to different film versions of 3.1. After a discussion students will compare film versions of the interaction between Hamlet and Ophelia in 1.3. These clips are short, so time may allow to show more than just two.[12]

The first of the four women, Ellen Terry, earned her fame playing Ophelia in the late nineteenth century in London. She visited asylums to study their female inhabitants, modeling her acting at least in part on a patient she saw there who sat vacantly staring at a wall; she saw Ophelia as a timid, weak woman who was not strong enough to stand up to Hamlet or her father.[13] Rebecca West, on the other hand, when she played Ophelia, emphasized Ophelia's sensuality; she saw in Ophelia a disreputable young woman, one who takes delight in Hamlet's affections and his bawdy jokes. Frances Barber emphasizes Ophelia's intelligence as her defining characteristic, and Fran Richmond, her genuine goodness.

All four provide nuance into the character, but none, a single definitive reading. These four women's ideas, though, serve to get students thinking more deeply about the possibilities for Ophelia. Together, as a whole class, spend fifteen minutes reading aloud, discussing each of the four critical perspectives and pointing out the key characteristics of each. Have students highlight keywords each woman uses to define Ophelia; do this either in pairs, on paper, with actual highlighters, or together, as a whole class, projected, as everybody thinks through these together. Next, on the whiteboard, have a student volunteer to summarize key ideas, which may look something like this (see table 3.1):

Table 3.1

Ellen Terry	Ophelia as timid, weak, and passive
Rebecca West	Ophelia as disreputable, but not scandalous
Frances Barber	Ophelia as intelligent, highly perceptive
Fran Richmond	Ophelia as good, too good for the world in which she finds herself

As the discussion progresses, have students compare the four perspectives and evaluate their preferences. Which ones most closely align with their own readings of Ophelia from 3.1? Is she a weak, timid character? Is she disreputable? Is she acutely intelligent and highly perceptive? Is she an innocent sacrificial lamb too pure for the world around her? Or is she some combination? Or, rather, something different entirely from these? If students were directing or performing Ophelia, which elements would they include in their portrayal?[14]

Afterward, compare at least two competing film versions of 3.1. Like in the previous chapters' film activities, divide students into groups of four, and assign students in each group one of the four watching roles:

- *Casting director:* Which elements of the four historical interpretations of Ophelia appear in the film actresses' portrayals? In what ways do they seem to incorporate weakness, disreputableness, intelligence, and goodness? In what ways do the film actresses find their own readings of Ophelia?
- *Set and props designer:* Pay attention to the set and props. Where are Hamlet and Ophelia when they talk? What do you notice about the room that makes it special (e.g., many mirrors)? What are the "remembrances" that Ophelia tries to give back to Hamlet? What do these say about the nature of their love? What other props do you see?
- *Special effects manager:* At what point does Hamlet realize he is being spied upon? What happens that alerts him that somebody is eavesdropping on him and Ophelia? How does he change as a result? How does this moment affect Ophelia?
- *Camera operator:* Pay special attention to the camera angles the production utilizes. How often does the scene utilize long-distance shots and how often close-ups? What is the emotional effect when the camera zooms in on their faces?

Table 3.2

Laurence Olivier as Hamlet; Jean Simmons as Ophelia (1948)	Starts at **55:40**; Ophelia exits at **1:00:10** (5 minutes)
Innokentiy Smoktunovskiy as Hamlet; Anastasia Vertinskaya as Ophelia (Russian-language film with English captions, 1964)	Starts at **49:30**; Ophelia exits at **53:30** (4 minutes)
Mel Gibson as Hamlet; Helena Bonham Carter as Ophelia (1990)	Starts at **45:25**; Ophelia exits at **48:35** (3 minutes)
Kenneth Branagh as Hamlet; Kate Winslet as Ophelia (1996)	Starts at **1:36:45**; Ophelia's speech ends at **1:43:25** (3 minutes)
Ethan Hawke as Hamlet; Julia Stiles as Ophelia (2000)	Starts at **48:00** and ends at **52:25** (5 minutes)
David Tennant as Hamlet; Mariah Gale as Ophelia (2009)	Starts at **1:00:35**; Ophelia's speech ends at **1:04:35** (4 minutes)

* *The Olivier, Smoktunovskiy, Gibson, and Hawke productions all cut Ophelia's last speech; choose the Branagh or Tennant version to keep these lines.*

As with previous chapters' film activities, watch one version to start, give five minutes for discussion, and then watch the same lines from the others. The start and end times are listed in the table (3.2) below:

Teachers should adapt this lesson over time as they teach it, bringing in other written perspectives of Ophelia that they may encounter in their own research. There are many places to find these: actress interviews from a current performance or excerpts from a program from local productions. One adaptation would be to have students research and present additional perspectives on performing Ophelia. Teachers can incorporate the best of these into future versions of the activity.

ELLEN TERRY
(1847–1928)

"But soft! The fair Ophelia! Sweet rose of May!" The whole tragedy of her life is that she is afraid; I think I am right in saying she is Shakespeare's only timid heroine. She is scared of Hamlet when trouble changes him from the "point-devise" lover—the "glass of fashion and the mould of form"—into a strange moody creature, careless of his appearance, bitter in his speech, scornful of society. She is scared of her father, and dare not disobey him, even when he tells her to play the spy on Hamlet. She is scared of life itself when things go wrong. Her brain, her soul and her body are all pathetically weak. It is not surprising that she should think Hamlet mad, for all he says in the scene in which she returns his presents is completely beyond her.

Ellen Terry, (1932), "Pathetic Women," in Four Lectures on Shakespeare, edited by Christopher St. John, (New York: Benjamin Bloom), 165–66.

REBECCA WEST
(1893–1983)

There is no more bizarre aspect of the misreading of Hamlet's character than the assumption that his relations with Ophelia were innocent and that Ophelia was a correct and timid virgin of exquisite sensibilities. She was not a chaste young woman. That is shown by her tolerance of Hamlet's obscene conversations, which cannot be explained as consistent with the customs of the time. If that were the reason for it, all the men and women in Shakespeare's plays, Romeo and Juliet, Beatrice and Benedict, Miranda and Ferdinand, Antony and Cleopatra would have talked obscenely together, which is not the case. The truth is that Ophelia was a disreputable young woman: not scandalously so, but still disreputable.

Rebecca West, (1957), The Court and the Castle (New Haven: Yale University Press), 18–19.

FRANCES BARBER
(B. 1958)

[Ophelia] is acutely intelligent and highly perceptive. Because of her position at court she has to choose her words even more carefully than, say, Miranda or Juliet. She recognises the potential repercussions of Hamlet's madness before anyone else in the play; albeit she is powerless to prevent them. My thoughts then ran to why she is therefore traditionally seen in such ineffective passive capacity, and I discovered that rather than being an extension of Hamlet's character, she actually presents the female counterpart and counterpoint to him. She provides the feminine qualities lacking in his sensibilities. Shakespeare uses her innocence and naivete to illustrate this imbalance and highlight its consequences: the destruction of a potent and feminine force, caught up in a male-dominated power struggle. However thin on paper, her function in the play is therefore vital: to suggest to the audience an alternative set of events, very much in the 'if only' tradition.

Frances Barber, (1988), "Ophelia in Hamlet," in Players of Shakespeare 2, edited by Russell Jackson and Robert Smallwood, (Cambridge: Cambridge University Press), 139.

FRAN RICHMOND

Ophelia is the sacrificial lamb: her innocence represents the values of an earlier time when Hamlet's father ruled as divinely ordained, and Gertrude was not yet false. The creeping corruption of the court at Elsinore does not taint the purity of her soul—far from it—but its workings act on those around her, threatening and then overcoming her sanity, leading ultimately to her death. Ophelia's tragedy is that she is too good for the corrupt world in which she finds herself.

A dutiful, obedient and loving daughter, she acts on Polonius's wishes not only out of what was for the time conventional obedience, but also from a deeply felt respect for her father's judgment and wisdom. Her involvement in her father's spy network is not malicious or self-interested: she truly believes that the grieving Hamlet has lost his senses. But, as a result, she suffers Hamlet's vile insults against herself personally and against women in general. Her . . . responses to Hamlet show not a weakness of character but rather indicate her depth of feeling for him. The pain Hamlet's comments inflict on Ophelia is real, but it stems not simply from their indisputable hurtfulness but also from what they reveal to her of his internal torment.

Qtd. in Bronwyn Mellor, (1999), Reading Hamlet (Urbana, IL: National Council of Teachers of English), 52–53.

FOLLOW-UP CREATIVE WRITING ASSIGNMENT: THE FOUR OPHELIAS

As a creative writing follow-up assignment, have students imagine a diary entry following the nunnery scene from the previous activity's four different perspectives of Ophelia. Have them first imagine what Ellen Terry's Ophelia (the weak, timid Ophelia) would write in her journal following her scene with Hamlet. Second, have them imagine what Rebecca West's Ophelia (the disreputable Ophelia) would write in her diary, then Frances Barber's Ophelia (intelligent and perceptive), and then Fran Richmond's Ophelia (the good Ophelia).

Since they are writing four of these, have them keep each one brief, maybe three to four sentences or a quarter page or so each. Instruct them to give enough details, though, in their short descriptions to make each of their four Ophelias unique from one another, as well as to write in a way so that it will be easy to match up each Ophelia to the actress/critic who wrote the initial description (e.g., make sure Rebecca West's Ophelia actually sounds disreputable in her journal entry).

DISCUSSION QUESTIONS AND WRITING PROMPTS

There is so much to talk about in act 3. Here are just a few starting points for conversation and writing:

1. Hamlet contemplates but ultimately rejects suicide in 3.1. On what grounds does he decide against suicide? Find specific lines in the speech where Hamlet gives his reasoning. What other reasons can you add for why Hamlet should carry on?
2. In what ways does the mousetrap resemble the actual story of how the king murdered his brother? In what ways is it different? What effect comes from having it be the *nephew* who kills the king instead of the *brother* in the play-within-a-play? In doing so what warning/threat does Hamlet send to the king?
3. Why can the king not ask God for mercy at the end of 3.3? Is it his pride, his unwillingness to admit even to God the murder he has committed? Is it his sense of guilt? Are people generally willing or unwilling to ask for forgiveness after doing something wrong? Why or why not? Are you generally willing to admit when you have made a mistake and ask for forgiveness?

4. Is it merciful or cruel, at the end of 3.3, that Hamlet decides to wait to kill the king? In what way is it merciful? In what way is he crueler for waiting? Do you think Hamlet is right or wrong to wait?[15]
5. In 3.4, in her first line to Hamlet, Gertrude chooses the familiar, second-person pronoun: "Hamlet, thou hast thy father much offended" (3.4.8), but Hamlet answers with formal pronouns, and Gertrude responds by switching to formal pronouns too. What does her shift suggest to an actress preparing to play Gertrude in this scene? What does it mean when she reverts to familiar pronouns later in the scene? What does it suggest that Hamlet never uses familiar pronouns with his mother throughout the play?

ACT 3 CULMINATING PROJECT: WORKING THROUGH THE PLAY LIKE A CRITIC

In this project, using Margaret Atwood's poem "Gertrude Talks Back" as a model—teachers can easily find the poem with a quick online search of the poet and title—students will write their own short, one-page first-person account of Gertrude. Literary critics like Atwood, a respected novelist perhaps most famous for *The Handmaid's Tale*, have had much to say about the women of *Hamlet*. Atwood sees a darker reading of Gertrude, whom she makes the primary agent in her husband's murder. Students will approach the play like Atwood, like a literary critic, synthesizing their own critical reading of Gertrude and then shaping that interpretation through either a creative or analytic lens.

First, take ten to twenty minutes to analyze Atwood's poem together as a class. Which of her two husbands does Atwood's Gertrude think was better looking, the old Hamlet or Claudius? Which one was more fun? Which matters more to her? What is her opinion of Ophelia? Of Hamlet? What secret does she reveal at the end? What makes Atwood's Gertrude an interesting character, albeit an evil one? What parts of her character come directly from Shakespeare, and which are Atwood's inventions? Why does Atwood give her poem the title she does? What does it mean to "talk back"?

Emphasize that Atwood draws on specific textual references in crafting her version of Gertrude: her Gertrude answers back to specific lines that Hamlet had said to her—about wringing her hands, the bloat king, about the rank sweat of an enseaméd sty—and turns those words back on him. Similarly, the four women describing Ophelia also made specific references back to the text of Hamlet. In their writing, whether analytic or creative, students should find at least two specific lines from the text, things that Hamlet or Gertrude say, and have their Gertrude mention them.

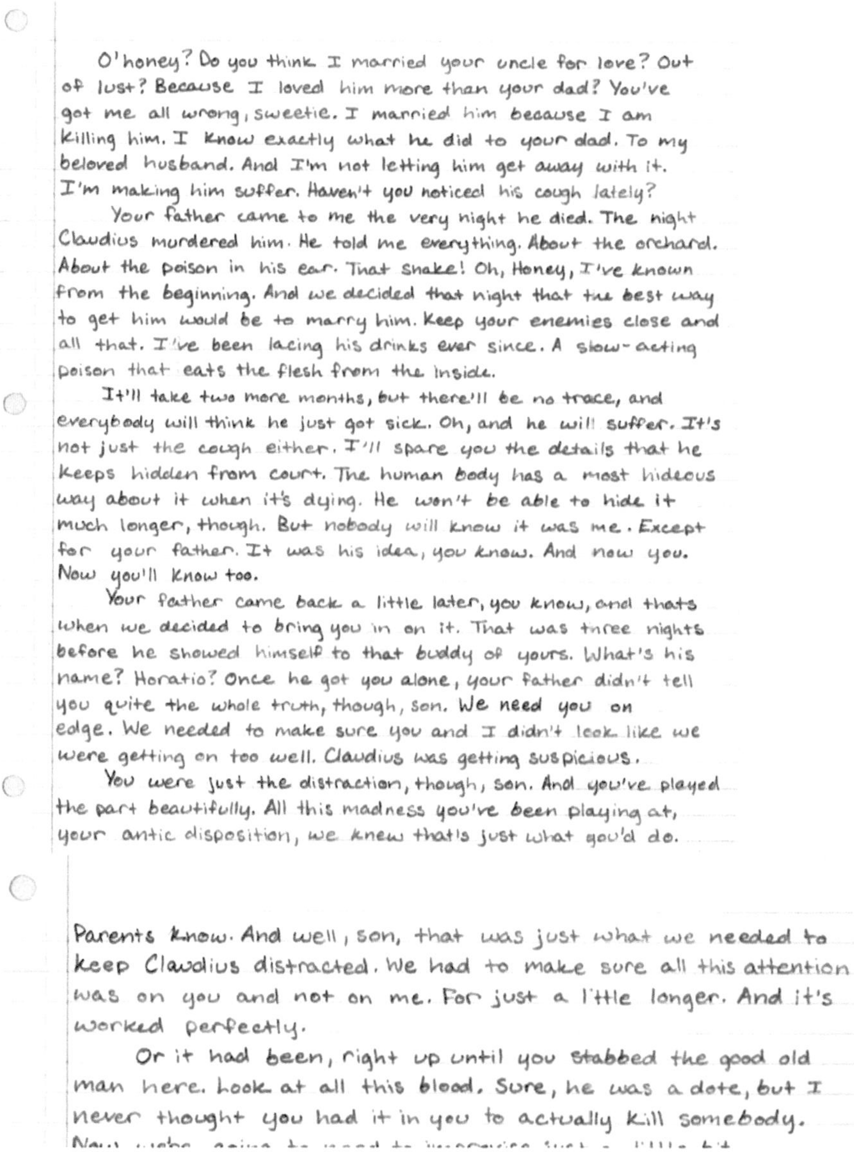

O' honey? Do you think I married your uncle for love? Out of lust? Because I loved him more than your dad? You've got me all wrong, sweetie. I married him because I am killing him. I know exactly what he did to your dad. To my beloved husband. And I'm not letting him get away with it. I'm making him suffer. Haven't you noticed his cough lately?

Your father came to me the very night he died. The night Claudius murdered him. He told me everything. About the orchard. About the poison in his ear. That snake! Oh, Honey, I've known from the beginning. And we decided that night that the best way to get him would be to marry him. Keep your enemies close and all that. I've been lacing his drinks ever since. A slow-acting poison that eats the flesh from the inside.

It'll take two more months, but there'll be no trace, and everybody will think he just got sick. Oh, and he will suffer. It's not just the cough either. I'll spare you the details that he keeps hidden from court. The human body has a most hideous way about it when it's dying. He won't be able to hide it much longer, though. But nobody will know it was me. Except for your father. It was his idea, you know. And now you. Now you'll know too.

Your father came back a little later, you know, and thats when we decided to bring you in on it. That was three nights before he showed himself to that buddy of yours. What's his name? Horatio? Once he got you alone, your father didn't tell you quite the whole truth, though, son. We need you on edge. We needed to make sure you and I didn't look like we were getting on too well. Claudius was getting suspicious.

You were just the distraction, though, son. And you've played the part beautifully. All this madness you've been playing at, your antic disposition, we knew that's just what you'd do.

Parents know. And well, son, that was just what we needed to keep Claudius distracted. We had to make sure all this attention was on you and not on me. For just a little longer. And it's worked perfectly.

Or it had been, right up until you stabbed the good old man here. Look at all this blood. Sure, he was a dote, but I never thought you had it in you to actually kill somebody.

Figure 3.2: In this example of the culminating project, Gertrude knows what Claudius did to her first husband and has been plotting a slow revenge ever since she found out.

Next, lead students as a whole class in a discussion of their perceptions of Gertrude. Brainstorm key adjectives that could describe her. Push them in directions other than Atwood's or their most obvious interpretations. What would it mean, for example, to craft a Gertrude drowning in sadness or one who spends all her time planning big social events? They would be very different characters. What about a philosophical Gertrude who is always lost in her thoughts, staring out a window? Or a doting mother obsessed with trying to make her son whole again? Students' final work needs to be grounded in textual examples, but students should take considerable liberties within those boundaries to craft their own reading.

In addition to the two specific lines students will reference, have them choose one defining characteristic they will emphasize in their writing, much like each of the four women above did in describing how they played Ophelia. These may be positive or negative attributes, depending on what kind of Gertrude they want to create. Atwood makes her Gertrude a strong-willed but devilish character capable of murder. If she were to describe Gertrude in one word or phrase, it might be "murderer" or "uses violence to get what she wants." Encourage your students to have very different takes on the character from one another; the project will prove far more interesting the more varied and creative students get.

Give students two options for writing about Gertrude like a critic: they are to write (1) a half-page analytical essay modeled after one of the four women who wrote of Ophelia in the chapter's previous activities or (2) a creative option in which they capture the voice of their Gertrude, modeled after Atwood as a poem or monologue. Either way, their writing should capture one specific reading of Gertrude—they should be able to summarize their Gertrude in a few words, as they did earlier with the four Ophelias—and it should refer to at least two specific lines from earlier in the play.

REFLECTING ON WRITING: TAKE THREE

As they did at the end of each of the previous two culminating projects, have students reflect on their writing and, specifically, on how their knowledge and skills have transferred (and will transfer) across different writing domains:

> Reflect on your writing thus far from the *Hamlet* unit. How was writing like a critic like writing a ghost story for act 1? What strategies did you use in both? How was writing like a critic similar to paraphrasing a speech from Shakespeare, like you did for act 2? Why is this kind of critical writing and thinking important? How will you use these skills in the future?

Again, reflect aloud as a whole class, then have students write for five to ten minutes, and, if time allows, close with further discussion after students have written. Adjust as necessary.

NOTES

1. The word "pajock" seems a typo for peacock, but modern editors have left it with an explanatory gloss because they are not certain what Shakespeare meant. "Pajock" was not a word in Shakespeare's time (and still is not, except when talking about this one line from *Hamlet*.) One twentieth-century scholar thinks Shakespeare meant "puttock," another word for a buzzard (Tannenbaum 1932, 127–30). While both birds would have carried negative connotations for Shakespeare's audiences, comparing Claudius to a buzzard is very different than comparing him to a peacock. Whether a "peacock" or "puttock" or something else, the verse works because it doesn't rhyme with "ass," which was Horatio's point in the next line. *Hamlet* leans heavily on bird imagery; Shakespeare mentions peacocks, sparrows, herons, hawks, and others. One resource for students and teachers to learn more about Shakespeare's use of bird imagery is https://www.birdsofshakespeare.com/.

2. Sarah Bernhardt's *Hamlet* opened on May 20, 1899. *Hamlet* had been popular in French theater through the nineteenth century, but Bernhardt was the first to do it in a translation true to Shakespeare's original. Before her, French productions of *Hamlet* had been looser adaptations that suited the show to French tastes. These played with key ideas from the play—like letting Hamlet live at the end—but Bernhardt's version made it *Hamlet* again, just in French. It was a success, and Bernhardt toured through England, Europe, and the USA. Gerda Taranow details Bernhardt's achievement in her 1996 book, *The Bernhardt Hamlet*.

3. Michael Byrnes and Siân Phillips played the title roles in a production of *Romeo and Juliet* at the Bristol Old Vic in 2010. Byrne was sixty-six years old, and Phillips was seventy-six.

4. Tony Howard (1997) writes of the women who have played Hamlet across the centuries in *Women as Hamlet: Performance and Interpretation in Theatre, Film and Fiction*, including several international female Hamlet actors in non-English performances. His research finds that Fanny Furnival, in 1741, was the first woman to play Hamlet but that Sarah Siddons was the first established actress to do so; Siddons first played the part in 1776 and would revive the role several times over a thirty-year span (Howard 1997, 16, 38–4; also see Boatner-Doane 2017 and Woo 2007). Early actresses, like Siddons and Bernhardt, mostly ignored gender and played as though they were men, carrying on the same stage traditions their male counterparts had before them. Later actresses, though, would make the performance a critique of what today would be called toxic masculinity. Angela Winkler, for example, a German actress, played Hamlet in 2000. She was fifty-five years old at the time, the same age as Bernhardt when she'd played in *Hamlet* a century before. Unlike Bernhardt, she exposed the toxicity inherent in earlier male-dominated performances done before her in Germany. Her Polonius was everything wrong with toxic men: "The male Hamlet

tradition gone rotten"; the actor playing him had been Hamlet himself years before, in a "pre-feminist production where Gertrude was half-naked with painted breasts, and Ophelia was a sex-toy" (Howard 2007, 288). Winkler made Rosencrantz and Guildenstern chorus boys who sang and danced. For teachers who would like a preview, Howard's first ten pages are included as an excerpt in the Norton *Hamlet* text.

5. Ralph Alan Cohen (2006/2018) adds the following for teachers to know: "Termagant was thought to be a noisy and violent Middle Eastern god. Thus a bad actor who outdoes Termagant is being superhuman in a bad way, an idea which is picked up in Hamlet's next speech, when he says they '[imitate] humanity so abominably" (61). Regarding Herod, he adds that "out-Herod" is word Shakespeare invented, "which refers to the ranting and raving stage impersonations of the king who ordered the murder of the baby Jesus" (61). Cohen's explanation is not just about the biblical reference, though; he is making the case that with the right scaffolding, even challenging components of Shakespeare's language are accessible to modern students.

6. Patrick Tucker (2016) explains that in Shakespeare's time, "instead of receiving a full copy of the play, the actor would be presented with a script that consisted just of his own lines, plus the cue words before each speech" (29). From this original practice, present-day theater makers and teachers use cue scripts to recreate the conditions in which Shakespeare's original actors learned their parts. Tucker (1990) argues that "using the same approach in teaching Shakespeare leads to fascinating insights and makes the whole subject much more accessible and interesting to all groups, from junior school pupils to post-graduates and professional actors" (25). Winston (2015) suggests, as an opening activity, having students stand back-to-back and read from cue scripts for Francisco and Bernardo; students are to work through the dialogue three times: first in whispers, then in shouts, and lastly, repeating and echoing words or phrases that stand out (60–61). Kevin Long and Mary T. Christel (2019), citing Tucker, offer strategies for using cue scripts to teach *A Midsummer Night's Dream* and for teachers making their own cue scripts (168–74). Miranda Fay Thomas (2019) makes the case for using cue scripts in the university classroom (128–37).

7. Paul Menzer (2008), in *The Hamlets: Cues, Qs, and Remembered Texts*, makes the case that studying just the cues in Hamlet reveals insights into text and meaning: "Scripts were distributed to players in parts. . . . Since players learned their lines in isolation, cues were the only textual fragments that overlapped between one player and another, and thus the only bits of text that more than one player had to commit to memory. Cues sutured a play's individual parts into a performable whole and were therefore the critical textual apparatus for turning a script into a performance" (18). His crux then is that in the original source texts for Hamlet, the First Quarto (Q1), the Second Quarto (Q2), and the First Folio (F1)—more on those in act 5—the cues provide textual stability. The internal words in a passage could shift across early performances, but the cues could not. If an actor alters a line in the middle of his speech but gets the cue right, the next actor still knows when it is his turn to speak. But if an actor fails to get the cue right, the performance breaks down. Menzer finds that cues remain stable, too, through print: "Of the thousands of cues that Q2 and F share, only around twenty significantly differ"; most lines differ at least in some small way between Q2 and F1, but hardly at all in their cues (41).

8. Menzer (2008) explains that "Ophelia's last cue, 'to a Nunry go,' is given prematurely.... It may threaten to prompt Ophelia's speech, 'Oh what a noble mind is here oerthrowne,' ten lines too soon, but that speech is prompted only by the "Nunry go' cue but also by Hamlet's exit ... Shakespeare varies the phrasing of Hamlet's repeated enjoinder to Ophelia" (64).

9. Peggy O'Brien ([1994] 2006) provides reading strategies for the nunnery scene, including having students read through the scene multiple times and comparing film versions (103–06).

10. Several scholars have explored issues related to cosmetics and makeup in Shakespeare's time. Farah Karim-Cooper (2019), for example, in *Cosmetics in Shakespearean and Renaissance Drama*, points out that women's use of cosmetics—a word that was not yet in everyday speech during Shakespeare's lifetime—was a complex subject; Hamlet may have critiqued women wearing makeup, but Shakespeare himself likely wore makeup on the stage (198). Scholars generally think that he played the ghost in *Hamlet*, and Karim-Cooper makes the case that the ghost would have worn such makeup (178–79). Boy actors, clown characters, twins, and spirits all likely wore makeup onstage (201–2). Karim-Cooper argues that Shakespeare engaged in the debate about women's cosmetics in his plays while simultaneously using makeup as part of the materiality of performance. Aileen Ribeiro (2011) in *Facing Beauty: Painted Women and Cosmetic Art* points out that Hamlet's line "let her paint an inch thick, to this favor she must come," while not intentional on Shakespeare's part, nonetheless provides an ironic, sad prologue for the women who died from cosmetic lead poisoning (188). Other recent scholars who have studied cosmetics in Shakespeare's time include Patricia Phillippy and her *Painting Women: Cosmetics, Canvases, and Early Modern Culture*, as well as Andrea Ria Stevens and her *Inventions of the Skin: The Painted Body in Early English Drama, 1400–1642*.

11. Emily Griffith Jones (2019) and her students, ask themselves the following about Ophelia: "What would it mean for her insanity, like Hamlet's, to be a sign not of powerlessness but of intent and savvy? ... Ophelia may not simply be mourning either Polonius or her loss of Hamlet; she may be signaling her choice to end her own life and leave the corrupt court" (61). She explains that the best part of that work with students was an "Ophelian transformation of traditional silence into critical and creative speech" (62).

12. My inspiration for having students compare these four actresses' perspectives started from a University of Windsor graduate course taught on-site by Dr. Donald Laing over a three-week period at the Stratford Shakespeare Festival in Ontario, Canada, in the summer of 2004. Bronwyn Mellor (1999) likely inspired that lesson in *Reading Hamlet* (52–53), which Dakin (2009) also cites as an example in her lesson on getting students to think about multiple readings of a character (135). Over the years of teaching *Hamlet*, I've tweaked it with many classes and now offer the activity here as a revision of what these earlier teacher-scholars shared with me.

13. Ellen Terry (1932) explains her process for preparing to play Ophelia: "I went to the madhouse to study wits astray. I was disheartened at first.... Then, just as I was going away, I noticed a young girl gazing at the wall. I went between her and the wall to see her face. It was quite vacant, but the body expressed that she was waiting,

waiting. Suddenly she threw up her hands and sped across the room like a swallow. I never forgot it. She was very thin, very pathetic, very young, and the movement was as poignant as it was beautiful" (161).

14. Ayanna Thompson and Laura Turchi (2016) make that case that "it is often very powerful when advanced learners have close readings modelled for them that contradict each other" and point to Hamlet's "Get thee to a nunnery" as an example (39; also see p. 16). They point out that "some read this line as a request to protect Ophelia's chastity among a group of celibate nuns, others read this line as an order for Ophelia to become a sex worker," explaining that "brothels in the early modern period were euphemistically called nunneries" (39).

15. Winston (2015) suggests using "interpolated questions" for teaching 3.3, a process actors use at the RSC. Students read their scripts but are interrupted by questions from the teacher. For example, the teacher would ask, "Why is your sword drawn?" To which students would answer, "Now might I do it pat, now he is praying"; the teacher would then ask, "And then?" And students would answer, "And now I'll do't. And so he goes to heaven" (71–72; 3.3.77–79). By working through the speech this way, teachers break the speech into parts and guide students to a deeper understanding of the soliloquy: "It is aimed at making the text as alive and relevant as possible, helping players feel they are thinking these thoughts and speaking them for the very first time" (Winston 2015, 71).

Chapter 4

"Like the Painting of a Sorrow"

Drawing Scenes from Hamlet— Getting Visual with the Text

Act 4 opens with Gertrude revealing to the king that Hamlet has murdered the "good old man," Polonius, but she keeps Hamlet's secret that he is only pretending to be mad (4.1.12). The king immediately realizes how easily it could have been him and has Hamlet brought before him, but Hamlet bests him in a witty battle of words, and he answers by having Hamlet sent to England that very night. He had planned to do so since act 3, but now he accelerates Hamlet's departure, and Hamlet disappears for the second half of act 4.

And the really good stuff of act 4 happens without Hamlet. This isn't his act. It belongs most of all to Ophelia and, to a lesser degree, to her brother, Laertes. With Hamlet gone, some days or even weeks pass between 4.4 and 4.5, and Ophelia breaks inside. Whereas Hamlet has been pretending to be mad, Ophelia slips into an awful mental place. Scholars sometimes refer to 4.5 as Ophelia's mad scene, but this book will refer to it instead as her flower scene. It is perhaps one of the best tests in Shakespeare's canon of an actor's skill.

Every production must find its own way to do Ophelia's flower scene, and when done well, the scene is perhaps Shakespeare's best at instilling pathos in audiences. Playgoers cannot help but pity her, seeing how the rancid Elsinore court—the king's treachery, Hamlet's misogyny, and her father's misdealing—has crushed Ophelia. Laertes speaks for centuries of playgoers and readers when he tenderly laments that her story can turn "thought and afflictions, passion," even "hell itself . . . to favor and prettiness" (4.5.211–12).

With Laertes's return—he had left in the play's second scene to return to university in France and has been absent since—he provides contrast to both Hamlet and Ophelia. Whereas Hamlet found out months ago that his father had been murdered and has brooded over how to proceed ever since, Laertes storms back from France, raises an army, and is ready to enact immediate revenge for his father's murder, even if it means killing the king. He needs no ghost to prod him. Whereas Ophelia slips from sanity after her father's death, Laertes slips from reason. This is a play about children who have lost their fathers and how they respond. Hamlet loses himself in thought. Laertes loses himself in rage. And Ophelia loses herself in grief.

This fourth chapter, following a similar format to the first three, will provide learning objectives for the play's fourth act that teachers can use in their planning, as well as suggestions for reading aloud as a class, an explanation of ecphonesis, a series of discussion questions and writing prompts, and a culminating project in which students consider the play like an artist would, recreating a moment or theme from the play through drawing or painting.

ACT 4 LEARNING OBJECTIVES

1. Students will define ecphonesis and analyze its possibilities for interpretation.
2. Students will compare a passage from *Hamlet* to a historical painting or illustration derived from that passage and make text-to-text connections between the two.
3. Students will compare and analyze film portrayals of Ophelia's flower scene.
4. Students will (like an artist) analyze a passage from *Hamlet* and synthesize its details to create a visual illustration depicting a scene from *Hamlet*.

READING SCENES OF ACT 4 TOGETHER

Teachers can gloss over the first four scenes for students and pick up again with an in-class reading of 4.5. Ophelia's flower scene (4.5) is ideal for acting out in class. Use artificial flowers as props; it is okay if they are not the exact flowers. Have students stand in groups of five, with one student reading Ophelia's flower lines aloud and passing out flowers according to the clues in the script.

- 4.1: Gertrude reveals that Hamlet has killed Polonius. She twice tells the king, though, that Hamlet is mad—as "mad as the sea and wind when both contend / Which is the mightier" and that it was in "his very madness" that he committed the murder (4.1.7–8, 26). In doing so, Gertrude either believes that Hamlet is still genuinely mad despite his

protestations, or she has decided to lie to her husband and keep her son's secret as he asked her to do.
- 4.2: Rosencrantz and Guildenstern find Hamlet and ask him where Polonius's body is hidden, but Hamlet toys with them instead of answering. Hamlet agrees, though, to go with them to see the king.
- 4.3: Hamlet toys with the king, too, but eventually divulges where Polonius's body is hidden—beneath the lobby stairs—and the king orders Hamlet to be sent to England that night for his own safety. After all the others exit, the king reveals in a soliloquy that he has made secret plans to have Hamlet killed in England.
- 4.4: The scene shifts outdoors. It is at least a day later, perhaps more. Hamlet encounters one of Fortinbras's captains on his way to England. He learns that there will be a battle over a worthless scrap of land, where thousands will die. The captain exits, and Hamlet soliloquizes that he is even more determined to revenge his father; if others can get themselves worked up over something as trivial as a useless plot of land, then it should be easy for him to rouse himself to revenge the murder of such a great king as his father.
- 4.5 (Ophelia's flower scene): Hamlet disappears from the action for the rest of act 4. Significant time passes, at least a week, probably a bit more. Ophelia has slipped into her own madness following her father's death, and Laertes has returned from France to Denmark. The scene opens with Ophelia making distracted conversation with the king and queen and singing nonsense songs; scholars have long puzzled over their melodies and lyrics. While such study is fascinating scholarship, it is better in a first or second reading to instead emphasize Ophelia's sadness and mental health.
    - In the second half of the scene, Laertes makes a warlike reappearance. He had been absent from Denmark since the first act. Laertes craves revenge for his father. The king, though, cools his wrath. Ophelia reenters, singing and passing out flowers. As with her songs, scholars have long sought symbolic meanings for her six types of flowers—rosemary, pansies, fennel, columbines, rue, and daisies—which will be the stuff of later activities and discussion in the chapter. In the students' first reading, though, teachers should focus on tone: the scene's overarching mood swings, starting with Ophelia's grief, through Laertes's rage, and then back to Ophelia.
- 4.6: In this short scene, Horatio receives a letter from Hamlet in which Hamlet reports that he is soon to return to Denmark: he has been abducted by pirates, but the pirates are "thieves of mercy" and have treated him kindly (4.6.21). Some scholars argue that Hamlet devised the scheme in advance and paid the pirates to rescue him.[1]

- 4.7: The action returns to the royal palace. The scene sets up the action of act 5: the king will devise a fencing match between Hamlet and Laertes, but Laertes will douse his foil in poison, and just to be sure, the king will prepare a poisoned chalice for Hamlet to drink midway. The tone changes, though, when Gertrude enters and narrates Ophelia's death. Laertes weeps for his lost sister, which ends act 4.

SOME NOTES ON SHAKESPEARE'S LANGUAGE: THE ECPHONESIS "O"

Shakespeare sometimes uses "oh" in a passage and, other times, "O." These are not the same thing. The first should be read as simply the word "oh" in whatever manner best fits the scene. But the capital "O" is different. It indicates *ecphonesis*, a device that playwrights have used since ancient times to create a vocal space for exclamation. It leaves room for an actor to insert more emotion into a line than the words by themselves make space for.

Actors may choose to use something like "oh" packed with their own unique emotional punch, but they may also choose an entirely different kind of sound, something that sounds nothing like "oh": perhaps something more like an "ack" or "ugh" or something that cannot even be spelled out as a word, whatever best suits their interpretation of the line.

For example, an actor playing the king might use *ecphonesis* to add a special oomph after learning that Hamlet has killed Polonius: "O heavy deed! / It had been so with us, had we been there" (4.1.13–14). An actor could choose to use the "O" to sigh heavily as he contemplates his mistakes, echoing his confessional from 3.3, giving an introspective flavor to the rest of his passage; he sees all the deaths adding up because of his treachery. Alternatively, and as most actors choose to do, he could fill the space with a disgusted snarl at the threat Hamlet has become; he doubles down on his first murder as he plans his second. There are countless possibilities. Shakespeare leaves the space open.

Another act 4 example comes later from Laertes, when he first sees what has happened to his sister: "O heat, dry up my brains! Tears seven times salt / Burn out the sense and virtue of mine eye" (4.5.177–78). Like the example with the king, the passage begins with ecphonesis; Shakespeare often begins a line or passage with ecphonesis. Imagine a burn seven times greater than salt in the eyes. Shakespeare is instructing the actor playing Laertes to craft a sound to match that torment. It is Laertes's first sound at seeing Ophelia, and Shakespeare leaves two other such spaces in the same passage to build on it further. The part is not timid; it is for an actor capable of portraying anguish.

"Like the Painting of a Sorrow"   85

There are many more examples of ecphonesis throughout *Hamlet*. As students encounter these, explain the creative freedom they offer. Many readers (and actors too) choose to fill the space with something that sounds like "oh," which is a fine choice, but students should be aware of other possibilities. Encourage them to get playful with the vocal space; their choice should fill roughly the space of a single syllable—or maybe just a little more—but Shakespeare leaves the rest to the imagination.[2]

Know that editors sometimes have differing views on when to include ecphonesis. Some use "oh" in a line, whereas others use "O," and vice versa. There is wiggle room for editors to decide. In the Laertes lines above, for example, Shakespeare's First Folio (F1) has "oh," but his Second Quarto (Q2) has "O." Both are respected textual sources, and editors must choose which to follow. Modern editors, in this case, have all chosen to follow the Second Quarto and keep the "O." These ideas about textual sources—the First Folio

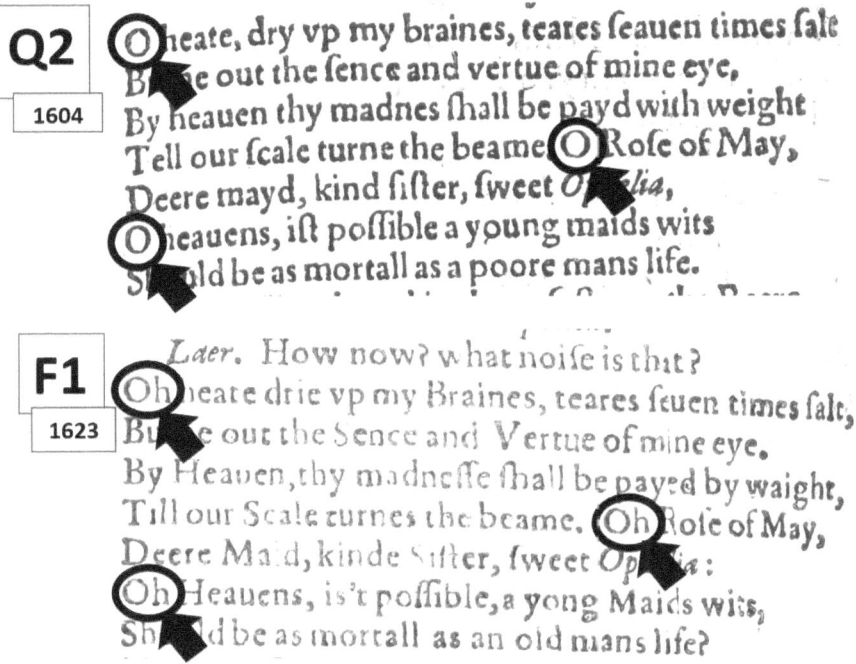

Figure 4.1: One of the first printings of Hamlet—the Second Quarto (Q2) from 1604—uses ecphonesis throughout Laertes's passage, whereas a later printing—the First Folio (F1) from 1623, which is the most influential volume of Shakespeare ever published—uses "oh" instead. Modern editors have all kept the ecphonesis, agreeing with the Q2 reading. These early printings and why they matter to teachers and students will be a central topic in chapter 5.
Source: British Library and Shakespeare Library website.

86   Chapter 4

and the Second Quarto—and how to use them with students will be the stuff of the next chapter. More on that soon.

ANTICIPATORY SET ACTIVITY: ANALYZING PAINTED SCENES FROM *HAMLET*

In this activity students will analyze a series of eight illustrations inspired by *Hamlet*, taking part in a long history of artists (and students) transforming scenes from Shakespeare into visual art.[3] Each image captures a specific line from the play and reveals its artist's particular reading of the play. Artists, like actors and directors, must make interpretative choices. There is no definitive reading of *Hamlet* but, rather, an infinite myriad of valid possibilities to explore. This does not make every reading valid, though. To be valid, a reading must still be rooted in the lines of the actual text.

The text leaves room for even the same artist—or actor or scholar or reader—to have varying interpretations. Henry Fuseli, for example, paints Hamlet's father's ghost in two different ways. In his first painting below (see figure 4.3), he gives his act 1 ghost a long, helter-skelter beard as he directs the action toward vengeance. In his second, though (see figure 4.7), Fuseli's act 3 ghost has a neatly trimmed beard and projects calmness; he gazes down with pity at his son and wife. Fuseli's first ghost induces action. His second subdues it. Delacroix, on the other hand, maintains consistency across his three prints: the king, for example, wears the same royal necklace in all three of his prints (see figures 4.2, 4.5, and 4.6). Hamlet also looks similar across the series.

The eight images below represent familiar tropes seen in *Hamlet* paintings and illustrations. Each represents but one possible visual reading of the scene it depicts. A simple online image search using the key terms from the captions will reveal many more. Before class find each image, then copy and paste it with its accompanying text and questions into an online document to share with students. All images are in the common domain or licensed under a Creative Commons license that permits their use for nonprofit, educational purposes. In class put students into pairs, and assign one image to each pair. Have them take ten to fifteen minutes to complete the following steps:

1. First, look at your assigned image carefully. Who are the characters in each? Are the characters standing or sitting? Who or what are they looking at? What are they doing? What do their facial expressions reveal?
2. Next, compare the image to the actual words from *Hamlet*. Highlight specific details in the text that the artist includes.

3. After that, take three minutes and conduct a quick online image search using these details from the original text. How many similar images can you find? Can you see any similarities between these and your image?
4. Last, work through the provided discussion questions with your partner(s).

After the anticipatory set activity, follow up with a whole-group discussion. Have each pair briefly present their images and findings with the rest of the class. The students' analyses of the eight images above and the tropes they represent provide a foundation for the culminating act 4 project in which students will create a visual response to Shakespeare's lines in the same vein that has inspired artists for centuries. More on that will come at the end of the chapter.

Figure 4.2: Eugene Delacroix. "Cast thy nighted color off." *The Queen Tries to Console Hamlet*. 1834. Lithograph.

Source: Metropolitan Museum https://www.metmuseum.org/art/collection/search/337353.

> *Gertrude:* Good Hamlet, cast thy nighted color off,
> And let thine eye look like a friend on Denmark.
> Do not forever with thy vailèd lids
> Seek for thy noble father in the dust.
> Thou know'st 'tis common; all that lives must die,
> Passing through nature to eternity
> *Hamlet*: Ay, madam, it is common.
> Gertrude: If it be,
> Why seems it so particular with thee?
> *Hamlet:* "Seems," madam, Nay, it is. I know not "seems."
> 'Tis not alone my inky cloak, good mother,
> Nor customary suits of solemn black, . . .
> That can denote me truly. These indeed "seem,"
> For they are actions that a man might play;
> But I have that within which passes show
> These but the trappings and the suits of woe. (1.2.70–89)

- Look closely at the queen's face. What emotion does she exhibit toward her son? By looking away from her, Hamlet portrays what emotion in response?
- Even though it is a black-and-white illustration, Hamlet's clothes are darker than the others; find the words in the passage that the artist read to decide on having Hamlet wear darker clothes than the rest. Did the artist get the details right? Does it matter?
- What does the king's facial expression suggest about the situation? Does he look like a concerned stepparent in the scene or a murderer-tyrant? What does that say about the artist's interpretation of the king?

Figure 4.3: After Henry Fuseli. "It beckons you to go away with it." *Hamlet, Horatio, Marcellus, and the Ghost* (Shakespeare, *Hamlet*, act 1, scene 4), 1796. Engraved by Robert Thew, 1852. Stipple Engraving.
Source: Metropolitan Museum https://www.metmuseum.org/art/collection/search/365584.

"Like the Painting of a Sorrow" 91

> *Horatio:* It beckons you to go away with it,
> As if it some impartment did desire
> To you alone.
> *Marcellus:* Look with what courteous action
> It waves you to a more removed ground.
> But do not go with it.
> *Horatio:* No, by no means.
> *Hamlet:* It will not speak; then I will follow it.
> *Horatio:* Do not, my lord.
> *Hamlet:* Why, what should be the fear?
> I do not set my life at a pin's fee,
> And for my soul, what can it do to that,
> Being a thing immortal as itself?
> It waves me forth again. I'll follow it. (1.4.63–76)

- Does the artist's Hamlet trust the ghost? Does Hamlet seem likely or unlikely to believe the story he will hear when the ghost does speak?
- In the image Horatio holds back Hamlet, while Marcellus is almost out of sight. What does their arrangement say about Hamlet's relationship with Horatio? With Marcellus? Why is Horatio more willing to use his body physically to hold Hamlet back?
- What does the artist do with shadow and texture to make his ghost different from the living characters? How does this ghost compare with the film versions you have seen?

Figure 4.4: Henry C. Selous. *Sleeping in My Orchard*. Book illustration. 1870.
Source: https://commons.wikimedia.org/wiki/File:Selous_-_Hamlet.jpg.

"Like the Painting of a Sorrow" 93

> *Ghost:* Sleeping in my orchard,
> My custom always in the afternoon,
> Upon my secure hour thy uncle stole,
> With juice of cursed hebona in a vial,
> And in the porches of my ears did pour
> The leprous distilment, . . .
> Thus was I, sleeping, by a brother's hand,
> Of life, of crown, of queen, at once dispatched . . .
> *Hamlet:* O all you host of heaven! O earth! What else?
> And shall I couple hell? Oh, fie! Hold, hold, my heart . . .
> O villain, villain, smiling, damnèd villain! . . .
> That one may smile and be a villain. (1.5.66–115)

- This image depicts events from before the play started; it is the scene in which the ghost tells his son how he was murdered, but that would not have appeared on stage. Why do you think the illustrator drew a scene that would not have appeared on stage? As a book illustration, how does the image help explain the ghost's narration of his death?
- What details from the original passage in 1.5 does the artist include? What does he add? Why do you think the artist invents a snake on the ground to watch the murder? What might the snake symbolize?
- Hamlet refers to his uncle as a smiling villain, but the artist chooses not to show him smiling in this illustration. Is that still consistent with the text? If you were to depict these lines in art, would you show Claudius smiling instead?

Figure 4.5: Eugene Delacroix. "Madam, how like you this play?" *The Play-within-a-Play.* 1835. Lithograph.
Source: Metropolitan Museum https://www.metmuseum.org/art/collection/search/337106.

Hamlet: Madam, how like you this play?

Queen: The lady doth protest too much, methinks.

Hamlet: O, but she'll keep her word.

King: Have you heard the argument? Is there no offense it in't?

Hamlet: No, no, they do but jest, poison in jest [ingest]. No offense i' th' world.

King: What do you call the play?

Hamlet: "The Mousetrap." Marry, how? Tropically. This play is the image of a murder done in Vienna. Gonzago is the duke's name, his wife Baptista. You shall see anon. 'Tis a knavish piece of work, but what of that? Your Majesty and we that have free souls, it touches us not. Let the galled jade wince, our withers are unwrung. (3.2.253–67)

- Identify the main characters in the painting: Gertrude, the king, Polonius, Ophelia, Hamlet, the players, and Horatio. What is each character doing with his or her hands? What does that say about each one? Who or what is each watching with his or her eyes? Why?
- Why is Hamlet sitting on the floor, resting on Ophelia's lap? Find the line in 3.2 where Hamlet says he will watch the play from this position.
- Why is Polonius not paying attention to the play? Find the line in 2.2 where Hamlet accuses Polonius of being a lousy audience member. What does Hamlet say in that scene that Polonius always does at the theater?
- Look carefully at the three actors in the background. Which scene are they reenacting? What does the king's face reveal about what he thinks of the play? Why is Horatio watching the king instead of the play? What is the king about to do in the moments just after this image?
- Do you think the mousetrap proves the king is guilty?

Figure 4.6: Eugene Delacroix. "O, my offense is rank, it smells to heaven." *Hamlet Attempts to Kill the King.* 1834. Lithograph.

Source: Metropolitan Museum https://www.metmuseum.org/art/collection/search/337348.

King: O, my offense is rank, it smells to heaven . . .
But, O, what form of prayer
Can serve my turn? "Forgive me my foul murder"?
That cannot be since I am still possessed
Of those effects for which I did the murder —
My crown, mine own ambition, and my queen.
May one be pardoned and retain th'offense? . . .
Hamlet: Now might I do it, now he is a-praying.
And now I'll do't. And so he goes to heaven,
And so am I revenged. That would be scanned:
A villain kills my father and for that,
I, his sole son, do this same villain send
To heaven . . .
And am I then revenged,
To take him in the purging of his soul,
When he is fit and seasoned for his passage?
No.
Up, sword, and know thou a more horrid hent.
King: My words fly up, my thoughts remain below;
Words without thoughts never to heaven go. (3.3.40–103)

- What does the artist reveal through Hamlet's facial expression? What's going through his mind? What keeps him from taking his revenge on his uncle?
- Why does the artist choose to have the king's eyes open? What else does the artist say about the king through his facial expression? Is he actually praying or not? What line in the text backs up this reading?
- Is Hamlet right or wrong to decide to wait to kill the king? Is it wrong that he wants to make sure the king's soul goes to hell and not heaven? Or is that fair?

Figure 4.7: Henry Fuseli. "Amazement on thy mother sits. / O, step between her and her fighting soul." *Gertrude, Hamlet, and the Ghost of Hamlet's Father.* 1793. Oil on Canvas.

Source: https://commons.wikimedia.org/wiki/File:F%C3%BCssli_-_Gertrud,_Hamlet_und_der_Geist_des_Vaters_-_1793.jpeg.

Ghost: Do not forget. This visitation
Is but to whet thy almost blunted purpose.
But look, amazement on thy mother sits.
O, step between her and her fighting soul . . .
Speak to her, Hamlet.
Hamlet: How is it with you, lady?
Queen: Alas, how is it with you?
That you do bend your eye on vacancy . . .
Whereon do you look?
Hamlet: On him, on him! . . .
Queen: To whom do you speak this?
Hamlet: Do you see nothing there?
Queen: Nothing at all; yet all that is I see.
Hamlet: Nor did you nothing hear?
Queen: No, nothing but ourselves. (3.4.126–153)

- Describe Hamlet's reaction to seeing the ghost in his mother's closet. How does the artist portray Hamlet to create a sense of his emotion?
- Who is Gertrude looking at? What do her facial expressions reveal? Find the textual evidence where Shakespeare makes it clear that she cannot see the ghost in this scene.
- Compare this version of Fuseli's Hamlet to his other version above (figure 4.3). How are their emotions different? Which of the two versions is more visually interesting?
- Next, describe the ghost's facial expression. In what ways is Fuseli's version of the ghost in this image different from his version of the ghost in figure 4.3?

Figure 4.8: After Robert Edge Pine. "There's rosemary, that's for remembrance?" *Ophelia* (Shakespeare, *Hamlet*, act 4, scene 5). Engraved by Caroline Watson. 1784. Stipple engraving.

Source: Metropolitan Museum https://www.metmuseum.org/art/collection/search/431236.

Ophelia: There's rosemary, that's for remembrance. Pray you, love, remember. And there is pansies, that's for thoughts.

Laertes: A document in madness: thoughts and remembrance fitted.

Ophelia: There's fennel for you, and columbines. There's rue for you, and here's some for me; we may call it herb of grace o' Sundays. You must wear your rue with a difference. There's a daisy. I would give you some violets, but they withered all when my father died. They say he made a good end . . .

Laertes: Thought and afflictions, passion, hell itself She turns to favor and prettiness. (4.5.199–212)

- Identify the four main characters from the scene: the king, Gertrude, Ophelia, and Laertes. Which ones are holding flowers? Which flower do you think each holds?
- What emotion does Pine put in the faces of the four main characters of the scene? What does the king's facial expression reveal as he watches Ophelia passing out flowers?
- The various characters in the background are invented. Who might they be, though? What do their faces reveal about what they are thinking?
- Why do you think the artist invented a little boy to add to the scene? How does having a child witness Ophelia's mental breakdown affect the scene?

Figure 4.9: Sir John Everett Millais. "Her garments, heavy with their drink." *Ophelia.* 1851–1852. Oil paint on canvas.
Source: © Tate https://www.tate.org.uk/art/artworks/millais-ophelia-n01506.

Queen: Your sister's drowned, Laertes.
Laertes: Drowned? O, where?
Queen: There is a willow grows askant the brook . . .
There on the pendent boughs her coronet weeds
Clamb'ring to hang, an envious sliver broke
When down her weedy trophies and herself
Fell in the weeping brook. Her clothes spread wide,
And mermaid-like awhile they bore her up,
Which time she chanted snatches of old lauds, . . .
But long it could not be
Till that her garments, heavy with their drink,
Pulled the poor wretch from her melodious lay
To muddy death.
Laertes: Alas, then she is drowned.
Queen: Drowned, drowned. (4.7.188–210)

- What specific details from Shakespeare's words does the painter capture in his painting?
- Look carefully at the flowers in the image; why must the artist include them? Would the image still be rooted in the text without flowers?
- What emotion does the painting cause for you? What does it make you feel? Why does Shakespeare include a character who makes us feel sad? Why is it important that authors include characters struggling with mental health?
- Paintings of Ophelia drowned in the water have long been popular with artists. If you do an online image search for "Ophelia drowning," dozens will pop up. Why do you think these images are such popular topics for artists? What do they say about *Hamlet* and about how Ophelia was treated in the play? What does her suicide teach us about helping those struggling with mental health?

ACT 4 BIBLICAL AND CLASSICAL REFERENCES: THE OWL AND THE BAKER'S DAUGHTER

Act 4 has fewer biblical and classical allusions than other acts. One, though, is a reference to a Bible-inspired (though not biblical) fairy tale familiar to those in Shakespeare's time: Ophelia's line, "They say the owl was a baker's daughter" (4.5.47–48). There are several versions of the story, but the gist is that Jesus once entered a bakery disguised as a beggar, asking for a gift of bread. The baker kindly begins to prepare some dough, but his daughter chides him for his charity and removes most of the dough so that the resulting loaf will be insultingly small. The dough, though, once in the oven, expands anyway into an impossibly enormous loaf, causing the baker's daughter to hoot in amazement. As punishment for her greed, she is transformed into an owl.

There are several possible interpretations. This is one of those rabbit holes into which scholars can dive deep.[4] In some ways, Ophelia's connection to the transformed baker's daughter resonates with the act 2 reference that Hamlet made earlier regarding Jephthah and his daughter (see chapter 2), whom Jephthah inadvertently promised to sacrifice in exchange for victory in battle. Both are lost daughters, though, in the baker's daughter's story, the daughter's selfishness, not her father's mistake, leads to her downfall.

The more quotable line from Ophelia's speech follows the baker's daughter's line: "Lord, we know what we are, but know not what we may be" (4.5.48–49). Ophelia acknowledges that none can know what will become of them, that, like Hecuba (also discussed in chapter 2), like Jephthah's daughter, and like the baker's daughter, mortals do not get to know their fates. And Ophelia, despite being born into privilege, could not have known the fall her life would take either. It is a sad reading, but Shakespeare intended Ophelia's breakdown to be moving. There is hope, too, though, in its reminder that since nobody can know their future, one should always live life to its fullest and take time to appreciate the blessings in the here and now.

INCORPORATING FILM: OPHELIA'S FLOWERS

This film activity, like in the previous chapter, will again focus on different actresses' interpretations of Ophelia, emphasizing Ophelia's declining mental health as she slips toward suicide.[5] Teachers should note that in the more recent film adaptations, Ophelia is dressed in her underwear in her flower scene, makes gestures that may be perceived as lewd, and appears briefly in a flashback making love in bed with Hamlet. Teachers should view these scenes before sharing them with students; more information for each production is included at the end of the section.

Divide students again into groups of four, and assign the four following watching roles to each group. For a shorter version of the activity, choose just one of the film versions below—they vary in length from eleven to twenty minutes—but if time allows, have students compare two different versions, stopping after each to discuss in small groups or as a whole class.

- *Casting director:* Pay special attention to the actress playing Ophelia. How does she portray madness? What emotions does her acting stir in you? Does she make you feel her pain? Does she make you feel sorry for her? Would you describe this actress's Ophelia as weak? Disreputable? Intelligent and highly perceptive? A genuinely good person broken by her world? How many people are in the room with her? How do they react?
- *Set and props designer:* Pay special attention to the set and props. Does the production use actual flowers for Ophelia's flower scene at the end? Or does she imagine them? Or does she use other props in place of flowers? What does such a choice say about her mental health? To whom does she distribute each flower? What does the production do for the setting for Ophelia's drowning?
- *Costume manager:* How is Ophelia dressed for act 4? How does it compare to how she was dressed in earlier acts? How does it compare to how the other characters dress in act 4?
- *Camera operator:* Does the camera spend more time looking at act 4 over the shoulder of male or female characters? That is, does the production privilege a male or female perspective of the play? Or does it provide a balanced perspective?

As with previous chapters' film activities, start and end times are listed in table 4.1; read the notes below and preview the Branagh and Tenant versions before showing them to high school students:

DISCUSSION QUESTIONS AND WRITING PROMPTS

Though act 4 is short, there is much for classroom discussion and writing. Guide students as they think critically through the nature of loyalty and revenge, grief and rage, and mental health:

1. In 4.1 Gertrude keeps Hamlet's secret, telling the king that Hamlet killed Polonius in "his very madness" (4.1.26). What does it suggest about her character that she keeps her son's secret? Two lines later, she adds that Hamlet "weeps for what is done," for having killed Polonius

Table 4.1

Laurence Olivier as Hamlet; Jean Simmons as Ophelia (1948) *Ophelia passes out actual flowers.*	4.5 begins at **1:38:15**, and 4.7 ends at **1:51:30** (13 minutes, with Gertrude in monologue over an image of the drowned Ophelia)
Innokentiy Smoktunovskiy as Hamlet; Anastasia Vertinskaya as Ophelia (Russian-language film with English captions, 1964) *Ophelia passes out twigs she picks up from the fireplace wood pile.*	4.5 begins at **1:38:30**, and 4.7 ends at **1:50:50** (13 minutes, again over an image of the drowned Ophelia; Gertrude's last lines of the scene are cut)
Mel Gibson as Hamlet; Helena Bonham Carter as Ophelia (1990) *Ophelia passes out various items in place of flowers.*	4.5 begins at **1:31:30**, and 4.7 ends at **1:44:30** (13 minutes, Gertrude reports Ophelia's death in monologue over images of Ophelia drowning)
Kenneth Branagh as Hamlet; Kate Winslet as Ophelia (1996) *Ophelia has no props for flowers but pretends she does and passes out imaginary flowers.*	4.5 begins at **2:38:00**, and 4.7 ends at **3:07:10** (29 minutes, with an image of the drowned Ophelia) (Note: includes *fifteen seconds of sexual innuendo* and a brief flashback of Ophelia and Hamlet being intimate in bed at **2:42:20–35**; teachers can avoid this by starting at **2:42:35**.)
Ethan Hawke as Hamlet; Julia Stiles as Ophelia (2000) *Ophelia has Polaroid photographs of flowers, which she passes out.*	4.5 begins at **1:17:30**, and 4.7 ends at **1:28:00** (11 minutes, with the drowned Ophelia)
David Tennant as Hamlet; Mariah Gale as Ophelia (2009) *Ophelia carries in a giant pile of weeds, which she passes out, but not actual flowers.*	4.5 begins at **2:15:50**, and 4.7 ends at **2:34:45** (19 minutes, there is no image of her as she drowns, only Gertrude's explanation) (Note: Ophelia takes off her clothes and appears in just her bra and underwear at the end of 4.5 from **2:18:00** until **2:18:55**. Later, she wears a revealing undergarment slip.)

(4.1.28). Is this an embedded stage direction? Does this line mean that Shakespeare wanted the actor playing Hamlet to have cried as he exited in the previous scene? Or is Gertrude lying to protect her son?

2. Why does Laertes want revenge? On whom does he want revenge? Compare his desire for revenge to Hamlet's; in what ways are the two sons similar in their desire for revenge for their murdered fathers? Do you see honor in their desire for revenge? If so, is Hamlet more

honorable for thinking things through before acting? Or is Laertes more honorable for wanting to take quick action?
3. Why does Ophelia break down mentally? What has happened? In what ways is her suffering like Hamlet's and Laertes's? In what ways does her place as a woman in a male-dominated world make her suffering harder for her to bear?
4. What plan in 4.7 do Claudius and Laertes devise to kill Hamlet? How will they do it? What is their backup plan to make sure Hamlet dies? Whose idea is it? Is it the king's idea, or are the two men equally responsible for coming up with the plot?
5. How does Gertrude feel about Ophelia at the end of 4.7, after her death? Have her feelings about her changed from the beginning of the play or remained consistent?

FOLLOW-UP FLOWER ACTIVITY AFTER READING 4.5

Have students reread Ophelia's flower lines and decide how Ophelia should pass out her flowers (4.5.199–212). She gives some clues. Rosemary is for remembrance; which character onstage with her in 4.5 most needs to remember something? She says that the pansies are for thoughts; which character most needs to do some thinking? Rue is an evergreen shrub, but the word also means to bitterly regret something you have done; which character might Ophelia think is experiencing bitter regret? Have students look up the other flowers and herbs and see if they can find references to their meanings. If they cannot find one, have them look at an online image of each and devise their own possible meaning. Have them organize the flowers and herbs in table 4.2, along with the

Table 4.2

Flower Name	*Flower meaning*	***Character to Receive the Flower/Herb***
Rosemary		
Pansies		
Fennel		
Columbines		
Rue		
Daisies		
Violets		

Note: Ophelia does not actually pass out any violets. She does not have any, because she says they "withered all when her father died" (4.5.208–9). But just before that, she says to somebody, "I would give you some violets, but . . . " (4.5.207–8). Who do you think she might say it to? (Or do you think she just says it wistfully aloud but to no one person in particular?)

characters who should receive the flowers. Some flowers might go to more than one character or to nonspeaking guards standing nearby.

ACT 4 CULMINATING PROJECT: WORKING THROUGH THE PLAY LIKE AN ARTIST

In this project students will analyze a passage and synthesize its details to create an illustration in the same fashion that visual artists have done with *Hamlet* for centuries, building on the work that began earlier in the chapter in the anticipatory set activity. Teachers and students need not worry that they are not very good at art; the objective is the analysis and synthesis of textual detail, not the artistic merit of the finished product. With that said, though, the activity offers space in the curriculum for students skilled in art to shine, an opportunity rarely provided and one these students will appreciate.

The act 4 culminating project also builds on learning from earlier chapters' culminating projects. These asked students to analyze Shakespeare's language and engage creatively, using Shakespeare as a lump of clay to shape their creative energies, first as a ghost story, then through performance, and in the third chapter, as a critical interpretation. The act 4 culminating project continues developing those skills by now emphasizing the interactions between readers and visual artists, and as readers become artists, reshaping the original and speaking to it critically, they ultimately transform their reading of *Hamlet* into a visual artifact.

For this activity assign pairs of students one of the following eight moments from the first four acts of *Hamlet*. These moments from the play align with the artistic tropes presented earlier in the chapter (and those images above can be used again for this project). Either keep students in the same pairs and with the same images as the earlier assignment, or mix things up for a fresh start.

Have the pairs use the provided quotations to find the scene in their books. Have them reread the provided lines and two to three passages before and after. Have students look up any unknown words, just as they did for the chapter two culminating project, and have them create a list of three specific details they will include in their art. Have students write these three details down. Next, have them draw out a sketch of the scene together. Provide students with paper, colored pencils, crayons, markers, paint, and so forth.

Explain that they should do their best, but assure those hesitant about their artistic skill that if they incorporate specific textual details, they will meet the learning objective for the project. Encourage them to get playful with their art. The idea is to create a representation of the scene rooted in Shakespeare's language, but the results should look very different from pair to pair.

- "Good Hamlet, cast thy nighted color off, / And let thine eye look like a friend on Denmark. / Do not forever with thy vailèd lids / Seek for thy noble father in the dust" (1.2.70–73).
- "It beckons you to go away with it, / As if it some impartment did desire / To you alone" (1.4.63–65).
- "Sleeping in my orchard . . . / with juice of cursèd hebona in a vial, / And in the porches of my ears did pour / The leprous distillment" (1.5.65–71).
- "Madam, how like you this play?" (3.2.253).
- "O, my offense is rank, it smells to heaven . . . " (3.3.40).
- "Amazement on thy mother sits. / O, step between her and her fighting soul" (3.4.112–13).
- "There's rosemary, that's for remembrance. Pray you, love, remember. And there is pansies, that's for thoughts" (4.5.199–201).
- "Her garments, heavy with their drink, / Pulled the poor wretch from her melodious lay / To muddy death" (4.7.206–8).

REFLECTING ON WRITING: TAKE FOUR

As they did at the end of previous culminating projects, have students reflect on their work and how their knowledge and skills have transferred (and will transfer) across different writing domains. The act 4 culminating project is a bit different from the earlier three chapters' culminating projects in that students have created a visual rather than a traditional written work. Still, students leaned on their textual analysis and synthesis skills to "write" a literary response to *Hamlet*. Ask them what they learned that they will apply in other writing contexts:

> How was this assignment different than a traditional writing assignment? How was it the same? In what ways are visuals important in conveying meaning? How did creating this drawing or painting help you think through these scenes? Are visual elements more important or less important than words? In what ways will you use visual elements in your future writing?

First, talk with students as a whole class, and generate ideas together. Then, have students freewrite individually. Last, bring the class together to discuss their reflections again as a whole group. As always, adjust the closing reflection to fit the available class time.

> **QUEEN:** Your sister's drowned, Laertes.
>
> **LAERTES:** Drowned? O, where?
>
> **QUEEN:** There is a willow grows askant the brook
> That shows his hoar [grey] leaves in the glassy stream.
> Therewith fantastic garlands did she make
> Of crowflowers, nettles, daisies, and long purples ...
> There on the pendent boughs her coronet weeds
> Clamb'ring to hang, an envious sliver broke
> When down her weedy trophies and herself
> Fell in the weeping brook. Her clothes spread wide,
> And mermaid-like awhile they bore her up,
> Which time she chanted snatches of old lauds,
> As one incapable of her own distress
> Or like a creature native and endued
> Unto that element. But long it could not be
> Till that her garments, heavy with their drink,
> Pulled the poor wretch from her melodious lay
> To muddy death.
>
> **LAERTES:** Alas, then she is drowned.
>
> **QUEEN:** Drowned, drowned. (4.7.188-210)

Handwritten annotations:
(1) a willow growing by the brook.
(2) her flower coronet and other flowers in the water
(3) her clothes all spread out wide

Figure 4.10: This example art includes three student-selected criteria from the text: (1) there's a willow growing by a brook, (2) Ophelia's flower coronet and other flowers are in the water with her, and (3) her clothes are all spread wide as she floats.
Source: Dakotah Haughey.

NOTES

1. One early scholar to suggest that Hamlet orchestrated his own rescue before leaving for England was George Henry Miles, in 1870. He made the case that Hamlet's line "O 'tis most sweet / Where in one line two *crafts* meet" (3.4.232–33, qtd. in Miles 1870, 70). According to Miles, Hamlet's double meaning is that the two ships/crafts will meet and facilitate his escape (i.e., he has arranged for the pirate ship to rescue him) and also that the two schemes/crafts, those of him and his uncle, are coming to a head but that he has anticipated his uncle's next move and will therefore emerge the victor. Horace Howard Furness outlines the larger critical discussion in his variorum edition of *Hamlet* ([1877] 1963, 353–54).

2. For more on teaching ecphonesis, see Long and Christel (2019, 75–76, 85–87).

3. Several teachers have proposed incorporating visual art—both analyzing it and creating it—in the teaching of Shakespeare. Mary Ellen Dakin (2009), for example, writes, "having students examine the art related to Shakespeare's plays holds the potential to enrich their comprehension of Shakespeare's text while introducing them to the grammar of images" (156). Long and Christel (2019) also offer strategies "appealing to visual intelligence" (4–5).

4. One good starting point for diving deeper into the story of the baker's daughter is Alison Chapman's "Ophelia's 'Old Lauds': Madness and Hagiography in *Hamlet*." Building on the work of Stephen Greenblatt's *Hamlet in Purgatory*—as discussed in the chapter 1 endnotes—and other scholars, Chapman makes the case for an Ophelia who draws on competing Protestant and Catholic theological underpinnings just as much as Hamlet does. Chapman explains (2007) how, in singing old lauds as she dies, Ophelia slips into a Catholic worldview; "her descent into grief and madness is marked by a surge of allusions of medieval Catholic forms of piety: St. James, St. Charity, 'old lauds,' pilgrimage to the shrine of Our Lady of Walsingham, and other pre-Reformation folklore" (111). Her reference to the baker's daughter's transformation to an owl similarly could be read as Ophelia's sense that she was wrong to favor obedience to her father earlier in the play instead of remaining truthful to Hamlet: "In act 3, Ophelia appears to think that cooperating with her father will help Hamlet's madness and thus secure her future marriage. What she cannot predict is the fact that Hamlet will read that choice of loyalties as an unforgivable rejection of him" (117). It is a choice she cannot now unmake; she could not have known then what would transpire afterward. The baker's daughter chose to decline a spiritual loyalty to Christ, and Ophelia chose to decline to side with Hamlet. The baker's daughter is physically transformed into an owl. Ophelia's mind is mentally transformed to madness.

5. Not all teachers and scholars agree that Ophelia died by suicide. Cohen ([2006] 2018) explains, "The gravedigger thinks so, but I don't . . . she was just taking a little lie down on the river. Your students may disagree, but it doesn't seem to me a profitable line of discussion" (147).

Chapter 5

"I Have Been Sexton/ Sixteene Here"

How Old Is Hamlet Anyway— Getting Gritty with Textual History

Act 5 is Hamlet's reckoning. With Shakespearean tragedy it is never a secret that the main characters will all be dead by the play's end; there is no need to avoid spoilers. With *Hamlet*, the play is not about whether Hamlet will survive but, rather, about his philosophical journey. And in the play's final scene, playgoers get Shakespeare's answer to Hamlet's most well-known philosophical question: to be or not to be? The answer is just "let be" (5.2.238).

Hamlet has had time to contemplate. He has seen his father's ghost twice, proven his uncle's guilt, confronted his mother about her marriage, stabbed a (mostly) innocent man, arranged for the deaths of two former friends, been sent away to England, escaped a plot that would have led to his own murder, and now returned to Denmark to find Ophelia dead by suicide. After all this Hamlet realizes that a content life comes from making peace with what life offers, both good and bad.

Hamlet's realization, perhaps Shakespeare's most insightful passage in the whole play, is in prose. It comes after he has been challenged to the fencing match against Laertes. He knows something is amiss. He suspects his uncle's treachery. Horatio tries to convince him to decline, to say he is unwell, but Hamlet is ready to accept what life will throw at him next:

> We defy augury. There is a special providence in the fall of a sparrow. If it be now, 'tis not to come; if it be not to come, it will be now; if it be not now, yet it will come. The readiness is all. Since no man of aught he leaves knows, what is 't to leave betimes? Let be. (5.2.233–38)

Augury is knowledge and fear of the future. Hamlet says he will defy augury. In saying there is special providence in the fall of a sparrow, Hamlet refers to a New Testament verse where Jesus explains to his disciples that even the sparrows, as well as their deaths, are part of God's larger plan.[1] All things exist as part of something collective that is bigger than any individual.

Hamlet knows that fate has dealt him a raw deal. After fighting against that fate the whole play, finally, in act 5, he accepts what will be and steps forward into that fate. He accepts Laertes's challenge and with it announces—to Horatio but also to the audience—that "the readiness is all," the readiness to just "let be" whatever is to happen at the match and whatever is to happen in life more broadly too (5.2.236–38).

This final chapter will provide learning objectives for the play's final act, which teachers can use in their planning, strategies for reading aloud together as a class, a series of discussion questions and writing prompts, and two follow-up activities that build on prior learning: more cue scripts (like those from chapter 3) and more art analysis (like that in chapter 4). The culminating project teaches students to analyze the play like an editor would,[2] as well as to synthesize key original textual sources for *Hamlet*—the Second Quarto (Q2) and First Folio (F1) and, to a far lesser degree, the First Quarto (Q1)—to make editorial choices and craft their own edition of a small part, some fifty lines, of the conversation between Hamlet and the gravedigger in 5.1.

ACT 5 LEARNING OBJECTIVES

1. Students will analyze the development of Hamlet's philosophical outlook from the play's beginning to its conclusion.
2. Students will compare the different reactions of Hamlet, Ophelia, and Laertes to their respective fathers' deaths.
3. Students will compare film versions of act 5 and evaluate production choices.
4. Students will describe how modern *Hamlet* texts derive from three historical textual sources—Q2, F1, and, to a lesser degree, Q1—and evaluate how differences between the two affect meaning.
5. Students will (like an editor) analyze the Q1, Q2, and F1 versions of the gravedigger scene and synthesize these into their own textual editions, complete with three to five footnotes.

READING SCENES OF ACT 5 TOGETHER

Act 5 has just two scenes, but both are long and complex. They include some of Shakespeare's best dialogue, and the imagery of Hamlet gazing at the skull of "poor Yorick" is perhaps the most iconic image in all of literature (5.1.190–91). There is not much here to be skipped, and teachers would be best served to allot two to three class periods for reading, acting, and discussing act 5 together in class.

- 5.1: Act 5 opens with two gravediggers at work. They are digging Ophelia's grave and debating whether a person who dies by suicide should be given a proper Christian burial. The first gravedigger is witty—he is the only character in the play who can match Hamlet's wordplay—and his riddle often gets skipped in performance but is too good not to analyze in class: who builds better houses than the mason (i.e., bricklayer), the shipwright (i.e., the ship maker), or the carpenter? His answer is the gravedigger because the "houses he makes" will last until "doomsday" (5.1.60–61).
  - Hamlet and Horatio arrive on the scene and engage with the witty gravedigger. (The other has been sent to fetch something to drink.) Their dialogue is humorous until the gravedigger hands Hamlet the skull of Yorick, the court jester of Hamlet's childhood. He holds it before him and contemplates mortality. It is some of the best stuff in all of Shakespeare. Have students read this part of the scene using the cue scripts provided later in the chapter. They follow the same format as those introduced in chapter 3. Invest in a cheap, plastic skull that students can use as a prop while reading together aloud. Alternatively, wad up a piece of paper and have students imagine it as a skull.
  - The three are interrupted when the king, the queen, and the rest of the funeral procession approach with the body of Ophelia. The gravedigger exits. Hamlet and Horatio watch from a distance at first, but when Laertes jumps into the grave in grief—as discussed in chapter 4, he is not a character who can contain his emotions—Hamlet steps forth and asserts that he loved Ophelia more than any brother ever could. The two exchange blows and are separated. All exit but the king and Laertes. The scene ends with the king reminding Laertes (and the audience) of their plan to kill Hamlet.
- 5.2: Hamlet and Horatio talk alone. Hamlet explains how, on his way to England, he discovered the king's plot to have him killed. Rosencrantz and Guildenstern had a secret, sealed message to have the English king execute Hamlet upon arrival, but he reversed the king's secret orders so

that Rosencrantz and Guildenstern instead would be killed. Hamlet does not feel bad for orchestrating their deaths. He asserts that "they did make love to this employment" (5.2.64). He does feel bad, though, for what he has done to Laertes.

- A new character, Osric, who seems to have taken over Polonius's role at court, interrupts Hamlet and Horatio with the challenge of facing Laertes in a fencing match. Hamlet is immediately suspicious but has come full circle philosophically and accepts both the match and, most significantly, whatever it is that is to come, even if it will be his own death.
- Hamlet faces Laertes in the fencing match. Laertes's rapier is poisoned, and Claudius further poisons the cup from which Hamlet is to drink, just as the two had planned out in act 4. It would have been a best-of-twelve bout, but after losing the first two points, Laertes cuts Hamlet with the poisoned rapier. However, Hamlet picks up Laertes's rapier and cuts him as well. Both are poisoned. Both have just minutes before death.
- The queen, by this time, has drunk from the poisoned cup despite the king's ordering her from across the room not to, and before dying, she declares that the drink had been poisoned. Laertes reveals all and then dies. In his last moments of life, Hamlet cuts the king with the poisoned rapier and forces him to drink from the cup. Horatio, the only major character who does not die, holds Hamlet in his arms until the end.

SOME NOTES ON SHAKESPEARE'S LANGUAGE: THE THREE *HAMLET* SOURCE TEXTS

The story of how Shakespeare's text came down through four centuries is both complex and fascinating. Teachers have a choice of a dozen modern editions (see the appendix at the end of this book for a selected list), and each is slightly different. Their apparatus, such as introductions, footnotes, and supplementary materials, differs depending on what the editor has thought is most important to explain and include. But the actual words also vary slightly from edition to edition. These differences are subtle, and while studying these textual choices should not be the focus of a study of *Hamlet*, students should know some basics.

They should know that all modern texts derive primarily from two textual sources: the Second Quarto (Q2), first published in 1604 during Shakespeare's lifetime, and the First Folio (F1), published in 1623, after Shakespeare's death.[3] Quartos were small books made from folding sheets of paper four times and were slightly larger than today's paperbacks. Folios were big books, some being three times the size of a modern hardcover book today.

Shakespeare's First Folio is perhaps the most celebrated secular book ever published.[4] Only 235 of them still survive. Because they are so rare, they are rarely sold, but they fetch millions of dollars when they sell. The First Folio is the definitive source for most of Shakespeare's plays, including eighteen that had not been published before and would otherwise have been lost. Without it, there would be no *Macbeth*, *Julius Caesar*, *The Tempest*, or *Twelfth Night*.

Hamlet would have survived, though, since it had also been published in quarto form. Editors treat the Q2 text as equal to or even superior to the F1 text. There was also a First Quarto (Q1) published a year before the Q2, but it contains only about half as much text as the other two, and the text that is there is quite different. Whereas the F1 and Q2, for example, both read "to be or not to be, that is the question," the Q1 reads "to be or not to be, aye that's the point."

Q1 is so different that it barely even feels like Shakespeare to some scholars. Its history is fascinating, though. Only two copies have survived, and even those were lost until over two hundred years after they were first printed.[5] Editors today mostly ignore Q1.[6] Students should be aware that modern editions usually combine elements of both Q2 and F1, and when the two sources differ, as students will explore in the next activity, editors must decide which version they will privilege. They often agree, but not always.

ANTICIPATORY SET ACTIVITY: CHOOSING BETWEEN SECOND QUARTO AND FIRST FOLIO READINGS

For this activity begin by working through the first six lines of Hamlet's first soliloquy from act 1 (1.2.133–38). Project images for students to examine. One easy textual problem is the matter of *seal slaughter* in Q2. Editors all agree it is a typo. There is simply a missing "f"; Shakespeare certainly did not promote the murder of marine mammals. Editors today all agree that the F1 reading here of *self-slaughter* should be privileged. (It was normal then to spell "seal," "self," and "seem" with an "e" at the end; those are not typos, just historical spelling variations). See figure 5.1.

Another easy problem is the question of *wary* or *weary* in the next line. The word "wary" describes a person who is anxious or cautious. It does not make sense for the "uses of this world" to seem "wary." Hamlet likely feels wary, but "the uses of this world," not being human, cannot feel "wary." And it just does not make sense to personify them as "wary." On the other hand, "weary" means tiresome. It makes sense to say that "all the uses of this world" are "weary"; they have worn Hamlet down. See figure 5.2.

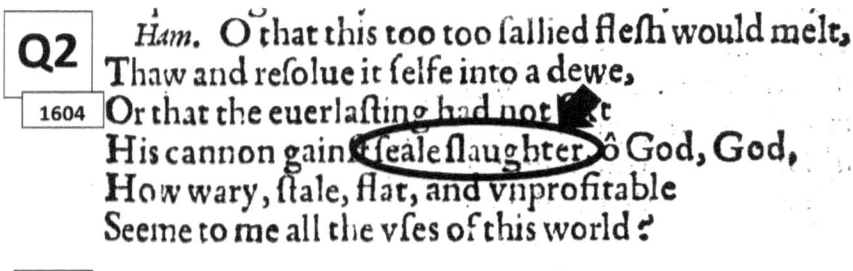

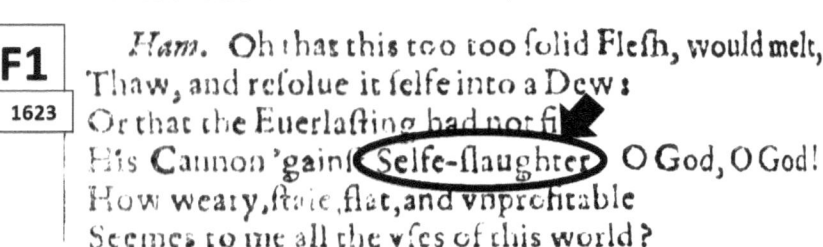

Figure 5.1: Modern editors all agree with the F1 reading of "selfe-slaughter" over the Q2 "seale-slaughter." Note that seventeenth-century print had some different formats than today. For example, the letter "s" was sometimes written like it is today, but other times, it was written more like what looks today like an "f" without the full crossbar. Also, the letters "u" and "v" were often used interchangeably in print, as were the letters "i" and "j."
Source: British Library and Folger Shakespeare.

There are many points, though, on which editors still disagree. For example, the first line of the soliloquy starts "O that this too, too *sullied* flesh would melt, thaw, and resolve itself into a dew," or, at least, that's how the modern Folger edition reads (1.2.133). Other modern editions have *sallied* or *solid* flesh. Choosing "sallied" here means following Q2. "Sallied" means assailed or attacked. It makes sense because Hamlet feels attacked after his father's death and his mother's marriage. Choosing "solid" here instead, though, means following F1. It fits too; it goes nicely and poetically with the passage's idea of melting and thawing. Editors do not agree on which is best.

Choosing "sullied"—as the Folger edition does, and the Folger text is the basis throughout this book for quotations and line numbers—is a variation of the Q2 reading. It assumes a typographical error: Shakespeare originally had "sullied," but the printer incorrectly put "sallied" instead. "Sullied" means defiled or polluted, so it works too. Hamlet feels his flesh, all flesh even, to be dirty metaphorically. Modern editors have never agreed on which of the three is best.[7] It remains open to debate. Ask students to weigh in and decide which they think is the best editorial choice. See figure 5.3.

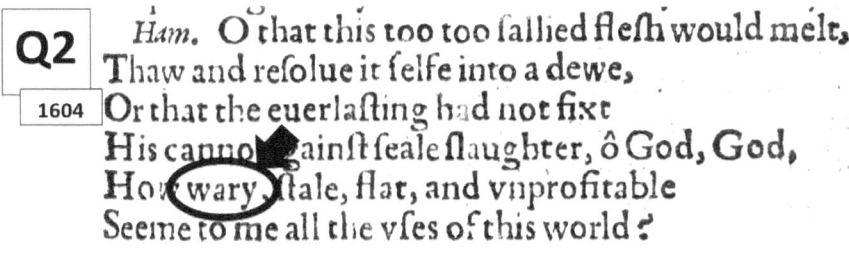

Figure 5.2: Similarly, modern editors again all choose F1's "weary" instead of Q2's "wary."

Source: British Library and Folger Shakespeare Library website.

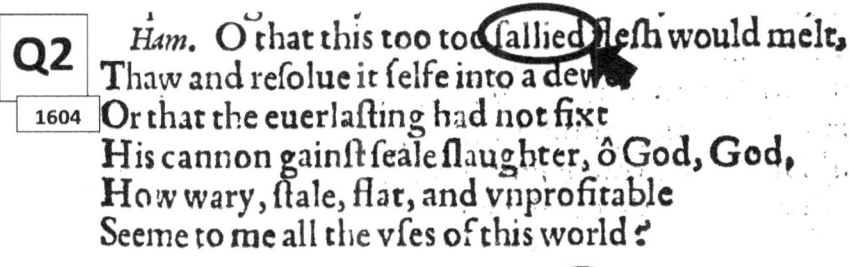

Figure 5.3: There is little agreement among editors on whether Q2's "sallied flesh" or F1's "solid flesh" is the better choice. Traditionally, editors from the nineteenth and early twentieth centuries privileged the F1 reading, but since the mid-twentieth century, many editors—though not all—have increasingly privileged the Q2 or the alternate "sullied."

Source: British Library and Folger Shakespeare Library website.

ANTICIPATORY SET ACTIVITY, PART TWO

After working through these six lines as a whole class, have students practice on the next example in pairs. Project the Q2 version of the passage for the class (figure 5.4). Have students take five minutes to work through the passage four to five times, each taking at least two turns as both characters. Praise the groups as they gain speed and fluency. Explain that they will need to change the "f" symbol to an "s" and the "u" to a "v."

Next, project an image for the class of the F1 version of the same dialogue (figure 5.5). Digital copies of F1 are available through the Folger Shakespeare Library website. Ask two student volunteers to read it aloud, one as Hamlet, the other as Gertrude. If time allows, have a second volunteer pair read it aloud again. Ask the class what differences they see. Students will note minor variations in spelling, capitalization, and punctuation. Point out

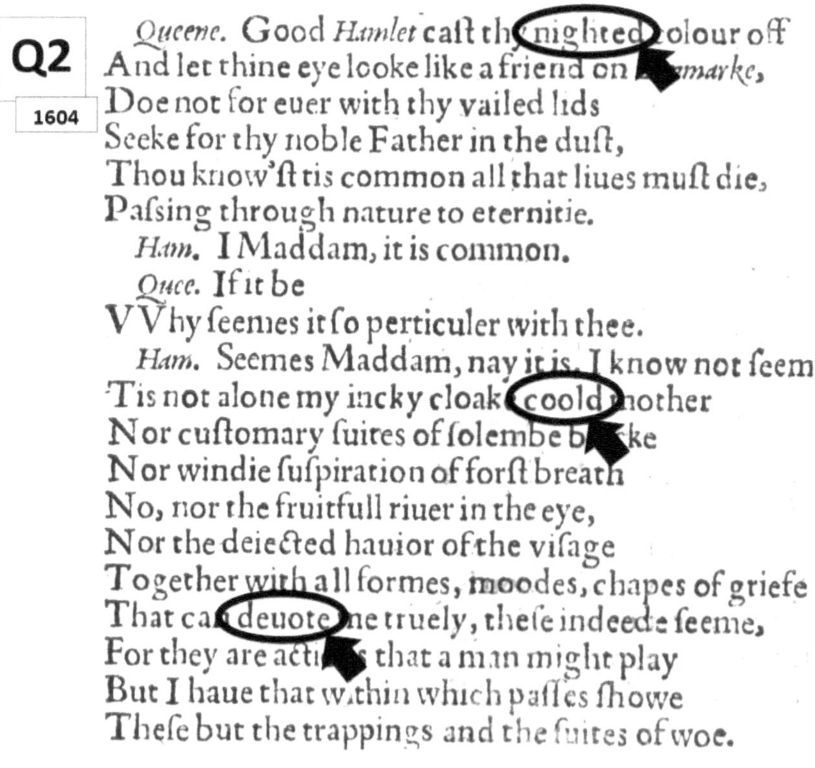

Q2 1604

> *Queene.* Good *Hamlet* caſt thy nighted colour off
> And let thine eye looke like a friend on Denmarke,
> Doe not for euer with thy vailed lids
> Seeke for thy noble Father in the duſt,
> Thou know'ſt tis common all that liues muſt die,
> Paſsing through nature to eternitie.
>   *Ham.* I Maddam, it is common.
>   *Quee.* If it be
> VVhy ſeemes it ſo perticuler with thee.
>   *Ham.* Seemes Maddam, nay it is, I know not ſeemes,
> 'Tis not alone my incky cloake coold mother
> Nor cuſtomary ſuites of ſolembe blacke
> Nor windie ſuſpiration of forſt breath
> No, nor the fruitfull riuer in the eye,
> Nor the deiected hauior of the viſage
> Together with all formes, moodes, chapes of griefe
> That can deuote me truely, theſe indeede ſeeme,
> For they are actions that a man might play
> But I haue that within which paſſes ſhowe
> Theſe but the trappings and the ſuites of woe.

Figure 5.4: Q2 version of act 1 dialogue between Gertrude and Hamlet. Few or no editors favor the Q2 version's "nighted," "cold," or "devote," even amongst those who privilege Q2 more generally than F1.
Source: Folger Shakespeare Library website.

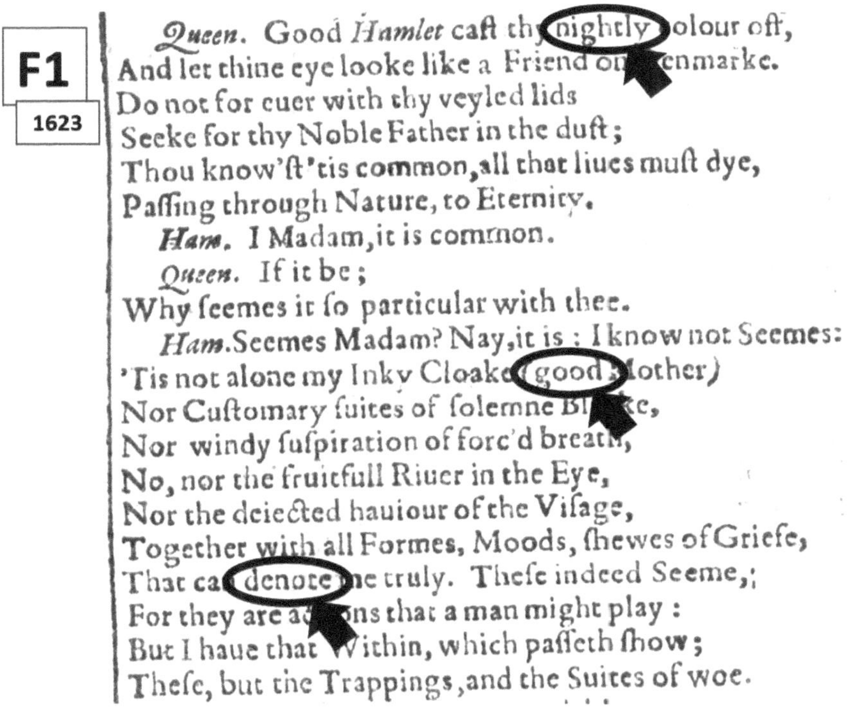

"I Have Been Sexton/Sixteene Here" 121

> **F1**
> **1623**
>
> *Queen.* Good *Hamlet* caſt thy nightly colour off,
> And let thine eye looke like a Friend on Denmarke.
> Do not for euer with thy veyled lids
> Seeke for thy Noble Father in the duſt;
> Thou know'ſt'tis common, all that liues muſt dye,
> Paſſing through Nature, to Eternity.
>   *Ham.* I Madam, it is common.
>   *Queen.* If it be;
> Why ſeemes it ſo particular with thee.
>   *Ham.* Seemes Madam? Nay, it is; I know not Seemes:
> 'Tis not alone my Inky Cloake good Mother)
> Nor Cuſtomary ſuites of ſolemne Blacke,
> Nor windy ſuſpiration of forc'd breath,
> No, nor the fruitfull Riuer in the Eye,
> Nor the deiected hauiour of the Viſage,
> Together with all Formes, Moods, ſhewes of Griefe,
> That can denote me truly. Theſe indeed Seeme,;
> For they are actions that a man might play:
> But I haue that Within, which paſſeth ſhow;
> Theſe, but the Trappings, and the Suites of woe.

Figure 5.5: F1 version of act 1 dialogue between Gertrude and Hamlet. Most editors privilege "nightly," "good," and "denote" over their Q2 counterparts. These word choices just make more sense compared to "nighted," "cold," and "denote."
Source: Folger Shakespeare Library website.

that modern editors have generally agreed on many of these—for example, the more modern spelling of "do" without the extra "e." Elsewhere, modern editors have also adopted the more modern spellings of "seems," "grief," "shows," and so forth, spelled without their extra "e" at the end. It is agreed that good editing modernizes such archaic spelling.

Some whole words are different, though, requiring some deeper thought on the part of an editor. Does one word make more sense than the other? Is one more likely to be what Shakespeare originally intended and the other, an error? In Q2, for example, Gertrude urges Hamlet, "Cast thy *nighted* color off," whereas, in F1, she urges him, "Cast thy *nightly* color off" (1.2.70). Point this out to students. Which does the editor choose in their modern edition? "Nighted" is not an actual dictionary word, but what might it mean if it was a word Shakespeare had invented? What color is night? Point out how "nightly color" aligns nicely with the idea of Hamlet's "inky cloak." What might the line mean if it's a misspelling and Shakespeare meant "knighted"?

Which would they choose—(k)nighted or nightly—if they were an editor? Explain afterward that modern editors have all privileged the F1 "nightly."

A more complicated choice is between Q2's "*cold* mother" and F1's "*good* mother." Hamlet certainly has some complex feelings about his mother, and it would make sense that he thinks of her as a "cold mother." But would he be so blunt in such a public space? The "good mother" is ambiguous. It leaves room for sincerity or sarcasm, giving more autonomy to readers and actors. Ask students which they would choose if they were an editor. Most editors have chosen "good." Another example comes between Q2's "*denote* me truly" and F1's "*devote* me truly." In this case, modern editors have overwhelmingly opted for the Q2 reading. See the extract as well as figures 5.4 and 5.5 above.

> *Queen:* Good Hamlet, cast thy (*nighted* or *nightly*) color off,
> And let thine eye look like a friend on Denmark.
> Do not forever with thy vailèd lids
> Seek for thy noble father in the dust.
> Thou know'st 'tis common; all that lives must die,
> Passing through nature to eternity
> *Hamlet:* Ay, madam, it is common.
> *Queen:* If it be,
> Why seems it so particular with thee?
> *Hamlet:* "Seems," madam, Nay, it is. I know not "seems."
> 'Tis not alone my inky cloak, (*cold* or *good*) mother,
> Nor customary suits of solemn black, . . .
> That can (*denote* or *devote*) me truly. These indeed "seem,"
> For they are actions that a man might play;
> But I have that within which passes show
> These but the trappings and the suits of woe. (1.2.70–89)

ACT 5 BIBLICAL AND CLASSICAL REFERENCES: ALEXANDER THE GREAT

As Hamlet gazes into the skull of poor Yorick, he contemplates that even the most remarkable historical figures, such as Alexander the Great and Julius Caesar, end up in the same state. Julius Caesar, who was discussed in chapter 3, was considered the greatest of the Romans in Shakespeare's time. Alexander the Great was just as well-known in Shakespeare's time as the greatest of the Greeks; he represents the epitome of Greek culture and military might. Born a prince some four centuries before Caesar, he inherited the Macedonian throne at age twenty. From there he led a series of campaigns over some ten years that forever changed the map, building an empire over a vast expanse that spread Greek culture east to India.

When Hamlet imagines neither Alexander's nor Caesar's skull being much different from Yorick's, he reminds playgoers how fragile and short all life is, that none escape death. All turn back to dust eventually. It does not matter how famous or powerful a person was in life; they all end up like Yorick. The stuff that was once Alexander is now dirt, and so is the matter that was once the body of Caesar, and now it might be packed together into loam as a plug to stop a hole in a barrel of beer:

Hamlet (gazing into the skull): Dost thou think Alexander looked o' this fashion i' th' earth?

Horatio: E'en so.

Hamlet: And smelt so? Pah!

Horatio: E'en so, my lord.

Hamlet: To what base uses may we return, Horatio! Why may not imagination trace the noble dust of Alexander till he find it stopping a bunghole [a hole in a barrel of beer that needs to be plugged up]?

Horatio: 'Twere to consider too curiously to consider so.

Hamlet: No, faith, not a jot; but to follow him hither, with modesty enough and likelihood to lead it, as thus: Alexander died, Alexander was buried, Alexander returneth to dust, the dust is earth; of earth we make loam; and why of that loam whereto he converted might they not stop a beer barrel? Imperious Caesar, dead and turned to clay, Might stop a hole to keep the wind away. (5.1.204–221)

One last classical reference comes in the final exchange between Hamlet and Horatio at the end of the play. Knowing Hamlet will die, Horatio reaches to drink from the poisoned cup, saying, "I am more an antique Roman than a Dane" (5.2.374). Hamlet stops him and insists that he live on to tell the story of what happened. Horatio is referring to the belief in Roman times that it was nobler to die by suicide than be taken prisoner by an enemy. It is how Brutus and Cassius both died in history and in Shakespeare's play *Julius Caesar*, which is also discussed previously in chapter 3.

INCORPORATING FILM: THROUGH TO THE END OF THE PLAY

The last act of *Hamlet* is important enough that if time allows, it is worth taking two full class periods to watch both scenes on film and discuss them. Make sure closed captions are turned on, and encourage students to read them as they watch. Like in previous film viewings, make groups of four, and within each group, assign watching roles. For each of the two class periods, watch one or two of the film versions together, give five minutes for group discussions, and then watch the same scenes from one of the other films. Afterward, use the remaining class time to lead a discussion based on the questions in the watching roles below. Start and end times are listed in the tables below.

Student Watching Assignments for 5.1

5.1 is shorter, so there should be enough time to watch at least two versions. If possible, pair one of the complete versions (Branagh or Tennant) with one of the shorter, abridged versions. Remind students how all productions make some cuts to keep the total production at a reasonable length for modern audiences.

- *Casting director:* Pay special attention to how the actors build on one another's performances. Do you think that the gravedigger knows who Hamlet is? Pay attention to the interaction between Hamlet and Laertes at the graveside: How does the production establish them as antagonists against one another? Which one do you feel most for? Are you convinced that Hamlet truly loved Ophelia?
- *Set and props designer:* How does the production create a graveyard as its set? Does the gravedigger "lie" in the grave (remember, too, that in Shakespeare's time, "lie" could also just mean to sit or stand in the grave) (5.1.125–31)? Does the production use one skull or several? How does the gravedigger handle them? How does Hamlet? Do Laertes and Hamlet actually get into the grave? How else do they use the grave/coffin as a part of the set?
- *Special effects manager:* Compare Hamlet's clothes to the gravedigger's—which is better dressed? Do Hamlet's clothes give away that he might be a prince? Pay special attention to how the production handles Ophelia's funeral. How does it incorporate flowers as a symbol of Ophelia? What else does the funeral say about her?
- *Camera operator:* How does the camera handle Hamlet's speech with the skull, mostly long shots or close-ups? What is Hamlet's emotion as he looks at it? How does the actor/production make Hamlet's memory of Yorick come to life?

Table 5.1

Laurence Olivier as Hamlet; Stanley Holloway as the gravedigger (1948)	Act 5.1 begins at **1:51:30** and ends at **1:59:30** (8 minutes).
Innokentiy Smoktunovskiy as Hamlet; gravedigger uncredited (Russian-language film with English captions, 1964)	Act 5.1 begins at **1:52:50** and ends at **2:03:00** (10 minutes).
Mel Gibson as Hamlet; Trevor Peacock as the gravedigger (1990)	Act 5.1 begins at **1:44:30** and ends at **1:51:40** (7 minutes).
Kenneth Branagh as Hamlet; Billy Crystal as the gravedigger (1996)	Act 5.1 begins at **3:07:15** and ends at **3:24:00** (17 minutes, keeps almost the entire script).
Ethan Hawke as Hamlet; Jeffrey Wright as the gravedigger (2000)	The Ethan Hawke production sadly *cuts the entire gravedigger scene*; there is just a few seconds' glimpse of him digging a grave at **1:29:10**—but none of his lines. It keeps a reduced version of the funeral scene, which begins at **1:28:45** and ends at **1:31:40** (3 minutes). The other four choices, if available, are better for this activity.
David Tennant as Hamlet; Mark Hadfield as the gravedigger (2009)	Act 5.1 begins at **2:34:45** and ends at **2:47:00** (12 minutes, keeps almost the entire script).

Student Watching Assignments for 5.2

The second scene is longer than the first, but there is some business at the beginning, the lines where Osric brings the challenge to the duel, that can be skipped to save time.

- *Casting director:* Pay attention to how the characters build on one another. Does Hamlet's apology before the duel seem sincere to you? Does Laertes accept it? How do the king and the queen react to Hamlet's apology? What about Laertes's apology at the very end—does it seem sincere? Does Hamlet accept it?
- *Set and props designer:* How does the production handle the poisoned cup? Is there an actual cup and an actual pearl that the king puts into it? What happens to the cup over the course of the scene? Who all drinks from it? Where is it at the end?
- *Special effects manager:* Pay close attention to the sword-fighting choreography. Does the production use actual swords? Does the fight between Hamlet and Laertes appear realistic? Is Hamlet or Laertes the better sword fighter? Or are they evenly matched? What happens just before Hamlet is poisoned by the unbated foil? How does Hamlet react?

Table 5.2

Laurence Olivier as Hamlet; Terence Morgan as Laertes (1948)	Hamlet's philosophical musings in 5.2 begin at **2:09:30**, and the scene lasts through the end of the recording (18 minutes); the swordplay choreography is excellent.
Innokentiy Smoktunovskiy as Hamlet; Stepan Oleksenko as Laertes (Russian-language film with English captions, 1964)	Hamlet's philosophical musings in 5.2 begin at **2:07:10**, and the scene lasts through the end of the recording (15 minutes).
Mel Gibson as Hamlet; Nathaniel Parker as Laertes (1990)	Hamlet's philosophical musings in 5.2 begin at **1:56:15**, and the scene lasts through the end of the recording (19 minutes); it's a powerful rendition of Gertrude as she realizes the king's villainy after drinking from the cup.
Kenneth Branagh as Hamlet; Michael Maloney as Laertes (1996)	Hamlet's philosophical musings in 5.2 begin at **3:35:00**, and the scene lasts through the end of the recording (27 minutes); this keeps the entire script, including the Fortinbras subplot.
Ethan Hawke as Hamlet; Liev Schreiber as Laertes (2000)	Hamlet's philosophical musings in 5.2 begin at **1:35:30**, and the scene lasts through the end of the recording (10 minutes); this uses guns at the end, and the gore is more explicit than in other productions.
David Tennant as Hamlet; Edward Bennett as Laertes (2009)	Hamlet's philosophical musings in 5.2 begin at **2:51:45**, and the scene lasts through the end of the recording, (10 minutes); this keeps almost the entire script.

- *Camera operator:* How does the production handle the duel between Hamlet and Laertes and the poisoning? Is the camera still, or does it move with the duel? If it moves, describe how it affects viewers' perspectives of the fight. What happens after Gertrude drinks from the cup? Which characters get close-ups?

REINFORCING SKILLS: MORE CUE SCRIPTS, THE GRAVEDIGGER SCENE

In this activity students will reinforce skills introduced in chapter 3, when they used cue scripts to read the parts of Hamlet and Ophelia in the nunnery scene. Put students in groups of three, and have them take turns reading the parts of Hamlet, the gravedigger, and Horatio. Each group will read through the scripts three times, giving each student a chance to do each part. For props, have groups make pretend skulls from wads of paper. Students should again highlight unfamiliar words, which will be part of the ensuing classroom discussion.

"The Gravedigger Scene" from 5.1: Hamlet's Cue Script
(Your lines are in bold; highlight words you
don't know. Listen for your cues)

[YOU START] That skull had a tongue in it and could sing once. How the knave jowls it to the ground as if 'twere Cain's jawbone, that did the first murder! This might be the pate of a politician, which this ass now overreaches; one that would circumvent God, might it not?

> *A "knave" is a scoundrel or rascal, and to "jowl" something is to knock it around. The gravedigger is knocking the dirt from the skulls he digs up with no consideration of the skulls may have once belonged to.*
>
> *And your "pate" is your head.*

. . . It might, my lord.

Or of a courtier, which could say "Good morrow, sweet lord! How dost thou, sweet lord?" This might be my Lord Such-a-one, that praised my Lord Such-a-one's horse when he went to beg it, might it not?

> *A "courtier" is a person at court, so a person with nobility.*

. . . Ay, my lord.

Why, e'en so. And now my Lady Worm's, chapless and knocked about the mazzard with a sexton's spade. . . . Did these bones cost no more the breeding but to play at loggets with them? Mine ache to think on 't.

> *"Mazzard" is just another old-fashioned word for your head.*
> *To be "chapless" is to be without your lower jaw.*
> *"To play at loggets" was a game in Shakespeare's time in which participants threw sticks at a target, like the game of horseshoes today.*

. . . For such a guest is meet.

There's another. Why may not that be the skull of a lawyer? . . . Why does he suffer this mad knave now to knock him about the sconce with a dirty shovel and will not tell him of his action of battery? Hum! This fellow might be in's time a great buyer of land . . . The very conveyances

"I Have Been Sexton/Sixteene Here"

of his lands will scarcely lie in this box, and must th' inheritor himself have no more, ha?

. . . Not a jot more, my lord.

I will speak to this fellow. Whose grave's this, sirrah?

. . . For such a guest is meet.

I think it be thine indeed, for thou liest in't.

. . . I do not lie in't, yet it is mine.

Thou dost lie in't, to be in't and say it is thine. 'Tis for the dead, not for the quick; therefore thou liest.

. . . 'twill away again from me to you.

What man dost thou dig it for?

For no man, sir.

What woman then?

. . . For none neither.

Who is to be buried in 't?

. . . our last king Hamlet overcame Fortinbras.

How long is that since?

. . . he that is mad, and sent into England.

Ay, marry, why was he sent into England?

. . . do not, 'tis no great matter there.

Why?

. . . the men are as mad as he.

How came he mad?

Some definitions and context:

- *The conversation is witty because there are two definitions for "lie": as a noun, it means an untruth, but as a verb, it is to recline or sit. Hamlet and the gravedigger keep playing with the two definitions to try to outwit one another. The gravedigger is the only character in the play who can keep up with Hamlet's wit.*

130 Chapter 5

	. . . Very strangely, they say.
How "strangely"?	
	. . . Faith, e'en with losing his wits.
Upon what ground?	
	. . . man and boy thirty years.
How long will a man lie i' th' earth ere he rot?	
	. . . tanner will last you nine year.
Why he more than another?	
	. . . earth three-and-twenty years.
Whose was it?	
	. . . Whose do you think it was?
Nay, I know not.	
	. . . was Yorick's skull, the King's jester.
This?	
	. . . E'en that.

Let me see. [Takes the skull.] Alas, poor Yorick! I knew him, Horatio. A fellow of infinite jest, of most excellent fancy. He hath borne me on his back a thousand times. And now how abhorred in my imagination it is! My gorge rises at it. Here hung those lips that I have kissed I know not how oft. Where be your gibes now? your gambols? your songs? your flashes of merriment that were wont to set the table on a roar? Not one now, to mock your own grinning? Quite chapfallen? Now get you to my lady's chamber, and tell her, let her paint an inch thick, to this favor she must come. Make her laugh at that. Prithee, Horatio, tell me one thing.

Some definitions and context:

- *Words like "jest" and "fancy" refer to fun and playfulness. When Hamlet says that Yorick was a "fellow of infinite jest, of most excellent fancy," he is simply saying that Yorick was a fun guy when he was alive.*

. . . What's that, my lord?

Dost thou think Alexander looked o' this fashion i' th' earth?

. . . E'en so.

And smelt so? Pah! [Puts down the skull.]

. . . E'en so, my lord.

To what base uses we may return, Horatio! Why may not imagination trace the noble dust of Alexander till he find it stopping a bunghole?

. . . to consider so.

No, faith, not a jot . . . Alexander died, Alexander was buried, Alexander returneth to dust; the dust is earth; of earth we make loam; and why of that loam whereto he was converted might they not stop a beer barrel? [Last line.]

Some definitions and context:

- *When Hamlet says that Yorick has **borne** him on his back a thousand times, he is saying that when he was a little boy, Yorick would often let him ride on his back.*
- *Think of "**gibes**" and "**gambols**" as playful insults and pranks (but not mean ones).*
- *Your chaps are your lower jaw bones. Yorick's skull is "chap-fallen" because the lower jaw is no longer connected to the rest of the skull. Hamlet is making a joke.*
- *Your "**gorge**" is your stomach. It is a similar word today to guts. Hamlet feels his guts rise up in himself when he imagines that a guy as nice as Yorick has to end up as just a skull in the ground.*
- *When Hamlet tells the skull "let her paint an inch thick, to this favor she must come," he is referring to makeup again. He's talking about Ophelia, his lady, and saying that no matter how much makeup she wears, her beauty and youth will still fade. Her fate, like Yorick's and everybody else's, is to one day be a skull in the ground.*

"Gravedigger Scene" from 5.1: Gravedigger's Cue Script
(Your lines are in bold; highlight words you
don't know. Listen for your cues.)

. . . Mine ache to think on 't

[Sings] ***A pickaxe and a spade, a spade,***
For and a shrouding sheet;
Oh, a pit of clay for to be made
For such a guest is meet. **[He throws another skull.]**

. . . Whose grave's this, sirrah?

Mine, sir.
[Sings again] ***O, a pit of clay for to be made***
For such a guest is meet.

. . . for thou liest in 't.

You lie out on't, sir, and therefore 'tis not yours. For my part, I do not lie in't, yet it is mine.

. . . therefore thou liest.

'Tis a quick lie, sir; 'twill away again from me to you.

. . . man dost thou dig it for?

For no man, sir.

. . . What woman then?

For none neither.

Some definitions and context:

- *Part of the humor between the gravedigger and Hamlet is the double meaning of the word "**quick**": it could mean fast, just like it still does today, but in Shakespeare's time, it also meant alive. When Hamlet says the grave is "not for the quick," he means that it is not for a living person. The gravedigger plays with the word and responds using the other meaning, that the lie is fast because it will go quickly back to Hamlet.*

>   . . . be buried in't?

One that was a woman, sir; but, rest her soul, she's dead.

>   . . . hast thou been a grave-maker?

Of all the days i' th' year, I came to 't that day that our last king Hamlet overcame Fortinbras.

>   . . . long is that since?

Cannot you tell that? Every fool can tell that. It was the very day that young Hamlet was born—he that is mad, and sent into England.

>   . . . was he sent into England?

Why, because he was mad. He shall recover his wits there. Or if he do not, 'tis no great matter there.

>   . . . Why?

'Twill not be seen in him there. There the men are as mad as he.

>   . . . How came he mad?

Very strangely, they say.

>   . . . How strangely?

Faith, e'en with losing his wits.

>   . . . Upon what ground?

Why, here in Denmark. I have been sexton here, man and boy thirty years.

Some definitions and context:

- *The joke about people all losing their wits in England is funny because Shakespeare was English himself, and he wrote the play for English people to see. He's poking fun at himself and his own people, joking that they all know they are a bit crazy.*
- *A "sexton" is a groundskeeper. He takes care of the churchyard cemetery. And he says he has been doing it for thirty years.*

> ... will a man lie i' th' earth ere he rot?

Faith, if he be not rotten before he die (as we have many pocky corses nowadays that will scarce hold the laying in), he will last you some eight year or nine year. A tanner will last you nine year.

> ... Why he more than another?

Why, sir, his hide is so tanned with his trade that he will keep out water a great while; and your water is a sore decayer of your whoreson dead body. Here's a skull now hath lien you i' th' earth three-and-twenty years.

> ... Whose was it?

A whoreson, mad fellow's it was. Whose do you think it was?

> ... I know not.

A pestilence on him for a mad rogue! He poured a flagon of Rhenish on my head once. This same skull, sir, was, sir, Yorick's skull, the King's jester.

> ... This?

E'en that.

Some definitions and context:

- A "tanner" was a person who worked with leather. Tanners turn animal skins into leather. The gravedigger is joking that by working with animal skins, the tanner also makes his own skin tougher and is therefore better at keeping out water after he dies.
- A "*flagon of Rhenish*" is a large container of Rhenish wine. The Rhine is a river in Germany, and Rhenish wine is wine that comes from that region. When Yorick was alive, he once poured a whole container of wine on the gravedigger's head, probably as a prank to make people laugh. The gravedigger seems to be reminiscing fondly on the memory. What does this suggest about the gravedigger and his relationship with Yorick and the old court under the old king? What does it suggest about Hamlet's childhood?

"The Gravedigger Scene" from 5.1: Horatio's Cue Script
(Your lines are in bold; helpful notes are in italics. Listen closely for your cues.)

                               . . . that would circumvent God, might it not?

It might, my lord.

                                    . . . he went to beg it, might it not?

Ay, my lord.

                     . . . and must th' inheritor himself have no more, ha?

Not a jot more, my lord.

                             . . . Prithee, Horatio, tell me one thing.

What's that, my lord?

                 . . . think Alexander lookd o' this fashion i' th' earth?

E'en so.

                                              . . . And smelt so? Pah!

E'en so, my lord.

                                       . . . stopping a bunghole?

'Twere to consider too curiously to consider so.

Some definitions and context:

- *Alexander the Great was one of the greatest military leaders in history. Hamlet contemplates how even somebody as great as Alexander eventually becomes dust after dying. All people share the same fate as Yorick: eventually they are to be reduced to a skull and, finally, to dust.*

REINFORCING SKILLS: ANALYZING MORE PAINTED SCENES FROM *HAMLET*

In this activity students will reinforce skills introduced in chapter 4, when they analyzed historical paintings and illustrations inspired by *Hamlet*. Have students look carefully at the two images below, which are inspired by the gravedigger scene, and take ten to fifteen minutes to answer the questions accompanying each. Though they refer to the same passage in *Hamlet*, they engender different moods.

The first image of Hamlet gazing into a skull is perhaps the most iconic in all of literature (figure 5.6). The second image (figure 5.7), Hamlet as a child riding on the back of Yorick, establishes the depth of Hamlet's and Yorick's affections for one another. Which better tells Yorick's story? Which better symbolizes Hamlet's philosophical quandaries? How do the two complement one another? Both images are in the public domain and accessible online.

As a whole group, conduct an online image search for "Hamlet with skull painting," and project the results so students can see the host of similar drawings, illustrations, paintings, and photographs that all capture the same moment. Look through these briefly with students. In what ways are they similar? Do they all create the same mood, or are some different? Ask students about which facial expressions work best.

Have them practice looking into a skull. A wad of paper makes an excellent impromptu skull, though it is always good for an English teacher to have invested in a plastic skull or two for their classroom. Cheap versions can be found around Halloween time. Start with the images and questions below, but as a follow-up activity, have students take selfies with a skull where they try to capture just the right facial expression as they enact Hamlet at the moment he contemplates his most profound philosophical questions (similar to figure 5.6).

Figure 5.6: Eugene Delacroix. *Hamlet Contemplating Yorick's Skull*. 1828. Lithograph.
Source: Metropolitan Museum https://www.metmuseum.org/art/collection/search/774286.

- The only motif more common from *Hamlet* in visual art than the drowned Ophelia is the image of Hamlet, from act 5, gazing into the skull of poor Yorick. Why do you think the idea of Hamlet looking into the skull is so iconic?
- How would it make you feel to hold an actual skull in your hand that had been buried in the ground for decades? How would it be different if you knew the skull was somebody you had known as a child? What if it was somebody who had been important to you?
- In the background you can see Ophelia's funeral procession; why does the artist include the image of the funeral too? What would have changed if he had not included it?

Figure 5.7: Phillip Hermogenes Calderon. *The Young Lord Hamlet*. 1868. Oil paint on canvas. Private collection.
Source: https://commons.wikimedia.org/wiki/File:The_Young_Lord_Hamlet.jpg.

- This image captures a scene from years before the play, when Hamlet was a young boy. He rides on the back of Yorick, the court jester. The artist was inspired by Hamlet's musing to Horatio that Yorick "bore [him] on his back a thousand times" (5.1.192–93). How is this idea of Yorick different from the more common motif of Hamlet gazing into Yorick's skull?
- How old do you think young Hamlet is in the painting? Who are the women depicted in the scene? One is likely Gertrude, but the others are the artist's invention. Who might the other two women be? Who might the baby be? Why does the artist choose to invent a dog to play alongside them?
- What does the overall scene suggest about Hamlet's childhood? Do you agree with the artist's reading that Hamlet had a happy childhood? What does it say about the play if Hamlet indeed had a happy childhood? What would it say if he did not have a happy childhood?

DISCUSSION QUESTIONS AND WRITING PROMPTS

Act 5 discussion and writing prompts bring together everything that students have been working on since starting their study: questions about language; conceptions of Ophelia and what she means to audiences today; themes of blame, cruelty, revenge, and forgiveness; and wading through the philosophical, existential angst that has made *Hamlet* the greatest of Shakespeare's plays. Use these for discussion and as starting points for writing assignments:

1. Go through the first half of the text of 5.1, and highlight the second-person pronouns. Do the two gravediggers use familiar or formal pronouns with one another? Which does the first gravedigger use with Hamlet? Which does Hamlet use with him? What does that suggest about the differences in the characters' status? Do you think this means that the gravedigger knows who Hamlet is?
2. At the end of his speech, holding the skull in 5.1, Hamlet suddenly switches from prose to verse in the middle of the speech (at 5.1.220). Why does he switch from prose to verse in the middle of this passage?
3. Go back through the second half of the text of 5.1, and highlight all the flower references at Ophelia's funeral in a different color. Which of these had already been mentioned in act 4? Which are new? What do these add to the way we think about Ophelia?
4. Do you think Hamlet was cruel to Rosencrantz and Guildenstern? Was it wrong for him to have changed the king's letter to have them killed when they got to England, or do you think they deserved it? Hamlet claims they "did make love to this employment" (5.2.64). Do you agree? Did they know what was happening? Do you think the king had told them they were taking Hamlet to England to be killed?
5. Do you believe Hamlet when he says he loved Ophelia in 5.1? If not, why not? If so, how do you reconcile his claims of love in 5.1 against the mean things he said to her earlier in the play (e.g., the nunnery scene, his comments about her makeup)?
6. Hamlet does not like it when women wear makeup. When he talks at the graveside with Yorick's skull, he jokes that the skull should go tell his lady (Ophelia) that even if she "paint[s] an inch thick" (i.e., puts on lots of makeup), she will eventually suffer the same fate—"to this favor she must come"—as everybody else (5.1.173–74). This is moments before he realizes that Ophelia died. How does hearing him make such mean comments just minutes before declaring his love for Ophelia influence your perception of Hamlet?
7. Do you think Hamlet is sincere when he apologizes to Laertes at 5.2.240? Do you think Laertes accepts his apology? If you were

directing this scene, how would you instruct Hamlet and Laertes to act to make the apology scene work the way you interpret it?
8. In what ways does Hamlet represent "thought" and Laertes represent "rage" through the earlier acts in the play? Upon Laertes's return to Denmark? At their skirmish at the graveside? During their duel? In which ways do the two change over time?
9. Would you accept Laertes's apology at the end of the play? Laertes says that "the King's to blame" (5.2.351). Is he right? Is the king entirely to blame for everything that has happened? Or do you put some blame on Laertes too? Do you put any blame on Hamlet? Gertrude? Explain why you think so.

ACT 5 CULMINATING PROJECT: WORKING THROUGH THE PLAY LIKE AN EDITOR (TWO DAYS)

In this project students will draft a short, scholarly text (complete with its own footnotes) of the thirty lines between Hamlet and the gravedigger. As discussed in the anticipatory set activity at the beginning of the chapter, editors have settled many textual issues with *Hamlet* that arise when comparing Q2 and F1, but not all, and having students work through the editorial process reveals insights into deeper questions. One such question revolves around Hamlet's age, and students will focus on this question as they complete this project.

Modern editions all make Hamlet's age clear. He is thirty. The gravedigger explains that he has been the sexton, or groundskeeper, at the churchyard for thirty years and that he started that work on the day young Hamlet was born. Ergo, Hamlet is now thirty. He further adds that Yorick's skull has been in the ground for twenty-three years; ergo, Hamlet was seven when poor Yorick died. The math is simple. However, even if modern editors agree on these details today, a careful reader could make the case by looking back at the three original sources (Q2, F1, and Q1) that Hamlet is actually just sixteen.

Here's the case: In Q2 the gravedigger states that he has been "sexten" at the churchyard for thirty years. "Sexten" was an accepted spelling from the time of "sexton," and modern editors unanimously agree that "sexton" is the correct editorial choice. However, "sexten" was also once a common spelling in Shakespeare's time for "sixteen"; this was before English spelling had been standardized.[8] F1, in fact, reads "sixteene," and if editors had chosen "sixteen" instead of "sexton," the gravedigger's line would read, "I have been sixteen here, man and boy thirty years."

In reply to Hamlet asking how long he has been a gravedigger, he would be replying, "I have been [working] sixteen [years] here [in this churchyard, digging graves], [in total, counting my years as both a man and a boy.] [I have been alive for] thirty years." If this were the case, it would make the gravedigger the one who is thirty years old, and he would have been fourteen when he started as an apprentice. In Shakespeare's time, the word "boy" could refer to someone in an apprenticeship, which usually started at age fourteen.

That still leaves the problem, though, that Yorick has been buried for twenty-three years. Both Q2 and F1 say so. Yorick would have died some seven years before Hamlet had been born and could never have born young Hamlet on his back a thousand times. Such inconsistency is part of the justification for privileging "sexton." Q1, though, offers a curious plausible alternate reading: in it, the gravedigger says, "Heres a scull hath bin here this dozen yeare [*sic*]." Editors rarely or never privilege Q1, and there are many reasons for that, but if they did here, it would mean that Yorick has been dead just twelve years. It would mean that Hamlet is now sixteen and remembers fondly a time twelve years before, when he was just some four years old, when Yorick would play with him. See figure 5.8.

Making Hamlet sixteen instead of thirty makes aesthetic sense too. He seems like a younger man.[9] It better explains why Hamlet did not become king upon his father's death: he was too young. It better explains why Hamlet, Horatio, Rosencrantz, and Guildenstern are all still in university. Adolescents in Shakespeare's time generally started university at some point between ages fourteen and sixteen and wrapped up some three to six years later. It would lend to the notion, too, that Laertes is also similar in age to Hamlet, as is himself off in France, attending university.

If Hamlet is sixteen, it also makes *Hamlet* a play about an adolescent, which immediately makes it more accessible to adolescents today too. That is not a good reason to make editorial choices—these should be driven instead by the textual source material (i.e., Q1, Q2, and F1) as well as what context and performance reveal—but it is a reason to make the editorial choice a discussion for high school and college-age students in the twenty-first century.

Performance can indeed drive editorial choices. Modern editors lean on what is learned in performance more today than historical editors. A moment in rehearsal or on stage can open up new ways of understanding a text. With that said, making Hamlet sixteen raises a question on stage. Historically, the part of Hamlet has been reserved for the best male actors of the age, who have proven themselves worthy of the role over many years.

And by the time they have proven themselves so, they are usually at least thirty years old. Chapter 2, in its film activities, mentions that Olivier, Gibson, Branagh, Hawke, and Tennant were all in their thirties and forties when they starred as Hamlet on film. None of these men looked like a sixteen-year-old. Richard Burbage was some thirty-two years old in 1599, when he played the very first Shakespearean Hamlet in the Globe Theatre. He would not have looked sixteen either. Virtually none of the men who played Hamlet on the

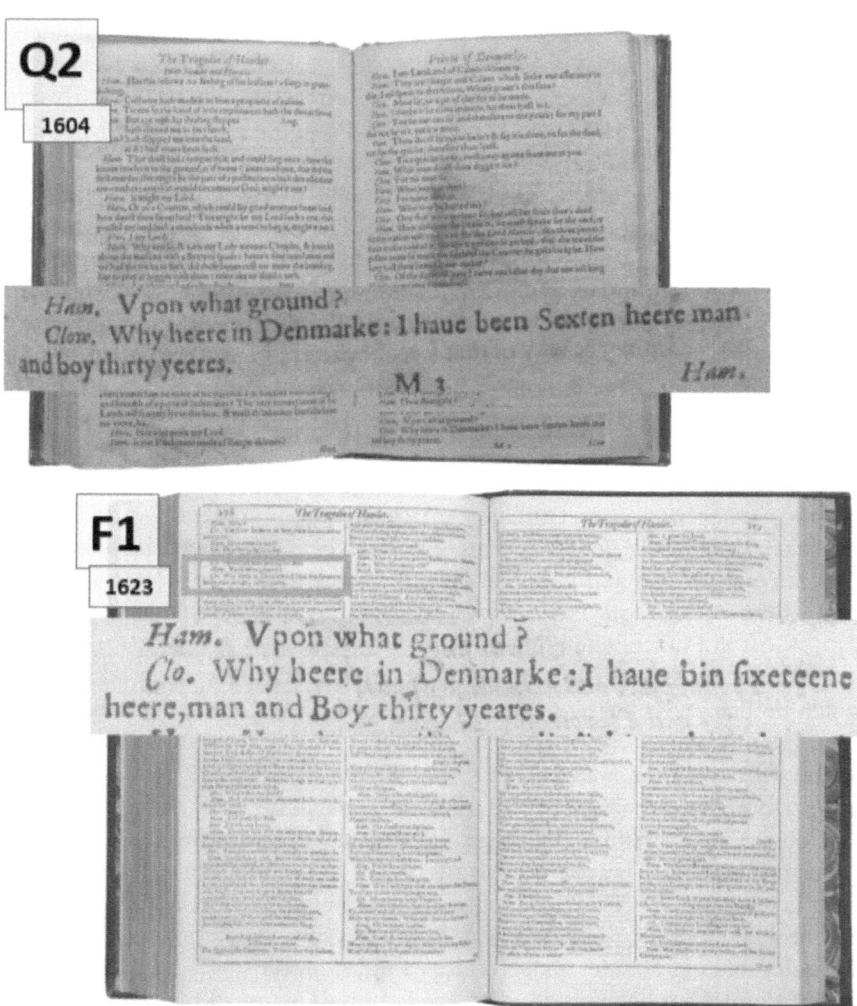

Figure 5.8: Modern editors have privileged the Q2 "sexten," or "sexton," over the F1 "sixteene." As a result, since Hamlet was born on the day he became a sexton, he would be thirty years old. If an editor privileged the F1 "sixteene," though, Hamlet would be just sixteen years old. Also, note that while we refer to him as the gravedigger, both Q2 and F1 refer to him as the clown; in Shakespeare's time, the word clown did not mean a funny fellow wearing makeup and a red nose (or his scary counterpart from a horror movie). It simply was the title given to a comic character.
Source: British Library and Folger Shakespeare Library website.

professional stage or screen over more than four centuries of performance looked sixteen.

Such a problem, though, does present an interesting justification for a woman playing Hamlet today. Chapter 3's anticipatory set activity had students complete preliminary research on some famous women who tackled the part. If Hamlet is only sixteen, then a mature female actor may be just as well or better suited to look the part than her male counterparts. She could be in her forties or fifties—Sarah Bernhardt was fifty-five when she played Hamlet in 1899—but still appear boyish on stage, particularly when seen from a distance.

DAY ONE: GETTING COMFORTABLE COMPARING THE SOURCE TEXTS

After taking some time to get comfortable with these issues and the three texts—they can be seen here as well as in their digital editions on the British Libraries and Folger Shakespeare Library websites—devote an entire class, or some fifty minutes of a longer period, to getting started with these conversations. Using the original three source texts, spend some ten minutes with each, thirty minutes total, having students read the speech between Hamlet and the gravedigger. Project the images of the texts for the whole class, or distribute copies to students digitally or on paper.

Have volunteer students read the passage from Q1, Q2, and F1. They have practiced these with the cue scripts before, but they will now face the additional challenge of deciphering their original versions. Offer support as students read. Have them compare the three texts and emphasize the possible editorial choices needed to convert them into a modern text. How does thinking about the issues like an actor or director affect their choices?

As the discussion progresses, avoid checking modern texts. Let students know that editors have overwhelmingly chosen the "sexton" option, but otherwise, compare the three source texts without leaning on modern editors' choices. Afterward, lead students in a discussion on the editorial issues the passage presents:

- Should an editor privilege an aesthetic approach to a strictly textual approach? That is, would it be okay for an editor to craft a sixteen-year-old Hamlet for their version, even if they didn't believe the three source texts supported it?
- What are the implications if Hamlet is thirty? What are the implications if he is sixteen? Which interpretation do students like better? Which

is best supported by the source texts? How much does it matter what editors have decided regarding this issue over the years? Is it wrong to challenge them?

If time allows at the end of the lesson, have students begin drafting their own modern text. These should all begin with Hamlet's "How long hast thou been a gravedigger" and end with his "Make her laugh at that"; their texts should end up being approximately fifty lines (5.1.145–201). The passage is prose, though, so this number will vary.

DAY TWO: MAKING THEIR OWN MODERN EDITIONS

Next, take another class period for students to write or finish writing their modern text of the Yorick lines between Hamlet and the gravedigger. Do not have them do the whole scene—it is too long—but just the lines described in the previous paragraph. Tell students they must choose one of the two interpretations for Hamlet's age: they can keep Hamlet as thirty years old or have Hamlet as sixteen years old (and as a result, challenge centuries of editorial practice). Either way, they will need to be able to justify their choices, considering the arguments that an editor would make from a textual approach as well as an aesthetic approach.

Explain that they should modernize archaic spellings and punctuation but stay as accurate as possible to what the original sources provide. In other words, they should become an editor and do the editorial work of converting a passage from these original texts into something modern that is readable to a twenty-first-century audience. Remind them what they know already about how editors lay out verse and prose on a page (from chapter 1). Also, emphasize that this is *not* a paraphrasing activity (like they completed for chapter 2): students should not put the text in their own words; rather, they should stay as accurate as possible to what they believe to be Shakespeare's original language based on their three source texts.

Remind them as well to keep their modern texts put away. The learning comes from working through the textual editorial problems instead of copying what modern editors have decided. After students have their modern text, have them add five footnotes. Four of these should be words or phrases that they think readers will find challenging. (They practiced this skill in the culminating project in chapter 2.) Instruct them to look these four words up and to provide definitions in their own words for their readers. For their fifth footnote, instruct them to provide context and expand upon Hamlet's age. It should summarize what the texts have to say about how old Hamlet is and explain their editorial choice.

REFLECTING ON WRITING: TAKE FIVE

Once again, have students reflect on their writing—specifically, on how their knowledge and skills have transferred (and will transfer) across different writing domains:

> Reflect on your work editing source texts into a modern text. What did you do when you encountered archaic spelling and punctuation? What did you do when you came across words you did not know? How did you decide which words to cut? How did you decide which needed footnotes? How will you use these skills in future writing?

Brainstorm together as a whole group—writing notes on the whiteboard—and then give students five to ten minutes to freewrite further ideas. After writing, bring the class together again to share new ideas and update the whiteboard. Adapt the time and format as needed.

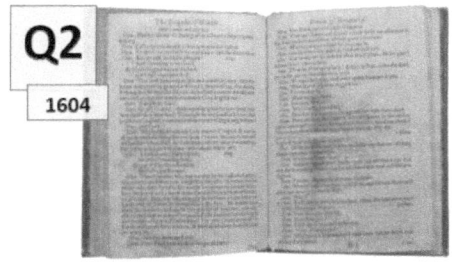

How long haſt thou been Graue-maker?

Clow. Of the dayes i'th yere I came too't that day that our laſt king *Hamlet* ouercame *Fortenbraſſe.*

Ham. How long is that ſince?

Clow. Cannot you tell that? euery foole can tell that, it was that very day that young *Hamlet* was borne: hee that is mad and ſent into *England.*

Ham. I marry, why was he ſent into *England*?

Clow. Why becauſe a was mad: a ſhall recouer his wits there, or if a doo not, tis no great matter there.

Ham. Why?

Clow. Twill not be ſeene in him there, there the men are as mad (as hee.

Ham. How came he mad?

Clow. Very ſtrangely they ſay.

Ham. How ſtrangely?

Clow. Fayth eene with looſing his wits.

Ham. Vpon what ground?

Clow. Why heere in Denmarke: I haue been Sexten heere man and boy thirty yeeres.

Figure 5.9: In the Q2 (1604) version of the passage, the gravedigger makes clear that he has been a sexton for thirty years total. That'd make him about forty-six years old—most boys started work as apprentices at age fourteen—and it would make Hamlet thirty years old since he began to work the day Hamlet was born.
Source: Folger Shakespeare Library and British Library websites.

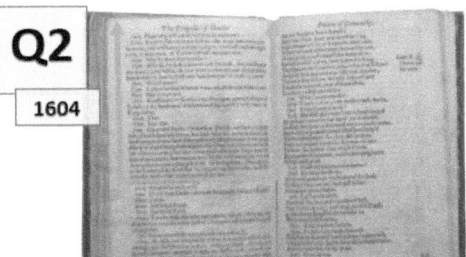

Ham. How long will a man lie i'th earth ere he rot?
Clow. Fayth if a be not rotten before a die, as we haue many pockie corses, that will scarce hold the laying in, a will last you som eyght yeere, or nine yeere. A Tanner will last you nine yeere.
Ham. Why he more then another?
Clow. Why sir, his hide is so tand with his trade, that a will keepe out water a great while; & your water is a sore decayer of your whorson dead body, heer's a scull now hath lyen you i'th earth 23. yeeres.
Ham. Whose was it?
Clow. A whorson mad fellowes it was, whose do you think it was?
Ham. Nay I know not.
Clow. A pestilence on him for a madde rogue, a pourd a flagon of Renish on my head once; this same skull sir, was sir *Yoricks* skull, the Kings Iester.
Ham. This?
Clow. Een that.
Ham. Alas poore *Yoricke*, I knew him *Horatio*, a fellow of infinite iest, of most excellent fancie, hee hath bore me on his backe a thousand times, and now how abhorred in my imagination it is: my gorge rises at it. Heere hung those lyppes that I haue kist I know not howe oft, where be your gibes now? your gamboles, your songs, your flashes of merriment, that were wont to set the table on a roare, not one now to mocke your owne grinning, quite chopfalne. Now get you to my Ladies table, & tell her, let her paint an inch thicke, to this fauour she must come, make her laugh at that.

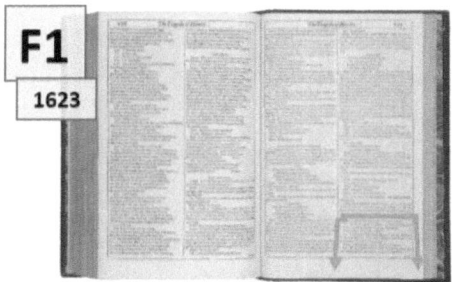

How long haſt thou been a Graue-maker?
Clo. Of all the dayes i'th' yeare, I came too't that day that our laſt King *Hamlet* o'recame *Fortinbras.*
Ham. How long is that ſince?
Clo. Cannot you tell that? euery foole can tell that: It was the very day, that young *Hamlet* was borne, hee that was mad, and ſent into England.
Ham. I marry, why was he ſent into England?
Clo. Why, becauſe he was mad; hee ſhall recouer his wits there; or if he do not, it's no great matter there.

Figure 5.10: F1, on the other hand, prints "sixteene." If that were the case, the gravedigger would have worked in the graveyard for sixteen years. That would make him thirty years old instead, and it would make Hamlet just sixteen. Editors across the centuries have all unanimously agreed, though, on the other reading. Even those who privileged the F1 as the better source over Q2 have changed "sixteene" to "sexton" in their editions. It just makes more sense given that, just ten lines later, the gravedigger reports that Yorick's skull has "laine in the earth three and twenty years." Hamlet couldn't have known Yorick if Yorick had died some seven years before Hamlet was born.
Source: Folger Shakespeare Library website.

Ham. Why?

Clo. 'Twill not be seene in him, there the men are as mad as he.

Ham. How came he mad?

Clo. Very strangely they say.

Ham. How strangely?

Clo. Faith e'ene with loosing his wits.

Ham. Vpon what ground?

Clo. Why heere in Denmarke: I haue bin sixeteene heere, man and Boy thirty yeares.

Ham. How long will a man lie 'ith' earth ere he rot?

Clo. Ifaith, if he be not rotten before he die (as we haue many pocky Coarses now adaies, that will scarce hold the laying in) he will last you some eight yeare, or nine yeare. A Tanner will last you nine yeare.

Ham. Why he, more then another?

Clo. Why sir, his hide is so tan'd with his Trade, that he will keepe out water a great while. And your water, is a sore Decayer of your horson dead body. Heres a Scull now: this Scul, has laine in the earth three & twenty years.

Ham. Whose was it?

Clo. A whoreson mad Fellowes it was; Whose doe you thinke it was?

Ham. Nay, I know not.

Clo. A pestilence on him for a mad Rogue, a pou'rd a Flaggon of Renish on my head once: This same Scull Sir, this same Scull sir, was *Yoricks* Scull, the Kings Iester.

Ham. This?

Clo. E'ene that.

Ham. Let me see. Alas poore *Yorick*, I knew him *Horatio*, a fellow of infinite Iest; of most excellent fancy, he hath borne me on his backe a thousand times: And how abhorred my Imagination is, my gorge rises at it. Heere hung those lipps, that I haue kist I know not how oft. VVhere be your Iibes now? Your Gambals? Your Songs? Your flashes of Merriment that were wont to set the Table on a Rore? No one now to mock your own Ieering? Quite chopfalne? Now get you to my Ladies Chamber, and tell her, let her paint an inch thicke, to this fauour she must come. Make her laugh at that:

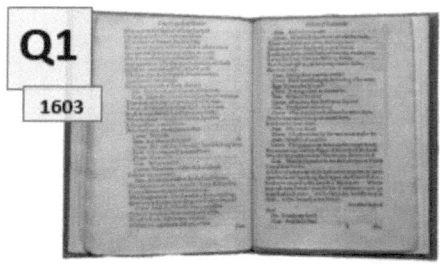

Ham. And why a tanner?
Clowne Why his hide is so tanned with his trade,
That it will holde out water, that's a parlous
Deuourer of your dead body, a great soaker.
Looke you, heres a scull hath bin here this dozen yeare,
Let me see, I euer since our last king *Hamlet*
Slew *Fortenbrasse* in combat, yong *Hamlets* father,
Hee that's mad.
Ham. I mary, how came he madde?
Clowne Ifaith very strangely, by loosing of his wittes.
Ham. Vpon what ground?
Clowne A this ground, in *Denmarke.*
Ham. Where is he now?
Clowne Why now they sent him to *England.*
Ham. To *England!* wherefore?
Clowne Why they say he shall haue his wittes there,
Or if he haue not, t'is no great matter there,
It will not be seene there.
Ham. Why not there?
Clowne Why there they say the men are as mad as he.
Ham. Whose scull was this?
Clowne This, a plague on him, a madde rogues it was,
He powred once a whole flagon of Rhenish of my head,
Why do not you know him? this was one *Torickes* scull.
Ham. Was this? I prethee let me see it, alas poore *Yoricke*
I knew him *Horatio,*
A fellow of infinite mirth, he hath caried mee twenty times
vpon his backe, here hung those lippes that I haue kissed a
hundred times, and to see, now they abhorre me : Wheres
your iests now *Yoricke?* your flashes of meriment : now go
to my Ladies chamber, and bid her paint her selfe an inch
thicke, to this she must come *Yoricke.*

Figure 5.11: Whereas Q2 and F1 differ in the scene in just a few words, Q1 provides a very different text for the conversation between the gravedigger and Hamlet. It entirely omits the lines about how long the gravedigger has been digging graves, and it also states that poor Yorick's skull has been buried just twelve years. If that were the case, then it would be possible for Hamlet to be just sixteen.
Source: British Libraries website.

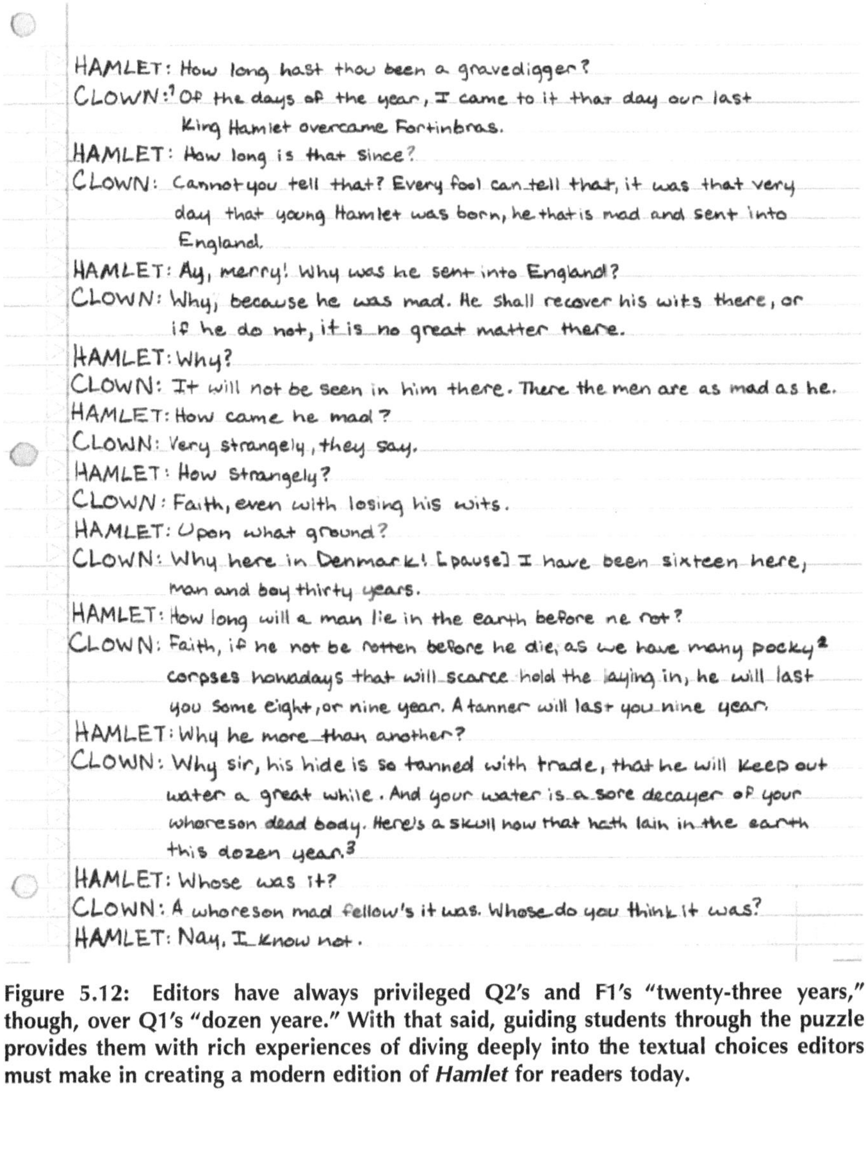

HAMLET: How long hast thou been a gravedigger?
CLOWN:[1] Of the days of the year, I came to it that day our last
   King Hamlet overcame Fortinbras.
HAMLET: How long is that since?
CLOWN: Cannot you tell that? Every fool can tell that, it was that very
   day that young Hamlet was born, he that is mad and sent into
   England.
HAMLET: Ay, merry! Why was he sent into England?
CLOWN: Why, because he was mad. He shall recover his wits there, or
   if he do not, it is no great matter there.
HAMLET: Why?
CLOWN: It will not be seen in him there. There the men are as mad as he.
HAMLET: How came he mad?
CLOWN: Very strangely, they say.
HAMLET: How strangely?
CLOWN: Faith, even with losing his wits.
HAMLET: Upon what ground?
CLOWN: Why here in Denmark! [pause] I have been sixteen here,
   man and boy thirty years.
HAMLET: How long will a man lie in the earth before he rot?
CLOWN: Faith, if he not be rotten before he die, as we have many pocky[2]
   corpses nowadays that will scarce hold the laying in, he will last
   you some eight, or nine year. A tanner will last you nine year.
HAMLET: Why he more than another?
CLOWN: Why sir, his hide is so tanned with trade, that he will keep out
   water a great while. And your water is a sore decayer of your
   whoreson dead body. Here's a skull now that hath lain in the earth
   this dozen year.[3]
HAMLET: Whose was it?
CLOWN: A whoreson mad fellow's it was. Whose do you think it was?
HAMLET: Nay, I know not.

Figure 5.12: Editors have always privileged Q2's and F1's "twenty-three years," though, over Q1's "dozen yeare." With that said, guiding students through the puzzle provides them with rich experiences of diving deeply into the textual choices editors must make in creating a modern edition of *Hamlet* for readers today.

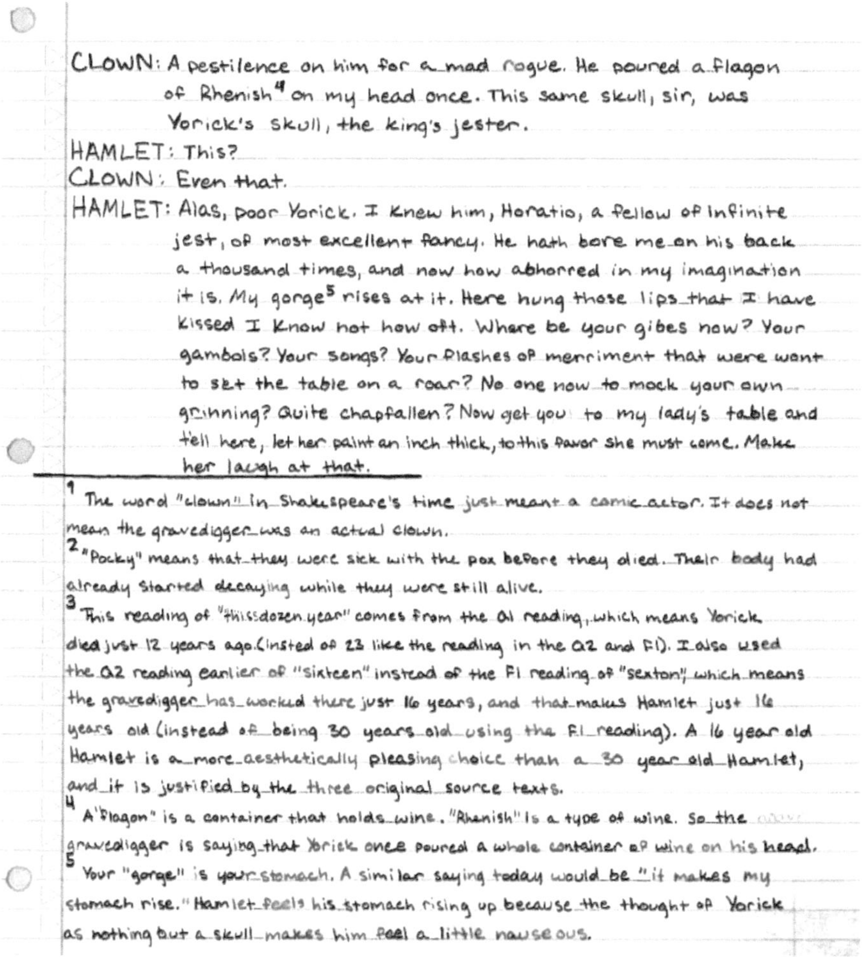

> CLOWN: A pestilence on him for a mad rogue. He poured a flagon of Rhenish[4] on my head once. This same skull, sir, was Yorick's skull, the king's jester.
> HAMLET: This?
> CLOWN: Even that.
> HAMLET: Alas, poor Yorick. I knew him, Horatio, a fellow of infinite jest, of most excellent fancy. He hath bore me on his back a thousand times, and now how abhorred in my imagination it is. My gorge[5] rises at it. Here hung those lips that I have kissed I know not how oft. Where be your gibes now? Your gambols? Your songs? Your flashes of merriment that were wont to set the table on a roar? No one now to mock your own grinning? Quite chapfallen? Now get you to my lady's table and tell her, let her paint an inch thick, to this favor she must come. Make her laugh at that.
>
> [1] The word "clown" in Shakespeare's time just meant a comic actor. It does not mean the gravedigger was an actual clown.
> [2] "Pocky" means that they were sick with the pox before they died. Their body had already started decaying while they were still alive.
> [3] This reading of "this dozen year" comes from the Q1 reading, which means Yorick died just 12 years ago (instead of 23 like the reading in the Q2 and F1). I also used the Q2 reading earlier of "sixteen" instead of the F1 reading of "sexton," which means the gravedigger has worked there just 16 years, and that makes Hamlet just 16 years old (instead of being 30 years old using the F1 reading). A 16 year old Hamlet is a more aesthetically pleasing choice than a 30 year old Hamlet, and it is justified by the three original source texts.
> [4] A "flagon" is a container that holds wine. "Rhenish" is a type of wine. So the gravedigger is saying that Yorick once poured a whole container of wine on his head.
> [5] Your "gorge" is your stomach. A similar saying today would be "it makes my stomach rise." Hamlet feels his stomach rising up because the thought of Yorick as nothing but a skull makes him feel a little nauseous.

Figure 5.13: This student exemplar edition of the gravedigger dialogue leans into a possible text that would make Hamlet just sixteen years old instead of the accepted thirty years old that modern editors have all agreed upon. It adopts the Q1 reading that Yorick has been dead just twelve years instead of twenty-three.

NOTES

1. Jesus says, "Do not be afraid of those who kill the body but cannot kill the soul. . . . Are not two sparrows sold for a penny? Yet not one of them will fall to the ground outside your Father's care. . . . So don't be afraid; you are worth more than many sparrows" (*New International Version Bible*, Matthew 10:28–31). A similar passage appears in Luke: "Do not be afraid of those who can kill the body and after that can

do no more. . . . Are not five sparrows sold for two pennies? Yet not one of them is forgotten by God. . . . Do not be afraid; you are worth more than many sparrows" (Luke 12:4–7).

2. Other teachers have advocated for strategies that push students to think like editors. Edward Rocklin (2005) makes the case that having students think about editorial choices (like in his segmenting activities; see chapter 1, endnote 2) pushes them to think about performance choices too: "It (re)opens discussion of the ways in which editors have worked with the text and, indeed, must be seen not only as editing the performance text but also as tacitly performing the text in the very act of editing it" (262; also see xvi–xvii). Mary Ellen Dakin (2009) has her students write their own stage directions for Shakespeare: she first removes the stage directions that editors provide, then has students analyze the remaining text for implicit stage directions and, finally, insert their own; she uses the fight between Tybalt and Mercutio from *Romeo* as an example, explaining that it changes the reading depending on when each character draws their sword (6–11). She explains, "I tell students they are editors, and in groups they translate their reading of the scene into stage directions" (9). Long and Christel (2019) likewise, in their *Folio* technique, ask students to think like editors by learning the skills necessary to find meaning through F1's textual clues (20–24).

3. There are many good sources for learning more about the textual history of Shakespeare's plays, but they are far too many to list here. The introductions to the Norton, Arden, and Bedford Hamlet editions are good starting points (Norton 2019, xxii–xxv; Arden [2006] 2016, 8–14, 76–88; Bedford 15–19). Another entry point is Stephen Orgel (2003), who makes the point that we have no original texts: "What we have of the Shakespeare text, all we have ever had, is a set of versions with no original" (xiv; note that this book includes images inappropriate for high school classrooms, qtd. in Dakin 2009, 59). The play quite possibly always has existed in multiple forms—much like the multiple cue scripts introduced in chapter 3—which would have been in flux over various performances, and so forth—and never as a single text (Thomas 2019, 129–30; also see Tiffany Stern's books on performance history: *Shakespeare in Parts* and *Documents of Performance in Early Modern England*). In another essay, Orgel (2002) adds, "Virtually all theatrical literature . . . must be seen as basically collaborative in nature" (4). The text was fluid before it was written down, and it remained so afterward.

4. The 235 First Folios themselves have rich material histories, as they have been passed down through the centuries. Eighty-two are in the Folger Shakespeare Library collection, more than are in any other library or collection. Several scholars have traced their history (the physical books themselves rather than the text they have transmitted). One recent scholar in this tradition is Emma Smith, who has several books on the First Folio: her 2015 *The Making of Shakespeare's First Folio* (second edition in 2023) and her 2016 *Shakespeare's First Folio: Four Centuries of an Iconic Book*. In the latter, Smith (2016) begins with Sir Edward Dering and his purchase of two copies of the First Folio on December 5, 1623 (he'd likely bought one copy for himself and the other as a gift); these two First Folios are the first recorded sales, and their story lends context to at least one type of reader from four hundred years ago (3). Dering was interested in both attending live productions—he records some

thirty theater visits from 1619 to 1626—and reading their printed scripts; he "bought playbooks in large quantities, often on the same day as a theatre visit, apparently constructing a complete collection from the back catalogue of the St. Paul's Churchyard booksellers" (7–8). Dering paid one pound each for them (4). Through her study Smith "proceeds through a range of associated examples and case studies," seeking "to connect the wider history of Shakespeare's critical transmission with the more specifically material history of a book" and how it "came to be so uniquely important to individuals, institutions, and nations (21, 23). Smith also edited the *Cambridge Companion to Shakespeare's First Folio*. Ben Higgins takes a different approach. Instead of detailing the story of the First Folio books themselves, he describes in *Shakespeare's Syndicate: The First Folio, and the Early Modern Book Trade* (2002) the four book-trade businesses that worked together to make all (or at least most) of Shakespeare's plays into one volume a reality. The story of the First Folios, as well as the various ways scholars have studied them, is not the subject matter for students in their first reading of *Hamlet*, but it is a fascinating study for those teachers (and advanced students) wishing to dive deeper into the history of how Shakespeare's plays made their way to the present day.

5. Zachary Lesser's 2015 *Hamlet after Q1: An Uncanny History of the Shakespearean Text* provides an excellent analysis of how Q1 made its way from Shakespeare's time to our own. First printed in 1603, it is the oldest version of Shakespeare's *Hamlet*, but all copies of it disappeared until 1823. For 220 years editors, scholars, and theater makers developed long-standing and stubborn traditions based on Q2 and F1, not knowing there even was a Q1, and when a copy was found, most chose to discredit or ignore it. Up through the late twentieth century, it was called the bad quarto. In the twenty-first century, though, editors have accepted it as a valid third source text, though they still privilege Q2 and F1. Another copy of Q1 surfaced later in the nineteenth century, but to date, only those two have been found to still exist; seven copies of Q2, on the other hand, made their way to the present (Shakespeare [2006] 2016, 9). This uncanny history fascinates Lesser (2015): Q1 "follows a wandering, echoic path that begins in the nineteenth century, reverberates back into the seventeenth and sixteenth, and returns to haunt the twentieth and twenty-first" (15). Lesser writes one chapter each on three key Q1 departures from Q2/F1: in the mousetrap scene, Hamlet says "contrary matters" instead of "country matters," undermining the interpretation of the line as the bawdiest in the play; Q1 adds a stage direction to the closet scene not found in Q2 nor F1, one in which the ghost enters in his nightgown, reinforcing an underlying domestic tone that Oedipal, psychoanalytic readings have since drawn from; and it fundamentally changes the "to be or not to be" speech. Lesser is most interested, though, in what Q1's critical reception reveals about "Shakespeare's authorship, his writing process, and even, given his paramount place in the literary canon, the nature of poetic genius itself" (58).

6. Many theater makers also ignore Q1, but not all. Ralph Alan Cohen directed a 2007 *Hamlet* at the American Shakespeare Center in their replica Blackfriars Playhouse. Cohen (2019) points out a comedic aspect more prevalent in Q1: "What made that 2007 production of Q1 so memorable during its run is not that it proved the 'bad' Quarto was playable and 'muscular'—a favorite word in reviews of it—but that, by

slightly disorienting us with its virtues, it reminded us of the 'play' and the muscles in the 'good' *Hamlets*" (179).

7. Editors through the nineteenth and early twentieth centuries often privileged the F1 text and, on that basis, generally opted for "solid flesh." More recent editions from the mid-twentieth century through today have leaned toward the Q2 text—it being the older of the two and the one printed in Shakespeare's lifetime—and favor "sullied flesh" or "sallied flesh" in their editions. The most recent Arden Revised Edition (Shakespeare [2006] 2016) aims not to privilege any of the three source texts over their counterparts. It prints all three texts in two volumes: Q2 gets its own volume, and F1 and Q1 share a second volume. Its editors explain, "We believe that each of the three texts has sufficient merit to be read and studied on its own" (11). Their introduction provides an excellent summary on how editors historically have weighed the three texts in their work (8–13). Similarly, the most recent Third Edition of the Norton Shakespeare (2015) prints the Q2 and Q1 texts and provides a digital version of the F1 text, also emphasizing again the value in each of the three source texts.

8. Robert Cohen (1973) outlines the case for a sixteen-year-old Hamlet that I have presented above: "Along with many other critics, I have always considered Prince Hamlet to have been a boy. A real boy, too, not a man at all, but an adolescent . . . as young as sixteen or so" (179). He adds speculatively that Shakespeare's son Hamnet, had he lived, would have been sixteen in 1601: "The first Elizabethan audience would have witnessed the author [on stage as the ghost] 'playing' the father of a sixteen-year-old boy named Hamlet—only in life it was the son who was a ghost, not the father . . . it may help to explain the general feeling . . . that *Hamlet* is Shakespeare's most personal play" (188). Ralph Alan Cohen ([2006] 2018), on the other hand, a different scholar from Robert Cohen, leaves no room for argument: "Thirty. The gravedigger says he has been sexton for thirty years and came to it 'the very day that young Hamlet was born.' Not much room for discussion" (147).

9. While Rocklin (2005) does not make the case for Hamlet being sixteen rather than thirty, he retells a classroom dialogue in which one of his students points to Hamlet's youthfulness: "And that's one reason why Hamlet seems like an adolescent early in the play! Because he can't accept a world that doesn't follow the patterns it's supposed to follow. He sounds like an adolescent because adolescents want the world to make sense, to live up to how things *should* be, and they have a very hard time accepting it when the world does not follow the rules" (262).

Epilogue

"This Business Is Well Ended"

Beginnings matter more than endings. If my hypothesis from early in the book holds, then there are no endings, at least not in the study of *Hamlet*. We are all our own "king of infinite space," and even the most veteran teacher still has as much left to learn as the greenest first-timer (2.2.274). That is how infinity works. My hope, all the same, is that this volume and its ideas have contributed something meaningful to that lifelong study for the teachers reading it and, by extension, for their students.

Take these ideas. They were not mine in the first place but inspirations from my teachers, colleagues, and students. Use them as you see fit to flame the love of this play for others. Mix them with your own and everything else you've gathered through your experiences. The point was never to finish; it was always to keep growing. Watch performances. Read more books about *Hamlet*. Visit other teachers' classrooms to see what they do to bring Shakespeare to life. And then keep giving the play your magic as you inspire your students to read broadly and deeply. Teach them likewise to make *Hamlet* their own.

Have fun in your teaching. Never forget that *Hamlet* is a ghost story. Leverage that with students. And keep finding ways for them to get creative with it. That can be through their creative writing but also through performance; teach your students to see the words actively through an actor's eyes, one getting ready to put those words on a stage for an audience. Teach them how Shakespeare's language works, but ensure they never doubt their capacity to understand it, even when it takes effort.

Teach students to think critically and open themselves to *Hamlet's* possibilities. Is Ophelia timid or strong? Did Gertrude want her former husband dead? Teach them to embrace the play's rich history, to get deep into how text functions as it passes through centuries, and to lean into but also to always question the apparatus that an edition provides. And to all these methods, as you teach, add your own. There are countless ways to craft a successful unit of *Hamlet*, far more than can be encompassed in this one meager volume. Go out and forge your path together with your students. The point is to enjoy the work and to convince adolescents to enjoy the work too. Make sure they know *Hamlet* matters.

Appendix A
"That You Must Teach Me":
Additional Hamlet Resources

HAMLET CLASSROOM TEXTS

Folger—The Folger *Hamlet* is the best classroom text for first-time readers. It is the text from which all the quotations in this book come. It presents the text with basic notes on the opposite page in an accessible format that will not overwhelm students. The Folger *Hamlet* has been around for a long time; its earlier editions are available online for free through the Folger Shakespeare Library website (along with tons of teaching and research resources), and its most recent print editions are affordably priced for purchase as classroom sets.

Arden—The Arden Shakespeare series is the gold standard in Shakespeare scholarly editions. Its most recent *Hamlet* editions come in two volumes. The first volume includes the Q2 text, and the second combines the F1 and Q1 texts. It includes a thorough introduction and copious footnotes. It is a phenomenal resource for teachers and college-level students but overwhelming to give to first-time students.

Norton—The Norton Shakespeare texts, like the Ardens, are also scholarly texts. Its *Hamlet* features Benedict Cumberbatch on the cover, who many younger readers will recognize. It has an excellent introduction and a rich collection of contextual artifacts and scholarly essays suitable for advanced students. Several of these provided inspiration for the activities in this book. It is another treasure chest for teachers and advanced students.

Cambridge—Initially edited by Rex Gibson in the 1990s to accompany his groundbreaking book on performance-based teaching (see below), the newly revised versions of the Cambridge Shakespeare Series provide all that is good in a textbook-like version of the play but without the baggage of a giant anthology. It provides a student-friendly apparatus that will not overwhelm: essential vocabulary defined, brief scene summaries, character-focused blurbs, an ongoing performance-based commentary, and lots of color photos from performances and films. It is the most visually appealing and highly recommended for first-time students. Its only downfall is its price, which is twice that of its cheaper paperback counterparts.

Penguin/Bantam/Pelican/Signet—These classic, cheap paperback editions have been used in their various editions in classrooms for decades now. They are well edited and provide a balance between the superscholarly Arden and Norton, but they still incorporate adequate introductions, notes, and apparatus for serious study.

The "Old" *New Variorum Hamlet* **(edited by Horace Henry Furness)**—This two-volume set is *not* a classroom edition. It is far too dense with notes to be helpful even to advanced college-level students. It is far denser than even the Arden or Norton. It is also out of print—its most recent reprinting was in 1963—and not easy to find. With that said, it is the best print version ever made for figuring out what an archaic word or phrase means in the context of *Hamlet*. It combines two centuries of textual and editorial work (through the nineteenth century, when Shakespeare scholarship focused on philological word history). If a teacher plans to teach *Hamlet* for years, it is an excellent reference for answering students' most challenging word questions. At the time of writing of this book, a digital New Variorum Hamlet edition has been in production, though, which will likely finally make the print version obsolete. Nonetheless, it is still recommended as an invaluable tool for advanced *Hamlet* study and is worthy of mention.

BOOKS ON TEACHING SHAKESPEARE

Mary Ellen Dakin, *Reading Shakespeare with Young Adults*—The first of two books Dakin has written on teaching Shakespeare—the other emphasizes strategies for incorporating film—this first volume shares the language-based, comprehension-based schema Dakin employed in her decades of high school teaching for getting students actively engaged with Shakespeare's texts. Lessons specific to *Hamlet* include guided readings of 1.1, 2.2, and 3.1

(88–101); a strategy for reading 3.2 and 3.3 in companies, in which students are assigned specific reading roles: questioner, clarifier, summarizer, predictor, connector, and so forth (103–32); and methods for incorporating visual art in 1.4–5, in which Hamlet first meets the ghost, as well as in 4.7, in which Gertrude describes Ophelia's watery death (151–65).

Ralph Alan Cohen, *ShakesFear and How to Cure it: The Complete Handbook for Teaching Shakespeare*—As a respected university professor and cofounder of the American Shakespeare Center (ASC), Cohen has spent a career bridging literary and theatrical approaches to studying Shakespeare. His work emphasizes the plurality of potential readings made possible through a performance-based approach in the classroom. His book covers general strategies as well as a chapter specific to *Hamlet*: having ghost tryouts, poking fun at Polonius, trying Claudius for the murder of his brother, and others.

Timothy J. Duggan, *Advanced Placement Classroom: Hamlet*—Duggan provides a host of ready-to-use lessons, activities, and copyable worksheets that teachers can use in teaching *Hamlet*; they are specifically designed for the Advanced Placement (AP) classroom and tests. Useful in the AP context and outside, his ideas provide a performance-based, language-based approach to get students to write effectively about *Hamlet*.

Rex Gibson, *Cambridge School Shakespeare: Teaching Shakespeare*— Gibson is a classic read in the performance-based approach to teaching Shakespeare. He argues for treating the plays like scripts. The study of Shakespeare should be learner-centered, physical, and social, a celebration of the imagination, and an exploration of the plurality of meaning found through classroom performance. The book accompanies his Cambridge School Shakespeare series, described above. Both volumes are highly recommended reading for anybody who teaches *Hamlet*.

Kevin Long and Mary T. Christel, *Bring on the Bard: Active Drama Approaches for Shakespeare's Diverse Student Readers*—Long and Christal have put together the best book for teachers wanting practical strategies for bridging the classroom and theater space. Ideal at both the high school and college level, their book provides a performance-based framework they've borrowed from theater called the *Folio* approach, and it includes a host of activities that get students on their feet and engaged immediately with Shakespeare's language. They include a phenomenal activity for applying their method for Hamlet's "too too solid flesh" speech (136–50).

Victor Maolo-Juvera, Paula Greathouse, and Brooke Eisenbach, *Shakespeare and Young Adult Literature: Pairing and Teaching*—The volume provides ten chapters from teachers, each suggesting practical strategies for pairing a young adult novel with a Shakespeare play. Two of its chapters offer companion young adult (YA) novels for *Hamlet*: Amy Connelly Banks and Chris Rowe write of pairing it with Walter Dean Myers's *Monster*, and Joseph Haughey (the author of the book you hold now in your hands) suggests pairing it with Matthew Quick's *Forgive Me, Leonard Peacock*.

Peggy O'Brien, ed., *Teaching Hamlet and Henry IV, Part 1: Shakespeare Set Free*—This is part of a series of three texts written by teachers, each covering two to three plays and suggesting practical strategies that are immediately useful in the classroom. Explicitly targeted to high school teachers but also with strategies that work well in an introductory college classroom, its twenty-two performance-based, language-centered lesson plans on teaching *Hamlet* cover a host of topics: Hamlet's mental state, the nunnery scene, a *Hamlet* festival, and more. The unit also includes seven ready-to-use, project-based, photocopiable student handouts. The *Shakespeare Set Free* series has long been the standard for teachers looking for inspiration for teaching Shakespeare; no Shakespeare teacher's shelf is complete without it.

Milla Cozart Riggio, ed., *Teaching Shakespeare through Performance*—This volume of essays is seminal reading for teachers wanting to understand the history and development of performance-based approaches to teaching Shakespeare. Targeting college-level instructors, it includes essays from the most formative minds of the late twentieth century regarding the teaching of Shakespeare. Both theoretical and practical, its offerings provide a rich read for those wanting a deeper dive into this shift in American education. Essays on teaching *Hamlet* include those by Sauer and Tribble, Ralph Alan Cohen, Richard Schechner, Robert Hapgood, David Bevington, Gavin Witt, and others.

Edward Rocklin, *Performance Approaches to Teaching Shakespeare*—Geared for teaching college-level Shakespeare classes, this book by Rocklin works through a series of performance-based approaches and analyses, including a chapter on *Hamlet* that is filled with a treasure trove of activities and insights. Rocklin never gives his students answers but, rather, privileges what they find in the text through their work. Rocklin has spent a lifetime studying and teaching Shakespeare, and the depth of his knowledge shows in the underlying scholarship he draws from in crafting his lessons. In one activity, based on an excerpt from an essay by Thomas F. VanLaan, Rocklin has students ponder, first, a *Hamlet* set in a providential universe (where natural forces push toward good), then one in a malign universe (where those forces push toward evil), and yet again, one in an amoral universe (where those forces do not care), experimenting with how each affects their larger understanding of the play (331–36). In another activity, adapted from a lesson by Sauer and Tribble, he divides his class into three groups; he gives one group a bouquet of flowers; another, a sword; and another, a bible (not an actual bible, but a notebook with "Bible" written on the cover). Students then work through 1.3 and analyze how each prop affects their reading (300–7). Rocklin also includes chapters on *Taming of the Shrew* and *Richard III*. It is all good stuff and is highly recommended reading for all Shakespeare teachers.

Sheridan Lynn Steelman, *Walking in Shakespeare's Shoes: Connecting His World and Ours Using Primary Sources*—Steelman brings decades of experience teaching Shakespeare to her documents approach. She makes the case that teachers should infuse their Shakespeare instruction with contemporary sixteenth- and seventeenth-century archival documents: pamphlets, letters, book excerpts, poems, paintings, drawings, and other materials that teachers can use to provide the necessary context for students to understand and relate to Shakespeare's plays. In her chapter on *Hamlet*, for example, she transcribes entries from *Gerard's Herbal*, a 1590s gardening book popular in Shakespeare's time that he likely knew, for each of the flowers Ophelia gifts in her flower scene: rosemary, pansies, and so forth. A website accompanies the book, hosting dozens of ready-to-use documents created over her successful teaching career.

Ayanna Thompson and Laura Turchi, *Teaching Shakespeare with Purpose: A Student-Centred Approach*—Thompson and Turchi provide a theoretical framework for teaching Shakespeare based on four foundational premises: (1) "participation in informal learning communities," (2) "explicit explorations of identity," (3) "following divergent paths to knowledge," and (4) "innovative performances of their knowledge" (3–6). They build on performance-based approaches but argue that a performance-based pedagogy alone is insufficient for twenty-first-century learners; teachers must also address race, gender, sexuality, and physical ability (2, 9, 77). They argue that Shakespeare's plays are ideal models for teaching students to read complex texts—skills necessary for twenty-first-century learners. Their volume includes chapters specific to *Hamlet*, *Othello*, *Romeo and Juliet*, *The Merchant of Venice*, *Julius Caesar*, *A Midsummer Night's Dream*, and *Macbeth*.

Along with a focus text, each chapter provides a specific pedagogical focus; for *Hamlet*, the pedagogical focus is establishing frames and entry points.

Thompson and Turchi walk through five frames and entry points for teaching *Hamlet*: "familial relations," "remembrance," "revenge," "purpose of playing," and "the problem with women," but also argue that the end goal is for students to craft their own frames (26–38). Subsequent chapters provide additional lenses: chapter 3 focuses on language; chapter 4, on embodiment; chapter 5, on history; chapter 6, on writing; and chapter 7, on assessment.

The book is one of the best on teaching Shakespeare that has been published thus far this century, both for its forward-thinking theoretical underpinnings and its practical, ready-to-use classroom applications.

Joe Winston, *Transforming the Teaching of Shakespeare with the Royal Shakespeare Company*—Winston outlines the history of education outreach at the Royal Shakespeare Company (RSC). His fourth chapter, "The Classroom as Rehearsal Room," offers performance-based strategies specific to *Hamlet* and based on a workshop from 2013 with teachers in conjunction with the 2013 RSC David Farr *Hamlet* production. His opening activity has five to six students create a tableau (i.e., a frozen image) of a family that has just lost a father. He has them then shift their image to a family that has lost a father and the mother has remarried, then to one in which the mother remarried her husband's brother, and then to one in which a grieving son is portrayed. Ultimately, his last shift is having them make the family royal (58–59). In other activities, students read together from cue scripts (60–61), compose personal histories for Marcellus and Barnardo (63–66), work through Hamlet's "Now might I do it" soliloquy from 3.3 (70–72), and other undertakings. All of the activities are rooted in RSC rehearsal practices. Winston explains, "The temperature of the room changes as soon as we say to young people that this is not work we have made up for them. This is what our actors and directors have to do to unlock the text . . . As soon as you put it on a professional footing, play becomes more serious" (66).

FOUR YA NOVELS THAT PAIR WITH *HAMLET*

***Ophelia* by Lisa Klein (2008)**—The book gives Ophelia a voice as she narrates the events of *Hamlet* from her perspective. Klein gives Ophelia nuance and agency. This Ophelia—think of chapter 3 and the activities diving into different readings of Ophelia—is resilient. She defies expectations, challenges societal norms, and finds her sense of purpose. Her ending is ambiguous; her mental state deteriorates as she moves through her narrative, but it is less clear how or even if she dies. The book was made into a film with the same name in 2019.

***Monster* by Walter Dean Meyers (1999)**—Sixteen-year-old Steve Harmon is accused of serving as a lookout during a liquor store robbery turned murder. As the story of his trial progresses, he grapples Hamlet-like with questions of identity and truth as he confronts a system bent against young Black men. Meyers interweaves a traditional narrative chapter by chapter against a mousetrap-like screenplay that Harmon writes, detailing his experiences. The book was made into a 2015 graphic novel and, later, a 2021 Netflix film.

***Forgive Me, Leonard Peacock* by Matthew Quick (2013)**—This book could be triggering for some; it includes sexual violence, threatened suicide, and gun violence against others in a school setting. Its protagonist, Leonard Peacock, has reached rock bottom. Feeling utterly alone in the world, with his dad gone, his absent mom always away to Manhattan for work, and nobody who understands him, Leonard plans, first, revenge against his former best friend for horrible things he did to Leonard, then his own suicide. Throughout the book, Shakespeare's *Hamlet* reverberates through Leonard's mind. He quotes from it at length and compares his situation to Hamlet's. It is dark and powerfully haunting but recommended only for mature students.

***Steep and Thorny Way* by Cat Winters (2016)**—The book reimagines *Hamlet* in 1920s Oregon as Hanalee struggles to cope after the death of her Black father and her White mother's hasty remarriage. When the man convicted of her father's murder is released early, she contemplates taking revenge into her own hands. Hers is a world, though, where the KKK reigns, and the intertwined systems of racism and homophobia distort justice. Much like Shakespeare's Hamlet's journey of self-discovery leads him down dark paths, Hanalee's search for self and truth leads her down an ugly road she cannot overcome.

SIX FILM VERSIONS OF *HAMLET*

Laurence Olivier and Jean Simmon's *Hamlet* (1948)—This is the classic, black-and-white version of Hamlet from the most famous Shakespearean actor from the early to mid-twentieth century. In his time nobody was more respected than Laurence Oliver. His heavily cut Hamlet feels dated by today's standards, but it was the first significant motion picture version of *Hamlet* and was groundbreaking.

Innokentiy Smoktunovskiy and Anastasiya Vertinskaya Hamlet (1964)—Directed by Grigoriy Kozintsev, this Russian-language version of Hamlet is considered by many scholars and critics the best non-English Hamlet on film. Renowned for its sets, lighting, and score, the black-and-white film has aged well over the past fifty years, and as a result, it provides an opportunity for students to engage cross-culturally with the play that contrasts against other English-language films.

Mel Gibson and Glenn Close's Hamlet (1990)—Franco Zeffirelli directs one of the shortest film versions of *Hamlet* and draws more on the First Quarto of 1603 than most productions. If you want the quickest version of *Hamlet*, then this is your best bet. One effect of this is that by cutting many males' speeches, this version gives the women of the play a more prominent role.

Kenneth Branagh and Kate Winslet's *Hamlet* (1996)—If Olivier ruled Shakespeare through most of the twentieth century, then Kenneth Branagh has ruled ever since. Though he is now getting older, he still makes films, and nobody has replaced him as the most respected Shakespearean actor of our time. In this four-hour marathon with virtually no cuts from Shakespeare's original, Branagh stars and directs a lavish film production featuring a star-studded cast rich with luxurious costumes and elaborate sets. It is a truly beautiful, albeit long, production.

Ethan Hawke and Julia Stiles's *Hamlet* (2000)—Set in Manhattan in 2000, the film, in its time, felt current and edgy; now it feels almost nostalgic as we look back some two decades. Hamlet, for example, films scenes for his own mousetrap play-within-a-play through a turn-of-the-century camcorder and, at one point, peruses VHS tapes in a Blockbuster store. It's a great example of a *Hamlet* performance of a specific historical moment, one that speaks back to how the play was perceived as we entered a new millennium.

David Tenant and Maria Gale's *Hamlet* (2008)—Following an RSC run, the film has the vibe of a stage production. It makes few cuts and is perhaps the best-acted *Hamlet* on the list. The skull in the gravedigger scene is real, as is explained in a 2023 BBC documentary where Tenant looks back on the production. The fellow it once belonged to bequeathed it to the RSC for that purpose years before so he could one day be part of an RSC production as Yorick.

Appendix A 167

SEVEN FILM ADAPTATIONS OF *HAMLET*

***The Bad Sleep Well* (1960)**—This Japanese adaptation is from renowned director Akira Kurosawa, who is also known for his samurai adaptations of *Throne of Blood* (*Macbeth*) and *Ran* (*King Lear*).

***Rosencrantz and Guildenstern Are Dead* (1990)**—Tom Stoppard's 1966 play comes to life on the screen. Told through the lens of Rosencrantz and Guildenstern, the two are more complex than in Shakespeare, and though more perceptive than their original namesakes, they are still unable to best Hamlet. They seem just on the edge, through the entire production, of realizing they are characters in a play/film and not actual people, but their/the end comes too soon for them to change their inevitable outcome. Stoppard takes his readers/viewers on a fantastic mind-bending and word-breaking side road to *Hamlet*. It is highly recommended.

The Lion King (1994 and 2019)—Almost everybody has seen *The Lion King*—either its animated original or its more recent live-action version. Uncle Scar (Claudius) kills Mufasa (King Hamlet), and Simba (Hamlet) must come to terms with his responsibility to right the kingdom. Another Shakespearean influence on the story was *1 Henry IV*, in which Prince Hal (Simba) takes on a surrogate father figure called Falstaff (Timon/Pumba), who lures him temporarily away from his royal obligations with the promise of a drunken, slovenly (and fun!) life.

***Legend of the Black Scorpion* (2006)**—Originally called *The Night Banquet* in its original Chinese (but renamed for its USA release), this is a lavish production with beautiful costumes, props, and sets. It's particularly fascinating for its focus on the relationship between Uncle Li (Claudius) and Wan (Gertrude); much of the film is shot from their perspective instead of Wu Luan's (Hamlet's). In this version, however, Wan is Wu Luan's stepmother, not his biological mother—he, in fact, is four years older than her—and the film explores her subtle deceptions to maneuver against Li and win Wu Luan in her quest to become empress. The ending isn't Shakespeare's, but it's a splendid watch nonetheless. Its DVD version (in Mandarin Chinese, with English subtitles) includes interviews and excellent bonus features.

***Rosencrantz and Guildenstern Are Undead* (2010)**—This fun spoof reveals an ancient plot in which the original Horatio, now, in the twenty-first century, a vampire living in New York City, puts on a production of his play

Rosencrantz and Guildenstern Are Undead with the intent of feeding on the audience after its opening night. The original Hamlet still lives, though, and intervenes at the end. Ridiculous in every way, it's a fun film that teases both Shakespeare and Stoppard.

Vishal Bhardwaj's *Haider* (2014)—Vishal Bhardwaj adapted three Shakespearean plays to an Indian setting: *Maqbool* (*Macbeth*) in 2003, *Omkara* (*Othello*) in 2006, and most recently, *Haider* (*Hamlet*) in 2014.

***Ophelia* (2019)**—Based on Lisa Klein's 2008 novel, the film follows the *Hamlet* story through the lens of Ophelia, starting in her childhood.

Appendix B
"I Have Some Rights of Memory": A Note on Fortinbras

Some teachers might have noticed that this book barely mentions Fortinbras. Earlier drafts did, but I removed them and glossed over his story to better focus on the play's main characters. That's not to say that advanced students should not eventually take some time with him. The Fortinbras story permeates *Hamlet*. He is referenced in four of the play's acts: Claudius sends ambassadors in act 1 to address his trespasses against Denmark, they report back in act 2, his captain talks with Hamlet in act 4, and he finally appears on stage in act 5 to end the play and order Hamlet's body carried away. Shakespeare constantly reminds playgoers that he is there.

Fortinbras's just-under-the-surface, behind-the-action presence also complicates the play in rich ways. Fortinbras's persistent presence reminds audiences that the actions of the royal family are not just domestic; what plays out in their court has far-reaching international repercussions that reverberate across Scandinavia. *Hamlet* is a play about adult children who have lost their fathers and how they respond. Fortinbras has lost his father too. When Hamlet loses his father, he loses himself in thought. Laertes loses himself in rage. And Ophelia loses herself in grief. Fortinbras, on the other hand, loses himself in conquest. He tries to right on the international stage what he sees as the wrong the older Hamlet committed against his father and country, as well as to regain what was taken.

In my teaching and this book, though, I have decided that first-time readers should focus mainly on the domestic elements of the play and save what Fortinbras adds for a later reading. Teachers and advanced students, though, should, in time, grapple with those complexities.

Glossary: "Words, Words, Words"

Teachers should study frequently used words and phrases from Shakespeare that are archaic today. This glossary is not comprehensive but, rather, a starting point. When time allows, teachers should dive into their scholarly editions with their detailed footnotes (such as those listed in Appendix A). There are also several excellent teaching books that include excellent lessons for Shakespeare's vocabulary. These are great resources for learning more. The following list can also be modified for classroom use.

adieu—goodbye

- The ghost closes his call for revenge with "*Adieu, adieu, adieu*! Remember me," which Hamlet echoes in the following speech (1.5.91). It is a common word throughout Shakespeare's plays.

antic disposition—feigned madness or pretended insanity

- Hamlet makes Horatio and the others swear that they will keep it secret when he puts on an *antic disposition*, which he will do for the rest of the play (1.5.179). Later in the play, he reveals his secret to his mother, that he is "not in madness, / But mad in craft" (3.4.190–91).

arras—a large, decorative tapestry that hangs on a wall

- In 3.1 Polonius and the king hide behind an *arras* so they can eavesdrop on Hamlet as he speaks with Ophelia. In 3.4 Polonius uses the same trick and hides behind another arras in the queen's closet, but this time, Hamlet thinks it is the king and stabs him through the arras, killing him.

augury—knowledge and fear of the future

- When Hamlet says he defies *augury*, he is saying he is ready to face his future even if it might mean his own death (5.2.233).

bark—ship or vessel

- Rarely used today, *bark* was a common word for a ship in Shakespeare's time. When the king says, "The bark is ready," he is saying the ship that will take Hamlet to England is ready to go (4.3.49). The king wants Hamlet to set sail that very night.

bawdry—lewdness, sexual lasciviousness

- When Hamlet complains of Polonius, saying, "He's for a jig or a tale of *bawdry*, or he sleeps," he is complaining of the low kind of theater that men like Polonius prefer. Hamlet says Polonius would rather see a silly dance, a lewd show filled with dirty jokes, or even go to sleep during the performance. It comes from the same root as *bawd*, which refers to a pimp who manages prostitutes.

board—to go and talk to somebody

- When Polonius says he will "*board* him presently," he means that he will go and talk to Hamlet right away (2.2.169). It is a word that appears often in Shakespeare's plays. It will appear again in *Hamlet* in act 5.

bodkin—a dagger

- In his "to be or not to be" speech, when Hamlet says he "might his quietus make / With a bare bodkin," he is saying he might bring himself some balance with a naked dagger, that he could even all his accounts in killing himself (3.1.76). He ultimately rejects suicide, though, later in the speech.

bore me on his back—when an adult carries a child on their back

- Hamlet says that Yorick had *borne him on his back* a thousand times (5.1.192–93). He means that when he was little, Yorick played with Hamlet and let him ride on him. Kids today might imagine themselves on horseback while riding aboard their parents or older siblings. It suggests Hamlet's close, almost paternal or familial, relationship with Yorick.

calumny—slanderous rumor; false words meant to injure another's reputation

- When Hamlet warns Ophelia that even if she "is chaste as ice" and as "pure as snow," she shall "not escape *calumny*," he is saying that no matter how pure she is, people will still make up and believe false rumors about her (3.1.136–37). Laertes had given her the same advice earlier: "Virtue itself cannot escape calumnious strokes" (1.3.37).

carouses—to toast somebody, to drink to their fortune

- Gertrude says she "*carouses* to thy fortune" just before she sips from the poisoned cup (5.2.315). She is saying that she wishes Hamlet luck and toasting his success.

closet—the private room of a noble person

- When Hamlet speaks with Gertrude in her closet, he speaks to her in her private room. In act 3, Rosencrantz reports to Hamlet that the queen "desires to speak with [him] in her closet," and a bit later, Polonius reports that Hamlet is "going to his mother's closet" (3.2.308; 3.3.27). Because it is set in the queen's closet, scholars often refer to 3.4 as the closet scene. Earlier in the play, Ophelia had been "sewing in her closet" when Hamlet had entered (2.1.75).

cozened—deceived, tricked

- The fear that devils trick people into doing terrible things is already well established in Hamlet's mind by the closet scene, when he questions his mother, "What devil was't / That thus hath cozened you at hoodman-blind?" (3.4.). Hoodman-blind, also known as blind man's bluff, was a physically violent game in which a blindfolded person was beaten and kicked until they could capture one of their tormentors. They would then switch places, and the game would continue. Hamlet asks his mother which devil managed to cozen her in such a game and turn her into the tormented one.

cuckold—a slang term for a man whose wife has been unfaithful sexually

- When the king urges Laertes to be calm, he answers by defending the chastity of his mother:

    > That drop of blood that's calm proclaims me bastard,
    > Cries *cuckold* to my father, brands the harlot
    > Even here between the chaste unsmirched brow
    > Of my true mother. (4.5.130–34)

- Laertes has an absolute obligation to avenge his father. For even one drop of his blood to remain calm after his father's murder would be like saying his father was not actually his father, that another man had sired him. There was great shame in Shakespeare's time for a man whose wife had cheated on him.

doublet—a close-fitting jacket worn by men in Shakespeare's time

- When Hamlet comes to Ophelia "with his *doublet* all unbraced," it means he comes to her with his jacket open. It would be like a man in modern times wearing his shirt unbuttoned. It would be unkempt.

ecstasy—madness, frenzied behavior

- The word appears four times in the play. Polonius first believes Hamlet's behavior is "the very *ecstasy* of love" (2.1.100). He is wrong, though. The second time, Ophelia laments at the end of the nunnery scene that Hamlet is "blasted with ecstasy," that the Hamlet she knew before has broken (3.1.159). The third and fourth times come in the closet scene, when Gertrude believes Hamlet's "ecstasy" to be the "coinage of his brain," the breakdown of his mind; he reveals to her, though, a few lines later, that he has been only pretending (3.4.140–41).

fishmonger—a person who sells fish

- Fish was generally food that poor people in Shakespeare's time ate, so when Hamlet pretends to be mad and calls Polonius a *fishmonger*, it is a sly insult that, when Polonius does not realize a few lines later that he had been insulted, suggests his lack of wit (2.2.173).

fell—mighty, terrible

- The player in act 2 describes Pyrrhus's "*fell* sword" as it kills the old king Priam (2.2.498). Similarly, Hamlet, just before he dies, calls death a "fell sergeant" who is "strict in his arrest" (5.2.368). Both are powerful and horrible.

flagon of Rhenish / stoups of wine—container of wine; cup of wine

- When the gravedigger complains that Yorick had "poured a *flagon of Rhenish*" on his head long ago, he is complaining that, in jest, Yorick had

poured a whole container of wine. Rhenish wine comes from Germany, named after the Rhine River. (5.1.185)
- A *stoup of liquor* or a *stoup of wine*, on the other hand, is a smaller vessel. When the gravedigger sends his mate for "a stoup of liquor," he sends him off to fetch something to drink (5.1.61–62). Similarly, when the king says, "Set me the stoups of wine upon that table," he orders his servants to bring wine and set it on the table (5.2.286).

fust—to become musty or moldy

- Hamlet argues that God gave humans discourse and reason and He meant for us to use them, not to let them *fust* away:

    > Sure He that made us with such large discourse,
    > Looking before and after, gave us not
    > That capability and godlike reason
    > To fust in us unused. (4.4.38–41)

- It is part of his ongoing inner struggle as he chastises himself for overthinking how to proceed against his uncle. A few lines later, he will counterargue that "thinking too precisely" is cowardly, and by the end of the speech, his only worthy thoughts will be his "bloody" ones (4.5.43, 69).

gambol—leap, jump

- The word appears twice in *Hamlet*. When Hamlet asks the skull where his *gambols* are, he sadly recollects how Yorick would leap and jump in his joking to make people laugh.

general gender—the ordinary people

- When the king bemoans the "great love the *general gender* bear him," he explains that the ordinary people of Denmark love Hamlet, further explaining to Laertes that holding Hamlet accountable for murdering Polonius would mean upsetting his people (4.7.20). Laertes does not push back, but there does seem to be a contradiction here in that the general gender must also have supported Laertes and his family to some degree, given that Laertes was able, in a short time, to raise his own militia to bring with him to Elsinore.

gibes—scoffs, taunts, jeers

- Hamlet asks Yorick's skull where his *gibes* are. Fools in Shakespeare were allowed to taunt the king and other royals to a degree not allowed from other subjects (the fool in *King Lear* is the best example of this). The taunting was playful, meant to make people laugh, but Shakespeare's fools were often given some of the wisest wit in their plays. There is no fool in *Hamlet* other than Hamlet's memory of Yorick and what would have been his witty gibes.

gilded—thinly covered with gold

- Claudius is contemplating as he tries unsuccessfully to pray that "in the corrupted currents of this world / Offence's *gilded* hand may shove by justice" (3.3.58). As king, he metaphorically wears a thin, protective layer of gold. He knows that on earth, his power and privilege permit him to get away with his brother's murder but that in heaven, he will be appropriately punished for it.

goblin—a malevolent demon

- The word *goblin* today refers to mischievous dwarf-like creatures, but it would have had demonic origins in Shakespeare's time. When Hamlet fears the ghost might be a "goblin damn'd," he fears the ghost might be a demon from hell that is trying to trick him into committing a horrible sin (1.4.44).

gorge—the stomach and its contents

- Pondering his own mortality troubles Hamlet but ultimately brings him inner peace. When he gazes into the skull and contemplates that it used to be Yorick, he reports, "My *gorge* rises at it"; he feels his stomach and its contents start to rise up inside him, as though he might be about to throw up (5.1.194).

hebona—a poisonous plant

- *Hebona* is a fascinating word because it appears Shakespeare made it up. It is not a real plant, though Shakespeare could have meant henbane, which is a real plant and quite poisonous. Either way, Claudius poured the "juice of cursed hebona" into his brother's ear to kill him (1.5.69).

hectic—a dangerous fever

- The king sees Hamlet in his rage as a dangerous disease that could kill him. In sending him to England with the secret order to have him killed there, he hopes to cure "the *hectic* in [his] blood" (4.3.75).

knavery—foolishness, trickery, roguery

- This is a must-know word for reading Shakespeare. It appears in almost all his plays. In its various forms, it appears some ten times in Hamlet. A *knave* is a scoundrel or a rascal, and *knavery* is the foolishness that he commits. In the nunnery scene, Hamlet declares that all men "are errant knaves" and that women should trust none of them (3.1.129). It is a mild insult, though it can also sometimes be so mild as to signify tenderness.

let her paint an inch thick—referring to women wearing makeup

- Hamlet is thinking of Ophelia when he gazes into Yorick's skull and suggests the skull should visit his lady and remind her of the following: "*Let her paint an inch thick*, to this favor she must come" (5.1.200–1). He is commenting on women's makeup. He is saying that no matter how much makeup a woman wears, one day, she will end up dead and a skull in the ground. He likely regrets such mean thoughts moments later, when he learns that Ophelia has died by suicide.

milch—moist, tearful

- When the player describes Hecuba's suffering, he says that her pain "made *milch* the burning eyes of heaven"; her suffering was so profound it would have made even the gods cry (2.2.442). The gods were rarely moved by the affairs of humankind, so for them to cry for Hecuba would have been an extraordinary occurrence.

niggard—grudging, reluctant

- This is a word often cut from performance and classroom use because it just sounds too much like the racial slur that has no place in speech today; Shakespeare's word *niggard*, though, is *not* the same word. It has variations as a noun, verb, or adjective and has to do with mean and miserly behavior. When Rosencrantz says Hamlet is "niggard of question," he means that Hamlet has not asked Guildenstern or him very many questions (3.1.13). Avoid saying the word aloud, or change it to "stingy" when you read it aloud. It is one of the few times it is best to change Shakespeare's language and paraphrase it with a more modern word.

orisons—prayers

- When Hamlet says that in seeing Ophelia's "*orisons* / Be all [of his] sins remembered," he is saying that when he sees her praying, he remembers his own sins (3.1.90–91).

pelican—the same bird as today, but in Shakespeare's time, it was believed she fed her hatchlings with her own blood

- When Laertes says that he will open his arms "and, like the kind life-rend'ring *pelican*, / Repast them [his friends] with [his] blood," he is saying that he will sacrifice for himself for his friends (4.5.67–68). Each act in *Hamlet* has a bird reference: in the first act, the ghost must depart when the "bird of dawning" sings, i.e. the rooster crows (1.1.175). Hamlet knows a hawk from a handsaw (another word for a heron; see 2.2.403). He calls the king a peacock after the mousetrap (3.2.310). Ophelia explains earlier that the owl was a baker's daughter (4.5.47–48). And in the next act, Hamlet philosophizes that "there is special providence in the fall of a sparrow" as discussed in chapter 5 (5.2.233–34).

providence—fate or destiny

- In 5.1 Hamlet senses that his fate might be to die when he faces Laertes in the duel. He has learned, though, that leading a good life means accepting what is to come; he states, "There is a special *providence* in the fall of sparrow," referring to a Bible verse in which Jesus reminds his disciples that there is a plan even for birds like sparrows; the idea gives Hamlet the resolve he needs to face his future (5.2.233–34).

purse—either money or a small bag for carrying money

- Those with wealth often carried their coins in a little bag. Shakespeare uses the word often in his plays. It appears three times in *Hamlet*. Polonius advises Laertes in act 1 that "costly thy habit [clothes] as thy *purse* can buy," meaning he should buy nice clothes, though, in the following line, he warns that they should not be "gaudy" (1.3.76–77).
- Hamlet uses the word twice in 5.2: first, in a literal sense, when he says that he had his father's royal signet in his purse, meaning that alongside

his coins, he had the signet, or royal seal, which he used to forge the order for Rosencrantz and Guildenstern to be killed in England (5.2.55); and second, metaphorically, to taunt that Osric's "purse is empty already," belittling him that "all his golden words are spent" when Osric cannot match his wit (5.2.143). Osric's mind is empty.

quick—alive

- Hamlet and the gravedigger exchange verbal play with the word in 5.1: Hamlet says that the grave is "for the dead, not for the *quick*" (5.1.129). This comedic idea takes tragic form later in the scene, when Laertes jumps into the grave with the body of Ophelia and orders attendants to "pile your dust upon the quick and dead" (5.1.263). He is pure emotion, declaring that he desires to be buried alive in the same grave as his dead sister.

quintessence—something in its purest form

- Hamlet thinks humankind is the greatest of nature's achievements, yet he remains unimpressed due to all humankind's faults. To him, humankind is a "*quintessence* of dust"; even in its purest form, it is still dust (2.2.269).

remembrances—love tokens, gifts, mementos

- Remembering is an essential theme throughout the play; the word appears in various forms some eighteen times in *Hamlet*. In the nunnery scene, when Ophelia offers Hamlet back the *remembrances* he had given her, this echoes his own words a few lines before, remembering his own sins in her orisons. It also echoes the ghost's last instructions from act 1: "Remember me," as well as foreshadowing Ophelia's act 4 lines, when she passes out flowers; she explains then that the rosemary she hands out is "for remembrance" (1.5.91; 4.2.170).

rose of May—a rose in its prime, at its best color, in its peak condition

- When Laertes sees that Ophelia is lost in a dark place inside, he calls her a "*rose of May*," one of many of the flower references that are used with and by Ophelia (4.5.181). May is when roses bloom. He is lamenting that at an age when she should be at her happiest, at the prime of her life, she is instead broken. In 3.1 Ophelia calls Hamlet the "rose of the fair state," which, along with her flower scene, is yet another example of her aligning people with flowers (3.1.166). It's most fitting for her brother to use similar symbolic language, comparing her to a rose.

sallied/solid—sallied means assailed or attacked, whereas solid means firm and stable in shape (as opposed to a liquid or a gas)

- Depending on your edition, in the first line of Hamlet's first soliloquy in 1.2, Hamlet will wish that his "too, too *sallied* flesh would melt" or that his "too, too *solid* flesh would melt" (1.2.129). They mean different things. The debate regarding which is the better choice here was discussed in chapter 5, when students explored the play as an editor would.

saws—wise sayings

- When Hamlet says he will "wipe away all trivial, fond records, / All *saws* of books," he says he will focus on only revenging his father's murder (1.5.100). It echoes back to the list of saws, or sayings, that Polonius gave his son, Laertes, two scenes previously. Hamlet, though, will have nothing to do with such empty maxims.

snatches of old lauds—verses from popular songs

- When Gertrude reports that Ophelia "chanted *snatches of old lauds*" before drowning, she says she was singing just before she died, much as she did in her other two appearances from act 4 (4.7.202). Lauds refer to songs of praise; perhaps she was again singing a song remembering her father.

stay—delay, defer, postpone

- Shakespeare uses this word sixteen times in *Hamlet*, and its meaning usually aligns closely with its definition today. In a more archaic use, though—which is not too difficult to puzzle out—the king asks Laertes, "Who shall *stay* you?" which means "Who will prevent you from getting your revenge?" (4.5.155).

strew—to scatter or spread loosely

- *Strew*, or its noun form, *strewment*, appears three times in *Hamlet* and is always about Ophelia. Horatio advises the queen to speak with Ophelia or else "she may strew / Dangerous conjectures in ill-breeding minds" (4.5.19–20). After her death, the priest complains that she has been allowed her "maiden strewments," that she has had flowers laid across her grave representing chastity (5.2.241). Gertrude laments that she had wanted those flowers her "bride-bed to have deck'd," rather than to "have strew'd [her] grave" (5.2.256–57).

unbated and envenomed—without a protective point on the top and poisoned

- The foils in the fencing match at the end of the play all should have been bated. They should have had protective points at the end to ensure nobody was stabbed. The king, though, plotted that Laertes's foil would be "a sword *unbated*" (4.7.157). Just before he dies, Laertes confirms that his sword indeed had been "unbated and *envenomed*"—that way, the point would stick and the poison be delivered (5.2.348).

unction of a mountebank—an ointment bought from a quack salesman

- Laertes has bought poison from a *mountebank* on his way back from France, and the king convinces him to lather it on the tip of his rapier during the duel to kill Hamlet. An *unction* should be a healing ointment, but instead, this one is a lethal poison. It is reminiscent of the poison Romeo buys from an apothecary in Romeo and Juliet; poisons bought from unsavory characters in Shakespeare lead to tragic and regrettable endings.
- Hamlet uses the word metaphorically earlier as well, with his mother, when he chides her: "Lay not that flattering unction to your soul / That not your trespass but my madness speaks"; he is telling her not to soothe herself with the idea that it is just his madness speaking and not her wrongs (3.4.166–67).

unhouseled, disappointed, uaneled—without having received the Eucharist, unprepared spiritually, and unanointed without having received the sacrament of the dying

- The ghost laments that he had been murdered "*unhouseled, disappointed, unaneled*," without having first been prepared to enter heaven, which is why he must hence endure painful penance in purgatory (1.5.77). Had he been prepared properly, he could have avoided such torment.

union—a large pearl

- The king declares that "in the cup an *union* shall he throw," then puts the pearl in the cup (5.2.291). He and Laertes are the only ones who know it is poison that the king is putting in the cup. Later in the scene, when the treachery has been revealed, Hamlet takes the cup, reviles, "Is thy union here?" and forces the king to drink his own poison (5.2.357).

visage—face

- The word appears often in Shakespeare's plays, including five times in *Hamlet*. It appears three times in act 3, often as part of a larger metaphor:

    > 'Tis too much prov'd, that with devotion's *visage*
    > And pious action we do sugar o'er
    > The Devil himself. (3.1.47–49)

- When Polonius delivers these lines to the king, he explains how people are inclined to let their devotion, or affection, blind them to the sins of those they love. The irony is that Polonius speaks these lines to the evilest character in the play, the king, whom he honors and loves, but whose wickedness he never sees.

wit—mental sharpness

- Hamlet makes yet another dig at Polonius when he retorts that "old men . . . have a plentiful lack of *wit*, together with most weak hams" (2.2.). He's slyly saying that Polonius lacks mental sharpness and has weak legs—though Polonius tellingly does not realize he has been insulted.

woodcock/springe—a bird and the trap used to catch it

- Shakespeare uses the metaphor of a *springe*, or trap, catching a *woodcock* twice in *Hamlet*. It comes first in 1.3, when Polonius compares Hamlet's kind words to Ophelia as "springes to catch woodcocks"; he is claiming that Hamlet only gave Ophelia kind words to trick her (1.3.124). His son, Laertes, echoes the same metaphor of his plan with the king to kill Hamlet: "As a woodcock to my own springe . . . I am justly killed with mine own treachery" (5.2.336–37).

wretch—a poor or unfortunate person to feel sorry for, or a person who is morally repugnant

- A complicated word, this has multiple connotations. Gertrude could simply be implying that she feels pity when she says that Ophelia's

garments, heavy with their drink,
Pulled the poor *wretch* from her melodious lay
To muddy death. (4.7.205–8)

- That is one valid reading: that Gertrude feels sympathy as she narrates how Ophelia died as she sang. Another, though, is that she felt Ophelia brought her fate upon herself. Most actors and scholars avoid this second interpretation.

Works Cited

Banks, Amy Connelly, and Chris Crowe. 2021. "Reading Hamlet and Monster to Study Identity." In *Shakespeare and Young Adult Literature: Pairing and Teaching*, edited by Victor Malo-Juvera, Paula Greathouse, and Brooke Eisenbach, 61–72. New York: Rowman and Littlefield.

Barber, Frances. 1988. "Ophelia in Hamlet." In *Players of Shakespeare 2*, edited by Russell Jackson and Robert Smallwood, 139. Cambridge: Cambridge University Press.

Bartsch, Virgil, and Shadi Bartsch. 2021. *The Aeneid*. Random House.

Bible Gateway. n.d. "New International Version Bible." Accessed October 19, 2023. https://www.biblegateway.com.

Boatner-Doane, Charlotte. 2017. "Sarah Siddons and the Romantic Hamlet." *Nineteenth Century Theatre and Film* 44, no. 2 (2017): 212–35. https://doi.org/10.1177/1748372718763621.

Chapman, Alison. 2007. "Ophelia's 'Old Lauds': Madness and Hagiography in 'Hamlet.'" *Medieval & Renaissance Drama in England* 20 (2007): 111–35. https://www.jstor.org/stable/24323015.

Cohen, Ralph Alan. (2006) 2018. *ShakesFear and How to Cure it: The Complete Handbook for Teaching Shakespeare.* 2nd ed. London: Arden.

———. 2019. "'Nothing Good or Bad': The 2007 American Shakespeare Center Production of Hamlet Q1." In *Hamlet*, 2nd Norton Critical ed., edited by Robert Miola, 170–79. New York: Norton.

Cohen, Robert. 1973. "Shakespeare's Sixteen-Year-Old Hamlet." *Educational Theatre Journal* 25, no. 2 (1973): 179–88. https://www.jstor.org/stable/3205867.

Dakin, Mary Ellen. 2009. *Reading Shakespeare with Young Adults*. Urbana: NCTE.

———. 2012. *Reading Shakespeare: Film First*. Urbana: NCTE.

Duggan, Tim. 2008. *Advanced Placement Classroom* Hamlet. Waco, TX: Prufrock Press.

Eklund, Hillary, and Wendy Beth Hyman. 2019. *Teaching Social Justice Through Shakespeare: Why Renaissance Literature Matters Now*. Edinburgh: Edinburgh University Press.

Gibson, Rex, and Janet Field-Pickering. 1998. *Discovering Shakespeare's Language: 150 Stimulating Activity Sheets for Student Work*. Cambridge: Cambridge University Press.

Gibson, Rex. (1998) 2016. *Cambridge School Shakespeare: Teaching Shakespeare*. 2nd ed. Cambridge: Cambridge University Press.

Greenblatt, Stephen. 2002. *Hamlet in Purgatory*. Princeton: Princeton University Press.

Greenblatt, Stephen. 2019. "Hamlet in Purgatory." In *Hamlet*, 2nd Norton Critical ed., edited by Robert Miola, 271–82. New York: Norton.

Hapgood, Robert. 1988. *Shakespeare The Theatre-Poet*. Oxford: Clarendon Press.

Haughey, Joseph. 2012. "What's Past Is Prologue: English Journal Roots of a Performance-Based Approach to Teaching Shakespeare." *English Journal* 101, no. 3 (January): 60–66.

———. 2021. "Revenge, Mental Health, and Suicide: Pairing Shakespeare's Hamlet and Matthew Quick's Leonard Peacock." In *Shakespeare and Young Adult Literature: Pairing and Teaching*, edited by Victor Malo-Juvera, Paula Greathouse, and Brooke Eisenbach, 43–59. New York: Rowman and Littlefield.

Higgins, Ben. 2002. *Shakespeare's Syndicate: The First Folio, Its Publishers, and the Early Modern Book Trade*. Oxford: Oxford University Press.

Howard, Tony. 2007. *Women as Hamlet: Performance and Interpretation in Theatre, Film and Fiction*. Cambridge: Cambridge University Press.

———. 2019. "Women as Hamlet (2007)." In *Hamlet*, 2nd Norton Critical ed., edited by Miola, Robert, 282–93. New York: Norton.

Jones, Emily Griffith. 2019 "Global Performance and Local Reception: Teaching Hamlet and More in Singapore." In *Teaching Social Justice Through Shakespeare: Why Renaissance Literature Matters Now* Hillary, edited by Hillary Eklund and Wendy Beth Hyman, 55–63. Edinburgh: Edinburgh University Press.

Karim-Cooper, Farah. 2019. *Cosmetics in Shakespearean and Renaissance Drama*, revised edition. Edinburgh: Edinburgh University Press.

Lesser, Zachary. 2015. *Hamlet After Q1: An Uncanny History of the Shakespearean Text*. Philadelphia: University of Pennsylvania Press.

Long, Kevin, and Mary T. Christel. 2019. *Bring on the Bard: Active Drama Approaches for Shakespeare's Diverse Student Readers*. Urbana: NCTE.

Malo-Juvera, Victor, Paula Greathouse, and Brooke Eisenbach, eds. 2021. *Shakespeare and Young Adult Literature: Pairing and Teaching*. New York: Rowman and Littlefield.

Mellor, Bronwyn. 1999. *Reading Hamlet*. Urbana, IL: National Council of Teachers of English.

Menzer, Paul. 2008. *The Hamlets: Cues, Qs, and Remembered Texts*. Newark: University of Delaware Press.

Miles, George Henry. 1870. *A Review of Hamlet*. Baltimore: Kelly, Piet & Company. https://www.google.com/books/edition/A_Review_of_Hamlet/jwo5AQAAMAAJ.

O'Brien, Peggy, ed. (1994) 2006. *Shakespeare Set Free: Hamlet and Henry IV Part One*. New York: Washinton Square Press.

Orgel, Stephen. 2003. *Imagining Shakespeare: A History of Texts and Visions*. New York: Palgrave.
Orgel, Stephen. 2002. "What Is a Text." In *The Authentic Shakespeare: And Other Problems of the Early Modern Stage*, 1–5. New York: Palgrave.
Palfrey, Simon, and Tiffany Stern. 2007. *Shakespeare in Parts*. Oxford: Oxford University Press.
Phillipy, Patricia. 2006. *Painting Women: Cosmetics, Canvases and Early Modern Culture*. Baltimore: John Hopkins University Press.
Rebeck, Theresa. 2019. *Bernhardt/Hamlet*. New York: Concord Theatricals.
Ribeiro, Aileen. 2011. *Facing Beauty: Painted Women and Cosmetic Art*. New Haven: Yale University Press.
Riggio, Milla Cozart, ed. 1999. *Teaching Shakespeare through Performance*. New York: Modern Language Association of America.
Rocklin, Edward L. 2005. *Performance Approaches to Teaching Shakespeare*. Urbana: NCTE.
Sauer, David Kennedy and Evylyn Tribble. 1999. "Shakespeare in Performance: Theory in Practice and Practice in Theory." In *Teaching Shakespeare through Performance*, edited by Milla Cozard Riggio, 33–47. New York: Modern Language Association of America.
Shakespeare, William. (1877) 1963. *Hamlet: A New Variorum Edition of Shakespeare*, 2 vols., edited by Horace Howard Furness. New York: Dover Publications.
———. (1992) 2000. *Hamlet*, Folger Shakespeare Library Paperback ed., edited by Barbara Mowat and Paul Werstine. New York: Washington Square Press.
———. 1994. "Hamlet," In Case *Studies in Contemporary Criticism*, edited by Susanne L. Wofford. Boston: Bedford.
———. (2006) 2016. *Hamlet*, Third Series, revised ed., 2 vols., edited by Ann Thompson and Neil Taylor. London: Bloomsbury Arden Shakespeare.
———. 2019. *Hamlet*, 2nd Norton Critical ed., edited by Robert Mioloa. New York: Norton.
Shakespeare, William, and G. Blakemore Evans. 1974. *The Riverside Shakespeare*. Boston: Houghton Mifflin.
Smith, Emma. (2015) 2023. *The Making of Shakespeare's First Folio*. Oxford: Bodleian Library, University of Oxford.
———, ed. 2016. *The Cambridge Companion to Shakespeare's First Folio*. Cambridge: Cambridge University Press.
———. 2016. *Shakespeare's First Folio: Four Centuries of an Iconic Book*. Oxford: Oxford University Press.
Snyder, Susan. (1994) 2006. "'Who's There?' Talking to Others and Talking About Yourself in Shakespeare." In *Shakespeare Set Free: Teaching Hamlet and Henry IV Part 1*, edited by Peggy O'Brien, 9–15. New York: Washington Square Press.
Steelman, Sheridan Lynn. 2022. *Walking in Shakespeare's Shoes: Connecting His World and*
Ours Using Primary Sources. Champaign, IL: NCTE.
Stern, Tiffany. 2009. *Documents of Performance in Early Modern England*. Cambridge: Cambridge University Press.

Stevens, Andrea Ria. 2013. *Inventions of the Skin: The Painted Body in Early English Drama, 1400–1642*. Edinburgh: Edinburgh University Press.

Tannenbaum, Samuel. 1932. "Hamlet's 'Pajock' Reconsidered." *The Shakespeare Association Bulletin* 7, no. 3 (July): 127–30. https://www.jstor.org/stable/23675777.

Taranow, Gerda. 1996. *The Bernhardt Hamlet: Culture and Context*. New York: Peter Lang Publishing.

Terry, Ellen. 1932. "Pathetic Women." In *Four Lectures on Shakespeare*, edited by Christopher St. John, 165–66. New York: Benjamin Bloom.

———. 2019. "'On Ophelia.' Excerpt from Ellen Terry's The Story of My Life: Recollections and Reflections. London, 1908." In *Hamlet*, 2nd Norton Critical ed., edited by Robert Miola, 161. New York: Norton.

Thomas, Miranda Fay. 2019. "'And So Everyone According to His Cue': Practice-Led Teaching and Cue-Scripts in the Classroom." In *How and Why We Teach Shakespeare: College Teachers and Directors Share How They Explore the Playwright's Works with Their Students*, edited by Sidney Homan, 128–37. New York: Routledge.

Thompson, Ayanna, and Laura Turchi. 2016. *Teaching Shakespeare with Purpose: A Student-Centred Approach*. London: Bloomsbury Arden Shakespeare.

Tucker, Patrick. 1990. "Teaching and Acting Shakespeare from Cue Scripts." *Shakespeare Bulletin* (Summer): 25–29. https://www.jstor.org/stable/44657118.

———. 2016. *Secrets of Acting Shakespeare: The Original Approach*. 2nd ed. New York: Routledge.

West, Rebecca. 1957. *The Court and the Castle*. New Haven: Yale University Press.

Winston, Joe. 2015. *Transforming the Teaching of Shakespeare with the Royal Shakespeare Company*. London: Bloomsbury Arden Shakespeare.

Woo, Celestine. 2007. "Sarah Siddon's Performances as Hamlet: Breaching the Breeches Part." *European Romantic Review* 18, no. 5 (December): 573–95. https://doi.org/10.1080/10509580701757219.

Yancey, Kathleen, Liane Robertson, and Kara Taczak. 2014. *Writing Across Contexts: Transfer, Composition, and Sites of Writing*. Logan, UT: Utah State University Press.

Index

The Aeneid, 34–37, 60–61
Alexander the Great, 122–23

the baker's daughter 104, 111, 178
bird imagery, 77, 104, 111–14, 152–53n1, 178, 182
Blackfriars Playhouse, x–xi, xivn3, 154n6

Caesar, Julius, 58–59, 117, 122–23, 163
Claudius, xivn3, 1, 4, 8, 9, 14, 21n5, 25–27, 29, 35, 44, 51–54, 59, 73–74, 75, 77, 78, 81–86, 88–89, 93–97, 100–1, 105–7, 115–16, 125, 138–39, 161, 167, 171, 172, 173, 174, 175, 176, 177 178, 180, 181–82
cue scripts, xii, 61–68, 126–35

ecphonesis, 82, 84–86, 111

fathers, coping with their death, 44, 106, 114–5, 169
films and adaptations, 12–14, 22, 38–43, 69–73, 104–5, 123–26, 164–68
flower imagery, xiii, 81–84, 100–1, 104–8, 163, 179, 179–80, 181
Folio technique, xv, 49n1, 49–50n3, 153n2
Fortinbras, 10, 83, 169

gender-blind casting, 55–57, 62
Gertrude, 1–3, 51–54, 74–76, 81–84, 89, 95, 99, 101, 105–7, 120–22, 173, 174, 180–81; compared to Dido, 60–61; compared to Niobe, 21; closet scene, 51, 54, 98–99, 105–6; Margaret Atwood's interpretation of, xii, 74–77
ghosts and ghost stories, xi, 1, 3–5, 7–8, 14–19, 90–93, 154n5
Globe Theatre, x–xi, xiv

Hamlet: age and maturation, 39, 42, 55–57, 140–52; mental health, xii, 5, 22–23n10, 25–26, 54, 81–83, 113–14, 171; mousetrap scene 21, 26, 41–44, 51, 53, 58, 59, 73, 95, 163, 178; intelligence and wit 21n6, 51–55, 81, 182
Hecuba, 32, 34–37, 40, 41, 42, 44–46, 50nn5–6, 104, 177
Hephaestus, 59. *See also* Vulcan
Herod, 59, 78
Horatio, 1–2, 5, 7–11, 49, 53, 55, 59, 77, 83, 90–91, 94–95, 113–14, 116, 123, 135, 171, 180

iambic pentameter, 28–34, 46

Jephthah, 34–36, 104

The Lion King, 14–15, 167

makeup, 131, 177

Nero, 58–59
Niobe, 21n6

Ophelia, 1, 3–4, 44, 164–65, 168, 169, 171, 172, 173, 174, 177–80, 182–83; compared to the baker's daughter 104; mental health vii–viii, 25, 30, 71, 81–84, 100–107, 111–15; nunnery scene 27–28, 51–53, 61–73, 79–80; flower scene xiii, 69–74, 81–84, 100–108, 163; death and burial, 100–103, 107, 110, 111, 115–16, 124, 136–39

paraphrasing, 45–46, 49
pronouns: second-person familiar and formal, 3, 5–8, 14, 16, 74, 138; royal we 9, 21

purgatory 10–12, 21–22, 96–97
Pyrrhus, 35–37

Q1, *Q2*, and *F1*, xiii, 20, 78, 84–86, 116–22, 141–55

Rosencrantz and Guildenstern, 25, 27, 29–30, 44, 52, 77–78, 83, 115–16, 139–41, 167–68
rhyme, 28, 52, 54–55, 77

Termagant, 59, 78
transfer theory, x, xviii, 16, 23, 49, 76, 109, 145

verse and prose, 26, 28–34, 44, 49–50, 113, 139, 144
Vulcan, 59. *See also* Hephaestus

Yorick, 115, 122–24, 136–44, 172
young adult literature, 15, 20, 160, 162–63, 165

About the Author

Dr. Joseph P. Haughey is an associate professor of English at Northwest Missouri State University, where he helps prepare future middle and high school English teachers. Before that he taught middle and high school himself—first, in the desert on the California/Arizona border and then, later, in a village in bush Alaska. Through all that time and before, he's wrestled with the question of whether Shakespeare is best experienced in text or on stage, and to that end, he spends much of his leisure time when classes are in session mulling about in Shakespeare's texts and, when they are not traveling to theaters around the USA and England, comparing the merit of each perspective. He hopes not to come to any answer too soon but, rather, to continue to enjoy pondering the question this way for many more years to come. When not reading or attending the theater, he enjoys traveling, hiking, star gazing, and contemplating the smallness of everything in comparison to the vastness of the universe.

When COVID uprooted everything in 2020, Haughey was in the midst of an altogether-different research project. He'd recently spent a week at the Harvard archives and had made a photo record of thousands of pages of nineteenth-century student notes that were taken during some of the earliest college Shakespeare classes. The idea had been to better understand the classroom experience of those first students who'd studied Shakespeare as a subject all its own, but the work derailed, as so many things did that spring, and transformed into something else. When he got to the student notes on *Hamlet*, he couldn't pull away. That was the play that most spoke to the moment, to the smallness and vastness of everything, and instead of moving on to the next play, he just kept reading more and more about what critics and actors and everybody else had to say about *Hamlet* over the last four centuries. That deep dive—reading everything he could find on *Hamlet*—combined with many years of experience teaching the play became the book you now hold in your hands. He hopes it will help the play speak to you and your students of the smallness and vastness of things in the way it does for him.

www.ingramcontent.com/pod-product-compliance
Lightning Source LLC
Chambersburg PA
CBHW020120010526
44115CB00008B/905